Elements of Criticism

CLASSICS IN ART
and
LITERARY CRITICISM

Editor: René Wellek

STERLING PROFESSOR OF COMPARATIVE LITERATURE

YALE UNIVERSITY

KAMES. *Elements of Criticism*. 3 vols. Reprinted 1967.
WARTON. *History of English Poetry*. 4 vols. With a new Introduction by René Wellek. 1968.

ELEMENTS

OF

CRITICISM.

In THREE VOLUMES.

VOLUME I.

EDINBURGH:

Printed for A. MILLAR, London;

AND

A. KINCAID & J. BELL, Edinburgh.

MDCCLXII.

JOHNSON REPRINT CORPORATION   JOHNSON REPRINT COMPANY LIMITIED
111 Fifth Avenue, New York, N.Y. 10003   Berkeley Square House, London, W. 1

First reprinting, 1967, Johnson Reprint Corporation

Second reprinting 1970, Johnson Reprint Corporation

Printed in the United States of America

TO THE

KING.

SIR,

THE fine arts have ever been encouraged by wife princes, not fingly for private amufement, but for their beneficial influence in fociety. By uniting different ranks in the fame elegant pleafures, they promote benevolence: by cherifhing love of order, they inforce fubmiffion to government: and by infpiring delicacy of feeling, they make regular government a double blefting.

THESE

THESE confiderations embolden me to hope for your Majefty's patronage in behalf of the following work, which treats of the fine arts, and attempts to form a ftandard of tafte by unfolding thofe principles that ought to govern the tafte of every individual.

IT is rare to find one born with fuch delicacy of feeling, as not to need inftruction: it is equally rare to find one fo low in feeling, as not to be capable of inftruction. And yet, to refine our tafte with refpect to beauties of art or of nature, is fcarce endeavoured in any feminary of learning; a lamentable defect, confidering how early in life tafte is fufceptible of culture, and how difficult to reform it if unhappily perverted. To furnifh materials for fupplying that defect, was an additional motive for the prefent undertaking.

To

To promote the fine arts in Britain, has become of greater importance than is generally imagined. A flourishing commerce begets opulence; and opulence, inflaming our appetite for pleasure, is commonly vented on luxury and on every sensual gratification: Selfishness rears its head; becomes fashionable; and infecting all ranks, extinguishes the *amor patriæ* and every spark of public spirit. To prevent or to retard such fatal corruption, the genius of an Alfred cannot devise any means more efficacious, than venting opulence upon the fine arts. Riches so employ'd, instead of encouraging vice, will excite both public and private virtue. Of this happy effect, ancient Greece furnishes one shining instance; and why should we despair of another in Britain?

In the commencement of an auspicious reign, and even in that early period of
life

life when pleafure commonly is the fole
purfuit, your Majefty has uniformly difplay'd to a delighted people, the nobleft
principles, ripened by early culture; and
for that reafon, you will be the more difpofed to favour every rational plan for
advancing the art of training up youth.
Among the many branches of education,
that which tends to make deep impreffions of virtue, ought to be a funda-
mental meafure in a well-regulated government: for depravity of manners will
render ineffectual the moft falutary laws ;
and in the midft of opulence, what other
means to prevent fuch depravity but
early and virtuous difcipline? The Britifh
difcipline is fufceptible of great improve-
ments; and if we can hope for them, it
muft be from a young and accomplifhed
Prince, eminently fenfible of their importance. To eftablifh a complete fyftem
of education, feems referved by providence for a Sovereign who commands
the

the hearts of his fubjects. Succefs will crown the undertaking, and endear GEORGE THE THIRD to our lateft pofterity.

THE moft elevated and moft refined pleafure of human nature, is enjoy'd by a virtuous prince governing a virtuous people; and that, by perfecting the great fyftem of education, your Majefty may very long enjoy this pleafure, is the ardent wifh of

Your Majefty's

Devoted Subject,

HENRY HOME.

CONTENTS.

b

Ch. 18.

In defcribing the fcale of founds made in pronouncing the five vowels, *vol.* 2. *p.* 239. it ought to have been mentioned, that the letter *i* muft be pronounced as in the word *intereft*, and other words beginning with the fyllable *in*; the letter *e* as in *perfuafion*; and the letter *u* as in *number*.

The reference intended, *vol.* 2. *p.* 419. is to *p.* 404. of the fame volume.

E L E-

INTRODUCTION.

THE five senses agree in the following particular, that nothing external is perceived till it first make an impression upon the organ of sense; the impression, for example, made upon the hand by a stone, upon the palate by sugar, and upon the nostrils by a rose. But there is a difference as to our consciousness of that impression. In touching, tasting, and smelling, we are conscious of the impression. Not so in seeing and hearing. When I behold a tree, I am not sensible of the impression made upon my eye; nor of the impression made upon my ear, when I listen to a song *. This difference in the manner of perception, distinguishes remarkably hearing and seeing from the other senses; and distinguishes still more remarkably the feelings of the former from those of the latter. A feeling pleasant or painful cannot exist but in the mind; and yet be-

* See the Appendix, § 13.

A caufe-

caufe in tafting, touching, and fmelling, we are confcious of the impreffion made upon the organ, we naturally place there alfo, the pleafant or painful feeling caufed by that impreffion. And becaufe fuch feelings feem to be placed externally at the organ of fenfe, we, for that reafon, conceive them to be merely corporeal. We have a different apprehenfion of the pleafant and painful feelings derived from feeing and hearing. Being infenfible here of the organic impreffion, we are not mifled to affign a wrong place to thefe feelings; and therefore we naturally place them in the mind, where they really exift. Upon that account, they are conceived to be more refined and fpiritual, than what are derived from tafting, touching, and fmelling.

The pleafures of the eye and ear being thus elevated above thofe of the other external fenfes, acquire fo much dignity as to make them a laudable entertainment. They are not, however, fet upon a level with thofe that are purely intellectual; being not lefs inferior in dignity to intellectual pleafures, than fuperior to the organic or corporeal.

They

They indeed refemble the latter, being like them produced by external objects : but they also refemble the former, being like them produced without any fenfible organic impreffion. Their mixt nature and middle place betwixt organic and intellectual pleafures, qualify them to affociate with either. Beauty heightens all the organic feelings, as well as thofe that are intellectual. Harmony, though it afpires to inflame devotion, difdains not to improve the relifh of a banquet.

The pleafures of the eye and ear have other valuable properties befide thofe of dignity and elevation. Being fweet and moderately exhilerating, they are in their tone equally diftant from the turbulence of paffion, and languor of inaction; and by that tone are perfectly well qualified, not only to revive the fpirits when funk by fenfual gratification, but alfo to relax them when overftrained in any violent purfuit. Here is a remedy provided for many diftreffes. And to be convinced of its falutary effects, it will be fufficient to run over the following particulars. Organic pleafures

have

have naturally a short duration : when continued too long, or indulged to excess, they lose their relish, and beget satiety and disgust. To relieve us from that uneasiness, nothing can be more happily contrived than the exhilerating pleasures of the eye and ear, which take place imperceptibly, without much varying the tone of mind. On the other hand, any intense exercise of the intellectual powers, becomes painful by overstraining the mind. Cessation from such exercise gives not instant relief : it is necessary that the void be filled with some amusement, gently relaxing the spirits *. Organic pleasure, which hath no relish but while we are in vigour, is ill qualified for that office : but the finer pleasures of sense, which occupy without exhausting the mind, are excellently well qualified to restore its usual tone after severe application to study or business, as well as after satiety from sensual gratification.

Our first perceptions are of external ob-

* Du Bos judiciously observes, that silence doth not tend to calm an agitated mind; but that soft and slow music hath a fine effect.

jects,

jects, and our firſt attachments are to them. Organic pleaſures take the lead. But the mind, gradually ripening, reliſheth more and more the pleaſures of the eye and ear; which approach the purely mental, without exhauſting the ſpirits; and exceed the purely ſenſual, without danger of ſatiety. The pleaſures of the eye and ear have accordingly a natural aptitude to attract us from the immoderate gratification of ſenſual appetite. For the mind, once accuſtomed to enjoy a variety of external objects without being conſcious of the organic impreſſion, is prepared for enjoying internal objects where there cannot be an organic impreſſion. Thus the author of nature, by qualifying the human mind for a ſucceſſion of enjoyments from the loweſt to the higheſt, leads it by gentle ſteps from the moſt groveling corporeal pleaſures, for which ſolely it is fitted in the beginning of life, to thoſe refined and ſublime pleaſures which are ſuited to its maturity.

This ſucceſſion, however, is not governed by unavoidable neceſſity. The God of nature offers it to us, in order to advance

our

our happiness; and it is sufficient, that he hath enabled us to complete the succession. Nor has he made our task disagreeable or difficult. On the contrary, the transition is sweet and easy, from corporeal pleasures to the more refined pleasures of sense; and not less so, from these to the exalted pleasures of morality and religion. We stand therefore engaged in honour, as well as interest, to second the purposes of nature, by cultivating the pleasures of the eye and ear, those especially that require extraordinary culture *, such as are inspired by poetry, painting, sculpture, music, gardening, and architecture. This chiefly is the duty of the opulent, who have leisure to improve their minds and their feelings. The fine arts are contrived to give pleasure to the eye

* A taste for natural objects is born with us in perfection. To relish a fine countenance, a rich landscape, or a vivid colour, culture is unnecessary. The observation holds equally in natural sounds, such as the singing of birds, or the murmuring of a brook. Nature here, the artificer of the object as well as of the percipient, hath suited them to each other with great accuracy. But of a poem, a cantata, a picture, and other artificial productions, a true relish is not commonly attained without study and practice.

and

and the ear, difregarding the inferior fenfes.
A tafte for thefe arts is a plant that grows
naturally in many foils; but, without culture, fcarce to perfection in any foil. It is
fufceptible of much refinement; and is, by
proper care, greatly improved. In this refpect, a tafte in the fine arts goes hand in
hand with the moral fenfe, to which indeed
it is nearly allied. Both of them difcover
what is right and what is wrong. Fafhion,
temper, and education, have an influence
upon both, to vitiate them, or to preferve
them pure and untainted. Neither of them
are arbitrary or local. They are rooted
in human nature, and are governed by
principles common to all men. The principles of morality belong not to the prefent
undertaking. But as to the principles of
the fine arts, they are evolved, by ftudying
the fenfitive part of human nature, and by
learning what objects are naturally agreeable,
and what are naturally difagreeable. The
man who afpires to be a critic in thefe arts,
muft pierce ftill deeper. He muft clearly
perceive what objects are lofty, what low,
what are proper or improper, what are man-
ly,

ly, and what are mean or trivial. Hence a foundation for judging of tafte, and for rea-foning upon it. Where it is conformable to principles, we can pronounce with certain-ty, that it is correct; otherwife, that it is incorrect, and perhaps whimfical. Thus the fine arts, like morals, become a rational fcience; and, like morals, may be cultiva-ted to a high degree of refinement.

Manifold are the advantages of criticifm, when thus ftudied as a rational fcience. In the firft place, a thorough acquaintance with the principles of the fine arts, redoubles the entertainment thefe arts afford. To the man who refigns himfelf entirely to fen-timent or feeling, without interpofing any fort of judgment, poetry, mufic, painting, are mere paftime. In the prime of life, indeed, they are delightful, being fupported by the force of novelty, and the heat of imagination. But they lofe their relifh gra-dually with their novelty; and are generally neglected in the maturity of life, which dif-pofes to more ferious and more important occupations. To thofe who deal in criticifm as a regular fcience, governed by juft prin-ciples,

ciples, and giving fcope to judgment as well as to fancy, the fine arts are a favourite entertainment; and in old age maintain that relifh which they produce in the morning of life *.

In the next place, a philofophic inquiry into the principles of the fine arts, inures the reflecting mind to the moft enticing fort of logic. Reafoning upon fubjects fo agreeable tends to a habit; and a habit, ftrengthening the reafoning faculties, prepares the mind for entering into fubjects more difficult and abftract. To have, in this refpect, a juft conception of the importance of criticifm, we need but reflect upon the common method of education; which, after fome years fpent in acquiring languages, hurries us, without the leaft preparatory difcipline, into the moft profound philofophy. A more effectual method to alienate the tender mind from abftract fcience, is beyond the reach of invention.

* " Though logic may fubfift without rhetoric or poetry, " yet fo neceffary to thefe laft is a found and correct logic, " that without it they are no better than warbling trifles." Hermes, p. 6.

With refpect to fuch fpeculations, the bulk
of our youth contract a fort of hobgoblin
terror, which is feldom, if ever, fubdued.
Thofe who apply to the arts, are trained in
a very different manner. They are led, ftep
by ftep, from the eafier parts of the operation, to what are more difficult ; and are
not permitted to make a new motion, till
they be perfected in thofe which regularly
precede it. The fcience of criticifm appears
then to be an intermediate link, finely qualified for connecting the different parts of
education into a regular chain. This fcience
furnifheth an inviting opportunity to exercife
the judgement : we delight to reafon upon
fubjects that are equally pleafant and familiar : we proceed gradually from the fim-
pler to the more involved cafes : and in a
due courfe of difcipline, cuftom, which improves all our faculties, beftows acutenefs
upon thofe of reafon, fufficient to unravel
all the intricacies of philofophy.

Nor ought it to be overlooked, that the
reafonings employed upon the fine arts are
of the fame kind with thofe which regulate
our conduct. Mathematical and metaphy-
fical

fical reafonings have no tendency to improve focial intercourfe : nor are they applicable to the common affairs of life. But a juft tafte in the fine arts, derived from rational principles, is a fine preparation for acting in the focial ftate with dignity and propriety.

The fcience of criticifm tends to improve the heart not lefs than the underftanding. I obferve, in the firft place, that it hath a fine effect in moderating the felfifh affections. A juft tafte in the fine arts, by fweetening and harmonizing the temper, is a ftrong antidote to the turbulence of paffion and violence of purfuit. Elegance of tafte procures to a man fo much enjoyment at home, or eafily within reach, that in order to be occupied, he is, in youth, under no temptation to precipitate into hunting, gaming, drinking; nor, in middle age, to deliver himfelf over to ambition ; nor, in old age, to avarice. Pride, a difguftful felfifh paffion, exerts itfelf without control, when accompanied with a bad tafte. A man of this ftamp, upon whom the moft ftriking beauty makes but a faint impreffion,

feels

feels no joy but in gratifying his ruling paſſion by the diſcovery of errors and blemiſhes.
Pride, on the other hand, finds in the conſtitution no enemy more formidable than a
delicate and diſcerning taſte. The man upon whom nature and culture have beſtowed
this bleſſing, feels great delight in the virtuous diſpoſitions and actions of others. He
loves to cheriſh them, and to publiſh them to
the world. Faults and failings, it is true, are
to him not leſs obvious : but theſe he avoids,
or removes out of ſight, becauſe they give
him pain. In a word, there may be other
paſſions, which, for a ſeaſon, diſturb the
peace of ſociety more than pride : but no
other paſſion is ſo unwearied an antagoniſt
to the ſweets of ſocial intercourſe. Pride,
tending aſſiduouſly to its gratification, puts
a man perpetually in oppoſition to others ;
and diſpoſes him more to reliſh bad than
good qualities, even in a boſom-friend.
How different that diſpoſition of mind, where
every virtue in a companion or neighbour,
is, by refinement of taſte, ſet in its ſtrongeſt light ; and defects or blemiſhes, natural

ral to all, are fuppreffed, or kept out of view?

In the next place, delicacy of tafte tends not lefs to invigorate the focial affections, than to moderate thofe that are felfifh. To be convinced of this tendency, we need only reflect, that delicacy of tafte neceffarily heightens our fenfibility of pain and pleafure, and of courfe our fympathy, which is the capital branch of every focial paffion. Sympathy in particular invites a communication of joys and forrows, hopes and fears. Such exercife, foothing and fatisfactory in itfelf, is productive neceffarily of mutual good-will and affection.

One other advantage of criticifm is referved to the laft place, being of all the moft important, that it is a great fupport to morality. I infift on it with entire fatiffaction, that no occupation attaches a man more to his duty than that of cultivating a tafte in the fine arts. A juft relifh of what is beautiful, proper, elegant, and ornamental, in writing or painting, in architecture or gardening, is a fine preparation for difcerning what is beautiful, juft, elegant,

or

or magnanimous, in character and behaviour. To the man who has acquired a taſte ſo acute and accompliſhed, every action, wrong or improper, muſt be highly diſguſtful. If, in any inſtance, the overbearing power of paſſion ſway him from his duty, he returns to it upon the firſt reflection, with redoubled reſolution never to be ſwayed a ſecond time. He has now an additional motive to virtue, a conviction derived from experience, that happineſs depends on regularity and order, and that a diſregard to juſtice or propriety never fails to be puniſhed with ſhame and remorſe *.

Rude ages exhibit the triumph of authority over reaſon. Philoſophers anciently were divided into ſects : they were either Epicureans, Platoniſts, Stoics, Pythago-

---

* Genius is allied to a warm and inflammable conſtitution, delicacy of taſte to calmneſs and ſedateneſs. Hence it is common to find genius in one who is a prey to every paſſion ; which can ſcarce happen with reſpect to delicacy of taſte. Upon a man poſſeſſed of this bleſſing, the moral duties, as well as the fine arts, make a deep impreſſion, ſo as to counterbalance every irregular deſire. And even ſuppoſing a ſtrong temptation, it can take no faſt hold of a calm and ſedate temper.

reans,

reans, or Sceptics. Men relied no farther upon their own judgement than to chufe a leader, whom they implicitly followed. In later times, happily, reafon hath obtained the afcendant. Men now affert their native privilege of thinking for themfelves, and difdain to be ranked in any fect, whatever be the fcience. I muft except criticifm, which, by what fatality I know not, continues to be not lefs flavifh in its principles, nor lefs fubmiffive to authority, than it was originally. Boffu, a celebrated French critic, gives many rules; but can difcover no better foundation for any of them, than the practice merely of Homer and Virgil, fupported by the authority of Ariftotle. Strange, that in fo long a work, the concordance or difcordance of thefe rules with human nature, fhould never once have entered his thoughts! It could not furely be his opinion, that thefe poets, however eminent for genius, were intitled to give laws to mankind, and that nothing now remains but blind obedience to their arbitrary will. If in writing they followed no rule, why fhould they be imitated? If they ftudied nature, and

were

were obfequious to rational principles, why fhould thefe be concealed from us?

With refpect to the prefent undertaking, it is not the author's intention to give a regular treatife upon each of the fine arts in particular; but only, in general, to apply to them fome remarks and obfervations drawn from human nature, the true fource of criticifm. The fine arts are calculated for our entertainment, or for making agreeable impreffions; and, by that circumftance, are diftinguifhed from the ufeful arts. In order then to be a critic in the fine arts, it is neceffary, as above hinted, to know what objects are naturally agreeable, and what naturally difagreeable. A complete treatife on that fubject would be a field by far too extenfive to be thoroughly cultivated by any one hand. The author pretends only to have entered upon the fubject fo far as neceffary for fupporting his critical remarks. And he affumes no merit from his performance, but that of evincing, perhaps more diftinctly than hitherto has been done, that the genuine rules of criticifm are all of them derived from the human heart. The

fenfitive

fenfitive part of our nature is a delightful
fpeculation. What the author hath difcovered or collected upon that fubject, he
chufes to impart in the gay and agreeable
form of criticifm; becaufe he imagines,
that this form will be more relifhed, and
perhaps be not lefs inftructive, than a regular and laboured difquifition. His plan
is, to afcend gradually to principles, from
facts and experiments, inftead of beginning
with the former, handled abftractly, and
defcending to the latter. But though criticifm be thus his only declared aim, he
will not difown, that all along he had it in
view, to explain the nature of man, confidered as a fenfitive being, capable of pleafure and pain. And though he flatters
himfelf with having made fome progrefs in
that important fcience, he is however too
fenfible of its extent and difficulty, to undertake it profeffedly, or to avow it as the
chief purpofe of the prefent work.

To cenfure works, not men, is the juft
prerogative of criticifm; and accordingly all
perfonal cenfure is here avoided, unlefs
where neceffary to illuftrate fome general
C proposition.

propofition. No praife is claimed on that
account; becaufe cenfuring with a view
merely to find fault, is an entertainment
that humanity never relifhes. Writers,
one would imagine, fhould, above all o-
thers, be referved upon that article, when
they lie fo open to retaliation. The author
of this treatife, far from being confident of
meriting no cenfure, entertains not even
the flighteft hope of fuch perfection. A-
mufement was at firft the fole aim of his
inquiries. Proceeding from one particular
to another, the fubject grew under his
hand; and he was far advanced before the
thought ftruck him, that his private medi-
tations might be publicly ufeful. In public, however, he would not appear in a
flovenly drefs; and therefore he pretends
not otherwife to apologife for his errors,
than by obferving, that, in a new fubject,
not lefs nice than extenfive, errors are in
fome meafure unavoidable. Neither pretends he to juftify his tafte in every particular. That point muft be extremely clear,
which admits not variety of opinion; and
in fome matters fufceptible of great refinement,

ment, time is perhaps the only infallible touch-ftone of tafte. To this he appeals, and to this he chearfully fubmits.

N. B. THE ELEMENTS OF CRITICISM, meaning the whole, is a title too affuming for this work. A number of thefe elements or principles are here evolved : but as the author is far from imagining, that he has completed the lift, a more humble title is proper, fuch as may exprefs any undetermined number of parts lefs than the whole. This he thinks is fignified by the title he has chofen, *viz.* ELEMENTS OF CRITICISM.

ELE-

ELEMENTS

OF

CRITICISM.

CHAPTER I.

Perceptions and ideas in a train.

A MAN while awake is senſible of a continued train of objects paſſing in his mind. It requires no activity on his part to carry on the train : nor has he power to vary it by calling up an object at will *. At the ſame time we learn

---

* For how ſhould this be done ? What object is it that we are to call up ? If this queſtion can be anſwered, the object is already in the mind, and there is no occaſion to exert the power. If the queſtion cannot be anſwered, I next demand, how it is poſſible that a voluntary power can be exerted without any view of an object to exert it upon ?

We

learn from daily experience, that a train of thought is not merely cafual. And if it depend not upon will, nor upon chance, we muft try to evolve by what law it is governed. The fubject is of import-ance in the fcience of human nature; and I promife beforehand, that it will be found of great importance in the fine arts.

It appears that the relations by which things are linked together, have a great in-fluence in directing the train of thought; and we find by experience, that objects are connected in the mind precifely as they are externally. Beginning then with things external, we find that they are not more remarkable by their inherent properties than by their various relations. We can-not any where extend our view without perceiving things connected together by certain relations. One thing perceived to be a caufe, is connected with its feveral

We cannot form a conception of fuch a thing. This argu-ment appears to me fatisfactory: if it need confirmation, I urge experience. Whoever makes a trial will find, that objects are linked together in the mind, forming a connect-ed chain; and that we have not the command of any object independent of the chain.

effects;

effects; fome things are connected by contiguity in time, others by contiguity in
place ; fome are connected by refemblance,
fome by contraft; fome go before, fome
follow. Not a fingle thing appears foli-
tary, and altogether devoid of connection.
The only difference is, that fome are intimately connected, fome more flightly ;
fome near, fome at a diftance.

Experience as well as reafon may fatisfy
us, that the train of mental perceptions is
in a great meafure regulated by the foregoing relations. Where a number of things
are linked together, the idea of any one fuggefts the reft ; and in this manner is a train
of thoughts compofed. Such is the law of
fucceffion ; whether an original law, or
whether directed by fome latent principle,
is doubtful ; and probably will for ever remain fo. This law, however, is not invio-
lable. It fometimes happens, though rarely, that an idea prefents itfelf to the mind
without any connection, fo far at leaft as can
be difcovered.

But though we have not the abfolute
command of ideas, yet the Will hath a confiderable

fiderable influence in directing the order of connected ideas. There are few things but what are connected with many others. By this means, when any thing becomes an object, whether in a direct furvey, or ideally only, it generally fuggefts many of its connections. Among thefe a choice is afforded. We can infift upon one, rejecting others; and we can even infift upon what has the flighteft connection. Where ideas are left to their natural courfe, they are generally continued through the ftrongeft connections. The mind extends its view to a fon more readily than to a fervant, and more readily to a neighbour than to one living at a diftance. This order may be varied by Will, but ftill within the limits of connected objects. In fhort, every train of ideas muft be a chain, in which the particular ideas are linked to each other. We may vary the order of a natural train; but not fo as to diffolve it altogether, by carrying on our thoughts in a loofe manner without any connection. So far doth our power extend; and that power is fufficient for all ufeful purpofes. To give us more

power,

power, would probably be detrimental inflead of being falutary.

Will is not the only caufe that prevents a train of thought from being continued through the ftrongeft connections. Much depends on the prefent tone of mind; for a fubject that accords with this tone is always welcome. Thus, in good fpirits, a chearful fubject will be introduced by the flighteft connection; and one that is melancholy, not lefs readily in low fpirits. Again, an interefting fubject is recalled, from time to time, by any connection indifferently, ftrong or weak. This is finely touched by Shakefpear, with relation to a rich cargo at fea.

My wind, cooling my broth,
Would blow me to an ague, when I thought
What harm a wind too great might do at fea.
I fhould not fee the fandy hour-glafs run,
But I fhould think of fhallows and of flats;
And fee my wealthy Andrew dock'd in fand,
Vailing her high top lower than her ribs,
To kifs her burial. Should I go to church,
And fee the holy edifice of ftone,
And not bethink me ftrait of dangerous rocks?

Which

Which touching but my gentle veſſel's ſide,
Would ſcatter all the ſpices on the ſtream,
Enrobe the roaring waters with my ſilks ;
And, in a word, but now worth this,
And now worth nothing.

Merchant of Venice, act I. ſc. I.

Another cauſe clearly diſtinguiſhable from that now mentioned, hath alſo a conſiderable influence over the train of ideas. In ſome minds of a ſingular frame, thoughts and circumſtances crowd upon each other by the ſlighteſt connection. I aſcribe this to a defect in the faculty of diſcernment. A perſon who cannot accurately diſtinguiſh betwixt a ſlight connection and one that is more ſolid, is equally affected with both. Such a perſon muſt neceſſarily have a great command of ideas, becauſe they are introduced by any relation indifferently ; and the ſlighter relations, being without number, muſt furniſh ideas without end. This doctrine is, in a lively manner, illuſtrated by Shakeſpear.

Falſtaff. What is the groſs ſum that I owe thee ?
Hoſteſs. Marry, if thou wert an honeſt man,
thyſelf

thyfelf and thy money too.   Thou didſt ſwear
to me on a parcel-gilt goblet, ſitting in my Dol-
phin chamber, at the round table, by a ſea-coal
fire, on Wedneſday in Whitſun-week, when the
Prince broke thy head for likening him to a
ſinging man of Windſor, thou didſt ſwear to me
then, as I was waſhing thy wound, to marry me,
and make me my Lady thy wife.   Canſt thou deny it?   Did not Goodwife Keech, the butcher's
wife, come in then, and call me Goſſip Quickly?
Coming in to borrow a meſs of vinegar; telling
us ſhe had a good diſh of prawns;   whereby thou
didſt deſire to eat ſome;   whereby I told thee
they were ill for a green wound?   And didſt not
thou, when ſhe was gone down ſtairs, deſire me
to be no more ſo familiarity with ſuch poor people, ſaying, that ere long they ſhould call me
Madam?   And didſt thou not kiſs me, and bid me
fetch thee thirty ſhillings?   I put thee now to thy
book-oath, deny it if thou canſt.

Second part, Henry IV. *act* 2. *ſc.* 2.

On the other hand, a man of accurate
judgement cannot have a great flow of ideas.
The ſlighter relations making no figure in
his mind, have no power to introduce ideas.
And hence it is, that accurate judgement is
not friendly to declamation or copious eloquence.

quence. This reasoning is confirmed by experience; for it is a noted observation, That a great or comprehensive memory is seldom connected with a good judgement.

As an additional confirmation, I appeal to another noted observation, That wit and judgement are seldom united. Wit consists chiefly in joining things by distant and fanciful relations, which surprise because they are unexpected. Such relations being of the slightest kind, readily occur to that person only who makes every relation equally welcome. Wit, upon that account, is, in a good measure, incompatible with solid judgement; which, neglecting trivial relations, adheres to what are substantial and permanent. Thus memory and wit are often conjoined: solid judgement seldom with either.

The train of thought depends not entirely upon relations: another cause comes in for a share; and that is the sense of order and arrangement. To things of equal rank, where there is no room for a preference, order cannot be applied; and it must be indifferent in what manner they be surveyed;
witness

witnefs the fheep that make a flock, or the trees in a wood. But in things of unequal rank, order is a governing principle. Thus our tendency is, to view the principal fubject before we defcend to its acceffories or ornaments, and the fuperior before the inferior or dependent. We are equally averfe to enter into a minute confideration of conftituent parts, till the thing be firft furveyed as a whole. In paffing from a part to the whole, and from an acceffory to its principal, the connection is the fame as in the oppofite direction. But a fenfe of order aids the tranfition in the latter cafe, and a fenfe of diforder obftructs it in the former. It needs fcarce be added, that in thinking or reflecting on any of thefe particulars, and in paffing from one to another ideally, we are fenfible of eafinefs or difficulty precifely as when they are fet before our eyes.

Our fenfe of order is confpicuous with refpect to natural operations ; for it always coincides with the order of nature. Thinking upon a body in motion, we follow its natural courfe. The mind falls with a heavy body, defcends with a river, and afcends with

with flame and fmoke. In tracing out a family, we incline to begin at the founder,
and to defcend gradually to his lateft pofterity. On the contrary, mufing on a lofty
oak, we begin at the trunk, and mount
from it to the branches. As to hiftorical
facts, we love to proceed in the order of
time ; or, which comes to the fame, to
proceed along the chain of caufes and effects.

But though, in following out a hiftorical
chain, our bent is to proceed orderly from
caufes to their effects, we find not the fame
bent in matters of fcience. There we feem
rather difpofed to proceed from effects to
their caufes, and from particular propofitions to thofe which are more general.
Why this difference in matters that appear
fo nearly related ? The cafes are fimilar in
appearance only, not in reality. In a hiftorical chain, every event is particular, the
effect of fome former event, and the caufe
of others that follow. In fuch a chain, there
is nothing to bias the mind from the order
of nature. Widely different is the cafe of
fcience, when we endeavour to trace out
                                                    caufes

caufes and their effects.   Many experiments
are commonly reduced under one caufe;
and again, many of thefe under fome one
ftill more general and comprehenfive.   In
our progrefs from particular effects to general caufes, and from particular propofitions
to the more comprehenfive, we feel a gradual dilatation or expanfion of mind, like
what is felt in proceeding along an afcending feries, which is extremely delightful.
The pleafure here exceeds what arifes from
following the courfe of nature; and it is
this pleafure which regulates our train of
thought in the cafe now mentioned, and in
others that are fimilar.   Thefe obfervations,
by the way, furnifh materials for inftituting
a comparifon betwixt the fynthetic and analytic methods of reafoning.   The fynthetic
method defcending regularly from principles to their confequences, is more agreeable to the ftrictnefs of order.   But in following the oppofite courfe in the analytic
method, we have a fenfible pleafure, like
mounting upward, which is not felt in the
other.   The analytic method is more agreeable to the imagination.   The other method
will

will be preferred by thofe only who with
rigidity adhere to order, and give no indul-
gence to natural emotions *.

It appears then that we are framed by nature to relifh order and connection. When
an object is introduced by a proper connection, we are confcious of a certain pleafure
arifing from that circumftance. Among
objects of equal rank, the pleafure is proportioned to the degree of connection; but
among unequal objects, where we require
a certain order, the pleafure arifes chiefly
from an orderly arrangement. Of this one
may be made fenfible, in tracing objects
contrary to the courfe of nature, or contrary to our fenfe of order. The mind proceeds with alacrity from a whole to its parts,
and from a principal to its acceffories; but
in the contrary direction, it is fenfible of a
fort of retrograde motion, which is unpleafant. And here may be remarked the great
influence of order upon the mind of man.
Grandeur, which makes a deep impreffion,

* A train of perceptions or ideas, with refpect to its uniformity and variety, is handled afterward, chap. 9.

inclines

inclines us, in running over any feries, to proceed from fmall to great, rather than from great to fmall. But order prevails over this tendency; and in paffing from the whole to its parts, and from a fubject to its ornaments, affords pleafure as well as facility, which are not felt in the oppofite courfe. Elevation touches the mind not lefs than grandeur doth; and in raifing the mind to elevated objects, there is a fenfible pleafure. But the courfe of nature hath ftill a greater influence than elevation; and therefore the pleafure of falling with rain, and defcending gradually with a river, prevails over that of mounting upward. Hence the agreeablenefs of fmoke afcending in a calm morning. Elevation concurs with the courfe of nature, to make this object delightful.

I am extremely fenfible of the difguft men generally have at abftract fpeculation; and for that reafon I would avoid it altogether, were it poffible in a work which profeffes to draw the rules of criticifm from human nature, their true fource. There is indeed no choice, other than to continue for fome

time in the fame track, or to abandon the
undertaking altogether. Candor obliges me
to notify this to my readers, that fuch of
them whofe averfion to abftract fpeculation
is invincible, may ftop fhort here; for till
principles be explained, I can promife no
entertainment to thofe who fhun thinking.
But I flatter myfelf with a different tafte in
the bulk of readers. Some few, I imagine,
will relifh the abftract part for its own fake;
and many for the ufeful purpofes to which
it may be applied. For encouraging the
latter to proceed with alacrity, I affure them
beforehand that the foregoing fpeculation
leads to many important rules of criticifm,
which fhall be unfolded in the courfe of
this work. In the mean time, for inftant
fatisfaction in part, they will be pleafed to
accept the following fpecimen.

It is required in every work of art, that,
like an organic fyftem, the conftituent parts
be mutually connected, and bear each of
them a relation to the whole, fome more
intimate, fome lefs, according to their deftination. Order is not lefs effential than connection; and when due regard is paid to
                                        thefe,

thefe, we have a fenfe of juft compofition, and fo far are pleafed with the performance. Homer is defective in order and connection; and Pindar more remarkably. Regularity, order, and connection, are painful reftraints on a bold and fertile imagination; and are not patiently fubmitted to, but after much culture and difcipline. In Horace there is no fault more eminent than want of connection. Inftances are without number. In the firft fourteen lines of ode 7. lib. 1. he mentions feveral towns and diftricts which by fome were relifhed more than by others. In the remainder of the ode, Plancus is exhorted to drown his cares in wine. Having narrowly efcaped death by the fall of a tree, this poet * takes occafion properly to obferve, that while we guard againft fome dangers, we are expofed to others we cannot forefee. He ends with difplaying the power of mufic. The parts of ode 16. lib. 2. are fo loofely connected as to disfigure a poem otherwife extremely beautiful. The 1ft, 2d, 3d, 4th, 11th, 24th, 27th odes of the

* Lib. 2. ode 13.

3d

3d book, lie open all of them to the same cenfure. The 1ſt ſatire, book 1. is ſo deformed
by want of unity and connection of parts, as
upon the whole to be ſcarce agreeable. It
commences with an important queſtion, How
it happens that perſons who are ſo much
ſatisfied with themſelves, are generally ſo
little with their condition? After illuſtra-
ting the obſervation in a ſprightly manner
by ſeveral examples, the author, forgetting
his ſubject, enters upon a declamation a-
gainſt avarice, which he purſues till the
line 108. There he makes an apology for
wandering, and promiſes to return to his
ſubject. But avarice having got poſſeſſion
of his mind, he follows out that theme to
the end, and never returns to the queſtion propoſed in the beginning.

In the Georgics of Virgil, though e-
ſteemed the moſt finiſhed work of that
author, the parts are ill connected, and
the tranſitions far from being ſweet and
eaſy. In the firſt book * he deviates from
his ſubject to give a deſcription of the five

* Lin. 231.

zones.

zones. The want of connection here is remarkable, as well as in the defcription of the prodigies that accompanied the death of Cæfar, with which the fame book is concluded. A digreffion upon the praifes of Italy in the fecond book *, is not more happily introduced. And in the midſt of a declamation upon the pleafures of hufbandry, that makes part of the fame book †, the author appears perfonally upon the ſtage without the flighteſt connection. The two prefaces of Salluſt look as if they had been prefixed by fome blunder to his two hiftories. They will fuit any other hiftory as well, or any fubject as well as hiftory. Even the members of thefe prefaces are but loofely connected. They look more like a number of maxims or obfervations than a connected difcourfe.

An epifode in a narrative poem being in effect an acceffory, demands not that ſtrict union with the principal fubject which is requifite betwixt a whole and its conſtituent parts. The relation however of prin-

* Lin. 136.   † Lin. 475.

cipal

cipal and acceffory being pretty intimate,
an epifode loofely connected with the principal fubject will never be graceful. I give
for an example the defcent of Æneas into
hell, which employs the fixth book of the
Æneid. The reader is not prepared for
this important event. No caufe is affigned,
that can make it appear neceffary or even
natural, to fufpend, for fo long a time, the
principal action in its moft interefting period. To engage Æneas to wander from
his courfe in fearch of an adventure fo extraordinary, the poet can find no better
pretext, than the hero's longing to vifit the
ghoft of his father recently dead. In the
mean time the ftory is interrupted, and the
reader lofes his ardor. An epifode fo extremely beautiful is not at any rate to be
difpenfed with. It is pity however, that it
doth not arife more naturally from the fubject. I muft obferve at the fame time, that
full juftice is done to this incident, by confidering it to be an epifode; for if it be a
conftituent part of the principal action, the
connection ought to be ftill more intimate.
The fame objection lies againft that elabo-

rate

rate defcription of Fame in the Æneid *.
Any other book of that heroic poem, or of
any heroic poem, has as good a title to that
defcription as the book where it is placed.

In a natural landfcape, we every day perceive a multitude of objects connected by
contiguity folely.   Objects of fight make an
impreffion fo lively, as that a relation, even
of the flighteft kind, is relifhed.   This however ought not to be imitated in defcription.
Words are fo far fhort of the eye in liveli-
nefs of impreffion, that in a defcription the
connection of objects ought to be carefully
ftudied, in order to make the deeper impreffion.   For it is a known fact, the reafon of which is fuggefted above, that it is
eafier by words to introduce into the mind
a related object, than one which is not connected with the preceding train. In the following paffage, different things are brought
together without the flighteft connection, if
it be not what may be called verbal, *i. e.*
taking the fame word in different meanings.

* Lib. 4. lin. 173.

Surgamus

Surgamus : folet effe gravis cantantibus umbra.
Juniperi gravis umbra : nocent et frugibus umbræ.
Ite domum faturæ, venit Hefperus, ite capellæ.
                              Virg. Buc. 10. 75.

The metaphorical or figurative appearance of an object, is no good caufe for introducing that object in its real and natural
appearance.   A relation fo flight can never
be relifhed.

Diftruft in lovers is too warm a fun ;
But yet 'tis night in love when that is gone.
And in thofe climes which moft his fcorching know,
He makes the nobleft fruits and metals grow.
                Part 2. *Conqueft of Granada*, *act* 3.

The relations among objects have a confiderable influence in the gratification of
our paffions, and even in their production.
But this fubject is referved to be treated in
the chapter of emotions and paffions *.

There is perhaps not another inftance of
a building fo great erected upon a foundation fo flight in appearance, as that which is

_____

* Part 1. fect. 4.

                                        erected

erected upon the relations of objects and their arrangement. Relations make no capital figure in the mind : the bulk of them are tranfitory, and fome extremely trivial. They are however the links that, uniting our perceptions into one connected chain, produce connection of action, becaufe perceptions and actions have an intimate correfpondence. But it is not fufficient for the conduct of life that our actions be linked together, however intimately : it is befide neceffary that they proceed in a certain order ; and this alfo is provided for by an original propenfity. Thus order and connection, while they admit fufficient variety, introduce a method in the management of affairs. Without them our conduct would be fluctuating and defultory ; and we would be hurried from thought to thought, and from action to action, entirely at the mercy of chance.

C H A P.

C H A P. II.

Emotions and Paſſions.

THE fine arts, as obſerved above *, are all of them calculated to give pleaſure to the eye or the ear ; and they never deſcend to gratify the taſte, touch, or ſmell. At the ſame time, the feelings of the eye and ear, are of all the feelings of external ſenſe, thoſe only which are honoured with the name of *emotions* or *paſſions*. It is alſo obſerved above †, that the principles of the fine arts are unfolded by ſtudying the ſenſitive part of human nature, in order to know what objects of the eye and ear are agreeable, what diſagreeable. Theſe obſervations ſhow the uſe of the preſent chapter. We evidently muſt be acquainted with the nature and cauſes of emotions and paſſions, before we can judge with any accuracy how far they are

* Introduction.　　　† Introduction.

under the power of the fine arts. The critical art is thus fet in a fine point of view.
The inquifitive mind beginning with criticifm the moft agreeable of all amufements, and finding no obftruction in its
progrefs, advances far into the fenfitive part
of our nature ; and gains infenfibly a
thorough knowledge of the human heart, of
its defires, and of every motive to action ;
a fcience which of all that can be reached
by man, is to him of the greateft importance.

Upon a fubject fo extenfive, all that can
be expected here, is a general or flight furvey. Some emotions indeed more peculiarly connected with the fine arts, I propofe to handle in feparate chapters ; a method that will fhorten the general furvey
confiderably. And yet, after this circum-
fcription, fo much matter comes under
even a general view of the paffions and
emotions, that, to avoid confufion, I find
it neceffary to divide this chapter into many
parts : in the firft of which are handled the
caufes of thofe emotions and paffions that are
the moft common and familiar ; for to explain

plain every paſſion and emotion, however
ſingular, would be an endleſs work. And
though I could not well take up leſs ground,
without ſeparating things intimately connected; yet, upon examination, I find the
cauſes of our emotions and paſſions to be
ſo numerous and various, as to make a ſub-
diviſion alſo neceſſary by ſplitting this firſt
part into ſeveral ſections. Human nature
is a complicated machine, and muſt be
ſo to anſwer all its purpoſes. There
have indeed been publiſhed to the world,
many a ſyſtem of human nature, that
flatter the mind by their ſimplicity. But
theſe, unluckily, deviate far from truth
and reality. According to ſome writers,
man is entirely a ſelfiſh being: according
to others, univerſal benevolence is his
duty. One founds morality upon ſympathy ſolely, and one upon utility. If any
of theſe ſyſtems were of nature's production, the preſent ſubject might be ſoon
diſcuſſed. But the variety of nature is not
ſo eaſily reached; and for confuting ſuch
Utopian ſyſtems without the intricacy of
reaſoning, it appears the beſt method to
enter

enter into human nature, and to set before the eye, plainly and candidly, facts as they really exist.

P A R T   I.

Causes evolved of the emotions and passions.

S E C T.   I.

Difference betwixt emotion and passion.——— Causes that are the most common and the most extensive.——— Passion considered as productive of action.

THese branches are so interwoven, as to make it necessary that they be handled together. It is a fact universally admitted, that no emotion nor passion ever starts up in the mind, without a known cause. If I love a person, it is for good qualities or good offices: if I have resentment against a man, it must be for some injury he has done me; and I cannot pity any one, who is under no distress of body or of mind.

The

The circumstances now mentioned, if they cause or occasion a passion, cannot be entirely indifferent: if they were, they could not move us in any degree. And we find upon examination, that they are not indifferent. Looking back upon the foregoing examples, the good qualities or good offices that attract my love, are antecedently agreeable. If an injury were not disagreeable, it would not occasion any resentment against the author; nor would the passion of pity be raised by an object in distress, if that object did not give us pain. These feelings antecedent to passion, and which seem to be the causes of passion, shall be distinguished by the name of *emotions*.

What is now said about the production of passion, resolves into a very simple proposition, That we love what is pleasant, and hate what is painful. And indeed it is evident, that without antecedent emotions we could not have any passions; for a thing must be pleasant or painful, before it can be the object either of love or of hatred.

As it appears from this short sketch, that passions are generated by means of prior e-motions,

motions, it will be neceffary to take firft under confideration emotions and their caufes.

Such is the conftitution of our nature, that upon perceiving certain external objects, we are inftantaneoufly confcious of pleafure or pain. A flowing river, a fmooth extended plain, a fpreading oak, a towering hill, are objects of fight that raife pleafant emotions. A barren heath, a dirty marfh, a rotten carcafs, raife painful emotions. Of the emotions thus produced, we inquire for no other caufe but merely the prefence of the object.

It muft further be obferved, that the things now mentioned, raife emotions by means of their properties and qualities. To the emotion raifed by a large river, its fize, its force, and its fluency, contribute each a fhare. The pleafures of regularity, propriety, convenience, compofe the emotion raifed by a fine building.

If external properties make a being or thing agreeable, we have reafon to expect the fame effect from thofe which are internal; and accordingly power, difcernment, wit,

wit, mildnefs, fympathy, courage, benevolence, render the poffeffor agreeable in a
high degree. So foon as thefe qualities are
perceived in any perfon, we inftantaneoufly
feel pleafant emotions, without the flighteft
act of reflection or of attention to confequences. It is almoft unneceffary to add, that
certain qualities oppofite to the former, fuch
as dullnefs, peevifhnefs, inhumanity, coward-
ice, occafion in the fame manner painful
emotions.

Senfible beings affect us remarkably by
their actions. Some actions fo foon as perceived, raife pleafant emotions in the fpectator, without the leaft reflection ; fuch as
graceful motion and genteel behaviour.
But as the intention of the agent is a capital
circumftance in the bulk of human actions,
it requires reflection to difcover their true
character. If I fee one delivering a purfe
of money to another, I can make nothing
of this action, till I difcover with what intention the money is given. If it be given
to extinguifh a debt, the action is agreeable
in a flight degree. If it be a grateful return,
I feel a ftronger emotion ; and the plea-
surable

furable emotion rifes to a great height when it is the intention of the giver to relieve a virtuous family from want.   Actions are thus qualified by the intention of the agent.   But they are not qualified by the event; for an action well intended is agreeable, whatever be the confequence.   The pleafant or painful emotion that arifeth from contemplating human actions, is of a peculiar kind.   Human actions are perceived to be *right* or *wrong*; and this perception qualifies the pleafure or pain that refults from them *.

Not

---

* In tracing our emotions and paffions to their origin, it once was my opinion, that qualities and actions are the primary caufes of emotions; and that thefe emotions are afterward expanded upon the being to which thefe qualities and actions belong.   But I have difcovered that opinion to be erroneous. An attribute is not, even in imagination, feparable from the being to which it belongs; and for that reafon, cannot of itfelf be the caufe of any emotion.   We have, it is true, no knowledge of any being or fubftance but by means of its attributes; and therefore no being can be agreeable to us otherwife than by their means.   But ftill, when an emotion is raifed, it is the being itfelf, as we apprehend the matter, which raifes the emotion; and it raifes it by means of one or other of its attributes.   If it be urged, That we can in idea abftract a quality from the thing to which it belongs; it might be anfwered,

Not only are emotions raiſed in us by the qualities and actions of others, but alſo by their feelings. I cannot behold a man in diſtreſs, without partaking of his pain ; nor in joy, without partaking of his pleaſure.

The beings or things above deſcribed, occaſion emotions in us, not only in the original ſurvey, but when they are recalled to the memory in idea. A field laid out with taſte, is pleaſant in the recollection, as well as when under our eye. A generous action deſcribed in words or colours, occaſions a ſenſible emotion, as well as when we ſee

That an abſtract idea, which ſerves excellently the purpoſes of reaſoning, is too faint and too much ſtrained to produce any ſort of emotion. But it is ſufficient for the preſent purpoſe to anſwer, That the eye never abſtracts. By this organ we perceive things as they really exiſt, and never perceive a quality as ſeparated from the ſubject. Hence it muſt be evident, that emotions are raiſed, not by qualities abſtractly conſidered, but by the ſubſtance or body ſo and ſo qualified. Thus a ſpreading oak raiſes a pleaſant emotion, by means of its colour, figure, umbrage, &c. It is not the colour ſtrictly ſpeaking that produces the emotion, but the tree as coloured : it is not the figure abſtractly conſidered that produces the emotion, but the tree conſidered as of a certain figure. And hence by the way it appears, that the beauty of ſuch an object is complex, reſolvable into ſeveral beauties more ſimple.

it performed. And when we reflect upon the diſtreſs of any perſon, our pain is of the ſame kind with what we felt when eye-witneſſes. In a word, an agreeable or diſagreeable object recalled to the mind in idea, is the occaſion of a pleaſant or painful emotion, of the ſame kind with that produced when the object was preſent. The only difference is, that an idea being fainter than an original perception, the pleaſure or pain produced by the former, is proportionably fainter than that produced by the latter.

Having explained the nature of an emotion and mentioned ſeveral cauſes by which it is produced, we proceed to an obſervation of conſiderable importance in the ſcience of human nature, that ſome emotions are accompanied with deſire, and that others, after a ſhort exiſtence, paſs away without producing deſire of any ſort. The emotion raiſed by a fine landſcape or a magnificent building, vaniſheth generally without attaching our hearts to the object; which alſo happens with relation to a number of fine faces in a crowded aſſembly. But the bulk of emotions are accompanied with deſire of

G 2   one

one fort or other, provided only a fit object for defire be fuggefted. This is remarkably the cafe of emotions raifed by human actions and qualities. A virtuous action raifeth in every fpectator a pleafant e-
motion, which is generally attended with a
defire to do good to the author of the action.
A vicious action, on the other hand, produceth a painful emotion; and of confequence a defire to have the author punifhed. Even things inanimate often raife defire. The goods of fortune are objects of
defire almoft univerfally; and the defire,
when more than commonly vigorous, obtains the name of *avarice*. The pleafant
emotion produced in a fpectator by a capital
picture in the poffeffion of a prince, feldom
raifeth defire. But if fuch a picture be expofed to fale, defire of having or poffeffing
is the natural confequence of the emotion.

If now an emotion be fometimes productive of defire, fomtimes not, it comes
to be a material inquiry, in what refpect a
paffion differs from an emotion. Is paffion
in its nature or feeling diftinguifhable from
emotion? I have been apt to think that
there

there muſt be a diſtinction, when the emotion ſeems in all caſes to precede the paſſion,
and to be the cauſe or occaſion of it.   But
after the ſtricteſt examination, I cannot
perceive any ſuch diſtinction betwixt emotion and paſſion.   What is love to a miſtreſs, for example, but a pleaſant emotion
raiſed by a ſight or idea of the perſon beloved, joined with deſire of enjoyment?   In
what elſe conſiſts the paſſion of reſentment,
but in a painful emotion occaſioned by the
injury, accompanied with deſire to chaſtiſe
the author of the injury ? In general, as to
every ſort of paſſion, we find no more in the
compoſition, but the particulars now mentioned, an emotion pleaſant or painful accompanied with deſire.   What then ſhall
we ſay upon this ſubject ?   Are *paſſion* and
emotion ſynonymous terms ?   This cannot
be averred.   No feeling nor agitation of the
mind void of deſire, is termed a paſſion;
and we have diſcovered that there are many emotions which paſs away without rai-
ſing deſire of any kind.   How is the difficulty to be ſolved ?   There appears to me
but one ſolution, which I reliſh the more,

as

as it renders the doctrine of the passions and emotions simple and perspicuous. The solution follows. An internal motion or agitation of the mind, when it passeth away without raising desire, is denominated *an emotion*: when desire is raised, the motion or agitation is denominated *a passion*. A fine face, for example, raiseth in me a pleasant feeling. If this feeling vanish without producing any effect, it is in proper language an emotion. But if such feeling, by reiterated views of the object, become sufficiently strong to raise desire, it is no longer termed an emotion, but a passion. The same holds in all the other passions. The painful feeling raised in a spectator by a slight injury done to a stranger, being accompanied with no desire of revenge, is termed an emotion. But this injury raiseth in the stranger a stronger emotion, which being accompanied with desire of revenge, is a passion. Again, external expressions of distress, produce in the spectator a painful feeling. This feeling is sometimes so slight as to pass away without any effect, in which case it is an emotion. But if the

feeling

feeling be so strong as to prompt desire of affording relief, it is a passion, and is termed *pity*. Envy is emulation in excess. If the exaltation of a competitor be barely disagreeable, the painful feeling is reckoned an emotion. If it produce desire to depress him, it is reckoned a passion.

To prevent mistakes, it must be observed, that desire here is taken in its proper sense, *viz*. that internal impulse which makes us proceed to action. Desire in a lax sense respects also actions and events that depend not on us, as when I desire that my friend may have a son to represent him, or that my country may flourish in arts and sciences. But such internal act is more properly termed a *wish* than a *desire*.

Having distinguished passion from emotion, we proceed to consider passion more at large, with respect especially to its power of producing action.

We have daily and constant experience for our authority, that no man ever proceeds to action but through the impulse of some antecedent desire. So well established is this observation, and so deeply rooted in

the

the mind, that we can scarce imagine a different system of action. Even a child will say familiarly, What should make me do this or that when I have no inclination to it? Taking it then for granted, that the existence of action depends on antecedent desire; it follows, that where there is no desire there can be no action. This opens another shining distinction betwixt emotions and passions. The former, being without desire, are in their nature quiescent : the latter, involving desire, have a tendency to action, and always produce action where they meet with no obstruction.

Hence it follows, that every passion must have an object, *viz.* that being or thing to which our desire is directed, and with a view to which every action prompted by that desire is performed. The object of every passion is that being or thing which produced it. This will be evident from induction. A fine woman, by her beauty, causes in me the passion of love, which is directed upon her as its object. A man by injuring me, raises my resentment; and becomes thereby the object of my resentment.

ment.   Thus the caufe of a paffion,
and its object, are the fame in different
views.   An emotion, on the other hand,
being in its nature quiefcent and merely a
paffive feeling, muft have a caufe ; but cannot be faid properly fpeaking to have an
object.

As the defire involved in every paffion
leads to action, this action is either ultimate,
or it is done as a means to fome end.
Where the action is ultimate, reafon and
reflection bear no part.   The action is performed blindly by the impulfe of paffion,
without any view.   Thus one in extreme
hunger fnatches at food, without the
flighteft reflection whether it be falutary or
not : Avarice prompts to accumulate wealth
without the leaft view of ufe ; and thereby
abfurdly converts means into an end :   Fear
often makes us fly before we reflect whether we really be in danger : and animal
love not lefs often hurries to fruition, without a fingle thought of gratification.   But
for the moft part, actions are performed as
means to fome end ; and in thefe actions
reafon and reflection always bear a part.

The end is that event which is defired; and the action is deliberately performed in order to bring about that end. Thus affection to my friend involves a defire to make him happy; and the defire to accomplish that end, prompts me to perform what I judge will contribute to it.

Where the action is ultimate, it hath a caufe, *viz.* the impulfe of the paffion. But we cannot properly fay it hath a motive. This term is appropriated to actions that are performed as means to fome end; and the conviction that the action will tend to bring about the end defired, is termed a motive. Thus paffions confidered as caufes of action, are diftinguifhed into two kinds; inftinctive, and deliberative. The firft operating blindly and by mere impulfe, depend entirely upon the fenfitive part of our nature. The other operating by reflection and by motives, are connected with the rational part.

The foregoing difference among the paffions, is the work of nature. Experience brings on fome variations. By all actions performed through the impulfe of paffion, defire

fire is gratified, and the gratification is pleafant. This leffon we have from experience.
And hence it is, that after an action has
often been performed by the impulfe merely
of paffion, the pleafure refulting from performance, confidered beforehand, becomes
a motive, which joins its force with the o-
riginal impulfe in determining us to act.
Thus a child eats by the mere impulfe of
hunger: a young man thinks of the pleafure of gratification, which is a motive for
him to eat: and a man farther advanced in
life, hath the additional motive that it will
contribute to his health.

Inftinctive paffions are diftinguifhed into
two kinds. Where the caufe is internal,
they are denominated *appetites:* where external, they retain the common name of
paffions. Thus hunger, thirft, animal love,
are termed *appetites*; while fear and anger,
even when they operate blindly and by
mere impulfe, are termed *paffions.*

From the definition of a motive above
given, it is eafy to determine, with the
greateft accuracy, what paffions are felfifh,
what focial. No paffion can properly be

termed

termed felfifh, but what prompts me to
exert actions in order for my own good;
nor focial, but what prompts me to exert
actions in order for the good of another.
The motive is that which determines a
paffion to be focial or felfifh. Hence it
follows, that our appetites, which make us
act blindly and by mere impulfe, cannot be
reckoned either focial or felfifh; and as
little the actions they produce. Thus eat-
ing, when prompted by an impulfe merely
of nature, is neither focial nor felfifh. But
add a motive, That it will contribute to my
pleafure or my health, and it becomes in a
meafure felfifh. On the other hand, when
affection moves me to exert actions to the
end folely of advancing my friend's happinefs, without the flighteft regard to my
own gratification, fuch actions are juftly
denominated *focial*; and fo is the affection
that is their caufe. If another motive be
added, That gratifying the affection will
contribute to my own happinefs, the actions I perform become partly felfifh. A-
nimal love when exerted into action by natural impulfe fingly, is neither focial nor
felfifh: when exerted with a view to gratification

tification and in order to make me happy, it is felfiſh. When the motive of giving pleaſure to its object is ſuperadded, it is partly ſocial, partly ſelfiſh. A juſt action when prompted by the love of juſtice ſole-ly, is neither ſocial nor ſelfiſh. When I perform an act of juſtice with a view to the pleaſure of gratification, the action is ſelfiſh. I pay my debt for my own ſake, not with a view to benefit my creditor. But let me ſuppoſe the money has been ad-vanced by a friend without intereſt, purely to oblige me. In this caſe, together with the inclination to do juſtice, there ariſes a motive of gratitude, which reſpects the cre-ditor ſolely, and prompts me to act in or-der to do him good. Here the action is partly ſocial, partly ſelfiſh. Suppoſe again I meet with a ſurpriſing and unexpected act of generoſity, that inſpires me with love to my benefactor and the utmoſt gratitude. I burn to do him good : he is the ſole object of my deſire ; and my own pleaſure in gra-tifying the deſire, vaniſheth out of ſight. In this caſe, the action I perform is purely ſo-cial. Thus it happens, that when a ſocial motive becomes ſtrong, the action is exerted

erted with a view singly to the object of the passion; and the selfish pleasure arising from gratification is never once considered. The same effect of stifling selfish motives, is equally remarkable in other passions that are in no view social. Ambition, for example, when confined to exaltation as its ultimate end, is neither social nor selfish. Let exaltation be considered as a means to make me happy, and the passion becomes so far selfish. But if the desire of exaltation wax strong and inflame my mind, the selfish motive now mentioned is no longer felt. A slight degree of resentment, where my chief view in acting is the pleasure arising to myself from gratifying the passion, is justly denominated *selfish*. Where revenge flames so high as to have no other aim but the destruction of its object, it is no longer selfish. In opposition to a social passion, it may be termed *dissocial* *.

Of

* When this analysis of human nature is considered, not one article of which can with any shadow of truth be controverted, I cannot help being surprised at the blindness of some philosophers, who, by dark and confused notions, are led to deny all motives to action but what arise from self-love.

Man,

Of self, every one hath a direct perception : of other things, we have no knowledge but by means of their attributes. Hence it is, that of self, the perception is more lively than of any other thing. Self is an agreeable object; and, for the reason now given, muft be more agreeable than any other object. Is not this sufficient to account for the prevalence of self-love?

In the foregoing part of this chapter, it is suggested, that some circumstances make beings or things fit objects for desire, others not. This hint muft be pursued. It is a truth ascertained by universal experience, that a thing which in our apprehension is beyond reach, never is the object of desire. No man, in his right senses, desires to walk in the air, or to descend to the centre of the earth. We may amuse ourselves in a reverie, with building castles in the air, and

Man, for ought appears, might possibly have been so framed, as to be susceptible of no passions but what have self for their object. But man thus framed, would be ill fitted for society. Much better is the matter ordered, by enduing him with passions directed entirely to the good of others, as well as with passions directed entirely to his own good.

wishing

wiſhing for what can never happen. But
ſuch things never move deſire. And indeed a deſire to act would be altogether ab-
ſurd, when we are conſcious that the action
is beyond our power. In the next place,
though the difficulty of attainment with reſpect to things within reach, often inflames
deſire; yet where the proſpect of attainment is faint and the event extremely uncertain, the object, however agreeable, ſeldom raiſeth any ſtrong deſire. Thus beauty or other good qualities in a woman of
rank, ſeldom raiſes love in any man greatly
her inferior. In the third place, different
objects, equally within reach, raiſe emotions in different degrees; and when deſire
accompanies any of theſe emotions, its
ſtrength, as is natural, is proportioned to
that of its cauſe. Hence the remarkable
difference among deſires directed upon beings inanimate, animate, and rational. The
emotion cauſed by a rational being, is out of
meaſure ſtronger than any cauſed by an animal without reaſon; and an emotion raiſed
by ſuch an animal, is ſtronger than what is
cauſed by any thing inanimate. There is a
                                    ſeparate

separate reason why desire of which a rational being is the object should be the strongest. Desire directed upon such a being, is gratified many ways, by loving, serving, benefiting, the object; and it is a well known truth, that our desires naturally swell by exercise. Desire directed upon an inanimate being, susceptible neither of pleasure nor pain, is not capable of a higher gratification than that of acquiring the property. Hence it is, that though every feeling which raiseth desire, is strictly speaking a passion; yet commonly those feelings only are denominated passions of which sensible beings capable of pleasure and pain are the objects.

S E C T.   II.

Causes of the emotions of joy and sorrow.

THis subject was purposely reserved for a separate section, because it could not, with perspicuity, be handled under the general head. An emotion involving desire is termed *a passion*; and when the desire is

VOL. I.   I   fulfilled,

fulfilled, the paffion is faid to be gratified.
The gratification of every paffion muft be
pleafant, or in other words produce a pleafant emotion ; for nothing can be more natural, than that the accomplifhment of any
wifh or defire fhould affect us with joy.   I
cannot even except the cafe, where a man,
through remorfe, is defirous to chaftife and
punifh himfelf.   The joy of gratification is
properly called an emotion; becaufe it makes
us happy in our prefent fituation, and is ultimate in its nature, not having a tendency
to any thing beyond.   On the other hand,
forrow muft be the refult of an event contrary to what we defire ; for if the accomplifhment of defire produce joy, it is equally
natural that difappointment fhould produce
forrow.

An event fortunate or unfortunate, that
falls out by accident without being forefeen
or thought of, and which therefore could
not be the object of defire, raifeth an emotion of the fame kind with that now mentioned.   But the caufe muft be different;
for there can be no gratification where there
is no defire.   We have not however far to
                                        feek

feek for a caufe. A man cannot be indifferent to an event that affects him or any of
his connections.   If it be fortunate, it gives
him joy; if unfortunate, it gives him forrow.

In no fituation doth joy rife to a greater
height, than upon the removal of any violent diftrefs of mind or body; and in no fituation doth forrow rife to a greater height,
than upon the removal of what makes us
happy.   The fenfibility of our nature ferves
in part to account for thefe effects.   Other
caufes alfo concur.   We can be under no
violent diftrefs without an anxious defire to
be free from it; and therefore its removal is
a high gratification.   We cannot be poffeffed
of any thing that makes us happy, without
wifhing its continuance; and therefore its
removal by croffing our wifhes muft create
forrow.   Nor is this all.   The principle of
contraft comes in for its fhare.   An emotion
of joy arifing upon the removal of pain, is
increafed by contraft when we reflect upon
our former diftrefs.   En emotion of forrow
upon being deprived of any good, is increa-

fed by contraſt when we reflect upon our former happineſs.

> *Jaffier*. There's not a wretch that lives on
>   common charity,
> But's happier than me.   For I have known
> The luſcious ſweets of plenty : every night
> Have ſlept with ſoft content about my head,
> And never wak'd but to a joyful morning.
> Yet now muſt fall like a full ear of corn,
> Whoſe bloſſom 'ſcap'd, yet's wither'd in the
>   ripening.
> *Venice preſerv'd, act* 1. *ſc.* 1.

It hath always been reckoned difficult to account for the extreme pleaſure that follows a ceſſation of bodily pain; as when one is relieved from the rack, or from a violent fit of the ſtone.   What is ſaid, explains this difficulty in the eaſieſt and ſimpleſt manner.   Ceſſation of bodily pain is not of itſelf a pleaſure; for a *non-ens* or a negative can neither give pleaſure nor pain.   But man is ſo framed by nature as to rejoice when he is eaſed of pain, as well as to be ſorrowful when deprived of any good.   This branch of our conſtitution, is chiefly the
                                        cauſe

caufe of the pleafure.   The gratification of defire comes in as an acceffory caufe; and contraft joins its force, by increafing the fenfe of our prefent happinefs.   In the cafe of an acute pain, a peculiar circumftance contributes its part.   The brifk circulation of the animal fpirits occafioned by acute pain, continues after the pain is vanifhed, and produceth a very pleafant feeling.   Sicknefs hath not that effect, becaufe it is always attended with a depreffion of fpirits.

Hence it is, that the gradual diminution of acute pain, occafions a mixt emotion, partly pleafant, partly painful. The partial diminution produceth joy in proportion ; but the remaining pain balanceth our joy.   This mixt feeling, however, hath no long endurance.   For the joy that arifeth upon the diminution of pain, foon vanifheth ; and leaveth in the undifturbed poffeffion, that degree of pain which remains.

What is above obferved about bodily pain, is equally applicable to the diftreffes of the mind ; and accordingly it is a common artifice, to prepare us for the reception of good news by alarming our fears.

S E C T.

S E C T.   III.

Sympathetic emotion of virtue, and its cause.

ONE feeling there is, that merits a deliberate view, for its fingularity, as well as
utility.   Whether to call it an emotion or a
paffion, feems uncertain.   The former it
can fcarce be, becaufe it involves defire ; and
the latter it can fcarce be, becaufe it has no
object.   But this feeling and its nature will
be beft underftood from examples.   A fignal act of gratitude, produceth in the fpectator love or efteem for the author.   The
fpectator hath at the fame time a feparate
feeling; which, being mixed with love or
efteem, the capital emotion, hath not been
much adverted to.   It is a vague feeling of
gratitude, which hath no object; but
which, however, difpofes the fpectator to
acts of gratitude, more than upon ordinary
occafions.   Let any man attentively confider his own heart when he thinks warmly
of any fignal act of gratitude, and he will
be confcious of this feeling, as diftinct from

the

the efteem or admiration he has for the grateful perfon. It merits our utmoft attention, by unfolding a curious piece of mechanifm in the nature of man. The feeling is fingular in the following refpect, that it involves a defire to perform acts of gratitude, without having any particular object; though in this ftate the mind, wonderfully difpofed toward an object, neglects no object upon which it can vent itfelf. Any act of kindnefs or good-will that would not be regarded upon another occafion, is greedily feized; and the vague feeling is converted into a real paffion of gratitude. In fuch a ftate, favours are returned double.

Again, a courageous action produceth in a fpectator the paffion of admiration directed upon the author. But befide this well-known paffion, a feparate feeling is raifed in the fpectator; which may be called *an emotion of courage*, becaufe while under its influence he is confcious of a boldnefs and intrepidity beyond ordinary, and longs for proper objects upon which to exert this emotion.

Spumantemque

Spumantemque dari, pecora inter inertia, votis
Optat aprum, aut fulvum defcendere monte leo-
 nem.

Æneid. iv. 158.

Non altramente 'il tauro, oue l' irriti
Gelofo amor con ftimoli pungenti
Horribilmente mugge, e co' muggiti
Gli fpirti in fe rifueglia, e l'ire ardenti:
E'l corno aguzza a i tronchi, e par ch' inuiti
Con vani colpi a' la battaglia i venti.

Taffo, canto 7. ft. 55.

So full of valour that they fmote the air
For breathing in their faces.

Tempeft, act. 4. fc. 4.

For another example, let us figure fome
grand and heroic action, highly agreeable
to the fpectator. Befide a fingular veneration for the author, the fpectator feels in
himfelf an unufual dignity of character,
which difpofeth him to great and noble actions. And herein principally confifts the
extreme delight every one hath in the hiftories of conquerors and heroes.

This fingular feeling, which may be
termed *the fympathetic emotion of virtue*, refembles,

fembles, in one refpect, the well-known appetites that lead to the propagation and prefervation of the fpecies. The appetites of
hunger, thirft, and animal love, arife in the
mind without being directed upon any particular object; and in no cafe whatever is
the mind more folicitous for a proper object,
than when under the influence of any of
thefe appetites.

The feeling I have endeavoured to e-
volve, may well be termed *the fympathe-*
tic emotion of virtue; for it is raifed in a
fpectator by virtuous actions of every kind,
and by no other fort. When we contemplate a virtuous action, which never fails to
delight us and to prompt our love for the
author, the mind is warmed and put into a
tone fimilar to what infpired the virtuous action. The propenfity we have to fuch actions is fo much enlivened, as to become
for a time an actual emotion. But no
man hath a propenfity to vice as fuch. On
the contrary, a wicked deed difgufts him,
and makes him abhor the author. This
abhorrence is a ftrong antidote fo long as

any impreſſion remains of the wicked action.

In a rough road, a halt to view a fine country is refreſhing; and here a delightful proſpect opens upon us. It is indeed wonderful to ſee what incitements there are to virtue in the human frame. Juſtice is perceived to be our duty, and it is guarded by natural puniſhments, from which the guilty never eſcape. To perform noble and generous actions, a warm ſenſe of dignity and ſuperior excellence is a moſt efficacious incitement*. And to leave virtue in no quarter unſupported, here is unfolded an admirable contrivance, by which good example commands the heart and adds to virtue the force of habit. Did our moral feelings extend no farther than to approve the action and to beſtow our affection on the author, good example would not have great influence. But to give it the utmoſt force, nothing can be better contrived than the ſympathetic emotion under conſidera-

* See Eſſays upon morality and natural religion, part 1. eſſay 2. ch. 4.

tion,

tion, which prompts us to imitate what we admire. This fingular emotion will readily find an object to exert itfelf upon; and at any rate, it never exifts without producing fome effect. Virtuous emotions of this fort, are in fome degree an exercife of virtue. They are a mental exercife at leaft, if they fhow not externally. And every exercife of virtue, internal and external, leads to habit; for a difpofition or propenfity of the mind, like a limb of the body, becomes ftronger by exercife. Proper means, at the fame time, being ever at hand to raife this fympathetic emotion, its frequent reiteration may, in a good meafure, fupply the want of a more complete exercife. Thus, by proper difcipline, every perfon may acquire a fet-tled habit of virtue. Intercourfe with men of worth, hiftories of generous and difin-terefted actions, and frequent meditation upon them, keep the fympathetic emotion in conftant exercife, which by degrees intro-duceth a habit, and confirms the authority of virtue. With refpect to education in particular, what a fpacious and commo-dious avenue to the heart of a young per-fon, is here opened?

S E C T. IV.

In many instances one emotion is productive of
another. The same of passions.

IN the first chapter it is observed, that the
relations by which things are mutually
connected, have a remarkable influence in
regulating the train of our ideas. I here
add, that they have an influence not less
remarkable, in generating emotions and
passions. Beginning with the former, it
holds in fact, that an agreeable object makes
every thing connected with it appear agreeable. The mind gliding sweetly and easily
through related objects, carries along the
beauty of objects that made a figure, and
blends that beauty with the idea of the present object, which thereby appears more
agreeable than when considered apart *

This

---

* Such proneness has the mind to this communication of
properties, that we often find properties ascribed to a related
object, of which naturally it is not susceptible. Sir Richard
Greenville in a single ship being surprised by the Spanish fleet,
was advised to retire. He utterly refused to turn from the e-
nemy;

This reason may appear obscure and meta-physical, but it must be relished when we attend to the following examples, which establish the fact beyond all dispute. No relation is more intimate than that betwixt a being and its qualities; and accordingly, the affection I bear a man expands itself readily upon all his qualities, which by that means make a greater figure in my mind than more substantial qualities in others. The talent of speaking in a friend, is more regarded than that of acting in a person with whom I have no connection; and graceful motion in a mistress, gives more delight than consummate prudence in any other woman.   Affection sometimes rises so high,

nemy; declaring, " he would rather die, than dishonour him-" self, his country, and her Majesty's ship." *Hakluyt, vol.* 2. *part* 2. *p.* 169. To aid the communication of properties in such instances, there always must be a momentary personifi-cation. A ship must be imagined a sensible being, to make it susceptible of honour or dishonour. In the battle of Mantinea, Epaminondas being mortally wounded, was carried to his tent in a manner dead. Recovering his senses, the first thing he inquired about was his shield; which being brought, he kissed it as the companion of his valour and glory. It must be remarked, that among the Greeks and Romans it was deemed infamous for a soldier to return from battle without his shield.

as

as to convert defects into properties.   The
wry neck of Alexander was imitated by his
courtiers as a real beauty, without intention to flatter.   Thus Lady Piercy, speaking of her husband Hotspur,

―――――――――――――――― By his light
Did all the chivalry of England move,
To do brave acts.   He was indeed the glass,
Wherein the noble youth did dress themselves.
He had no legs that practis'd not his gait:
And speaking thick, which Nature made his ble-
  mish,
Became the accents of the valiant:
For those who could speak low and tardily,
Would turn their own perfection to abuse,
To seem like him.

     Second part, *Henry* IV. *act* 2. *sc*. 6.

 When the passion of love has ended its
course, its object becomes quite a different
creature.――― Nothing left of that genteel
motion, that gaiety, that sprightly conversation, those numberless graces, that formerly, in the lover's opinion, charmed all
hearts.

 The same communication of passion ob-
            tains

tains in the relation of principal and acceſſory.   Pride, of which ſelf is the object, expands itſelf upon a houſe, a garden, ſer-
vants, equipage, and every thing of that
nature.   A lover addreſſeth his miſtreſs's
glove in the following terms :

Sweet ornament that decks a thing divine.

A temple is in a proper ſenſe an acceſſory of
the deity to which it is dedicated.   Diana
is chaſte, and not only her temple, but the
very iſicle which hangs on it, muſt partake
of that property :

The noble ſiſter of Poplicola,
The moon of Rome; chaſte as the iſicle
That's curdled by the froſt from pureſt ſnow,
And hangs on Dian's temple.
                    Coriolanus, act 5. *ſc.* 3.

  Thus it is, that the reſpect and eſteem,
which the great, the powerful, the opulent
naturally command, are in ſome meaſure
communicated to their dreſs, to their manners, and to all their connections.   It is this
                              principle,

principle, which in matters left to our own choice prevails over the natural taste of beauty and propriety, and gives currency to what is called *the fashion*.

By means of the same easiness of transition, the bad qualities of an object are carried along, and grafted upon related objects. Every good quality in a person is extinguished by hatred; and every bad quality is spread upon all his connections. A relation more slight and transitory than that of hatred, may have the same effect. Thus the bearer of bad tidings becomes an object of aversion:

Fellow begone, I cannot brook thy sight,
This news hath made thee a most ugly man.
King John, act 3. sc. 1.

Yet the first bringer of unwelcome news
Hath but a losing office: and his tongue
Sounds ever after, as a sullen bell
Remember'd, tolling a departing friend.
Second part, Henry IV. act 1. sc. 3.

This disposition of the mind to communicate the properties of one object to another,

ther, is not always proportioned to the intimacy of their connection. The order of the tranfition from object to object, hath alfo an influence. The fenfe of order operates not lefs powerfully in this cafe, than in the fucceffion of ideas *. If a thing be agreeable in itfelf, all its acceffories appear agreeable. But the agreeablenefs of an acceffory, extends not itfelf fo readily to the principal. Any drefs upon a fine woman is becoming ; but the moft elegant ornaments upon one that is homely, have fcarce any effect to mend her appearance. The reafon will be obvious, from what is faid in the chapter above cited. The mind paffes more eafily from the principal to its acceffories, than in the oppofite direction.

The emotions produced as above may properly be termed *fecondary*, being occafioned either by antecedent emotions or antecedent paffions, which in this refpect may be termed *primary*. And to complete the prefent theory, I muft now remark a difference betwixt a primary emotion and a

* See chap. 1.

primary paffion in the production of fecondary emotions. A fecondary emotion cannot but be more faint than the primary;
and therefore, if the chief or principal object have not the power to raife a paffion,
the acceffory object will have ftill lefs power.
But if a paffion be raifed by the principal
object, the fecondary emotion may readily
fwell into a paffion for the acceffory, provided the acceffory be a proper object for defire. And thus it happens that one paffion
is often productive of another. Examples
are without number: the fole difficulty is a
proper choice. I begin with felf-love, and
the power it hath to generate other paffions.
The love which parents bear their children,
is an illuftrious example of the foregoing
doctrine. Every man, befide making part
of a greater fyftem, like a comet, a planet,
or fatellite only; hath a lefs fyftem of his
own, in the centre of which he reprefents
the fun difperfing his fire and heat all a-
round. The connection between a man
and his children, fundamentally that of
caufe and effect, becomes, by the addition of
other circumftances, the completeft that can
be

be among individuals; and therefore, felf-
love, the moſt vigorous of all paſſions, is
readily expanded upon children. The ſe-
condary emotion they at firſt produce by
means of their connection, is, generally
ſpeaking, ſufficiently ſtrong to move deſire
even from the beginning; and the new paſſion ſwells by degrees, till it rival in ſome
meaſure ſelf-love, the primary paſſion. The
following caſe will demonſtrate the truth of
this theory. Remorſe for betraying a friend,
or murdering an enemy in cold blood,
makes a man even hate himſelf. In this
ſtate, it is a matter of experience, that he
is ſcarce conſcious of any affection to his
children, but rather of diſguſt or ill-will.
What cauſe can be aſſigned for this change,
other than the hatred which beginning
at himſelf, is expanded upon his children?
And if ſo, may we not with equal reaſon
derive from ſelf-love the affection a man
for ordinary has to them?

The affection a man bears to his blood-
relations, depends on the ſame principle.
Self-love is alſo expanded upon them; and
the communicated paſſion, is more or leſs

vigorous in proportion to the connection. Nor doth self-love reft here: it is, by the force of connection, communicated even to things inanimate. And hence the affection a man bears to his property, and to every thing he calls his own.

Friendſhip, leſs vigorous than ſelf-love, is, for that reaſon, leſs apt to communicate itſelf to children or other relations. Inſtances however are not wanting, of ſuch communicated paſſion ariſing from friendſhip when it is ſtrong. Friendſhip may go higher in the matrimonial ſtate than in any other condition: and Otway, in *Venice preſerv'd*, ſhows a fine taſte in taking advantage of that circumſtance. In the ſcene where Belvidera ſues to her father for pardon, ſhe is repreſented as pleading her mother's merit, and the reſemblance ſhe bore to her mother.

Priuli. My daughter!
Belvidera. Yes, your daughter, by a mother
Virtuous and noble, faithful to your honour,
Obedient to your will, kind to your wiſhes,
Dear to your arms. By all the joys ſhe gave you,
When

When in her blooming years fhe was your trea-
　　　　　fure,
Look kindly on me; in my face behold
The lineaments of hers y' have kifs'd fo often,
Pleading the caufe of your poor caft-off child.

And again,

　　Belvidera. Lay me, I beg you, lay me
By the dear afhes of my tender mother.
She would have pitied me, had fate yet fpar'd her.
　　　　　　　　　Act 5. *fc.* 1.

This explains why any meritorious action or
any illuftrious qualification in my fon or
my friend, is apt to make me overvalue myfelf. If I value my friend's wife or his fon
upon account of their connection with him,
it is ftill more natural that I fhould value
myfelf upon account of my own connection
with him.

　Friendfhip, or any other focial affection,
may produce oppofite effects. Pity, by interefting us ftrongly for the perfon in diftrefs,
muft of confequence inflame our refentment
againft the author of the diftrefs. For, in
general, the affection we have for any man,
　　　　　　　　　　　　　　　　　generates

generates in us good-will to his friends and ill-will to his enemies. Shakefpear fhows great art in the funeral oration pronounced by Antony over the body of Cæfar. He firft endeavours to excite grief in the hearers, by dwelling upon the deplorable lofs of fo great a man. This paffion raifed to a pitch, interefting them ftrongly in Cæfar's fate, could not fail to produce a lively fenfe of the treachery and cruelty of the confpirators; an infallible method to inflame the refentment of the multitude beyond all bounds.

> *Antony.* If you have tears, prepare to fhed them
>   now.
> You all do know this mantle; I remember
> The firft time ever Cæfar put it on,
> 'Twas on a fummer's evening in his tent,
> That day he overcame the Nervii——
> Look! in this place ran Caffius' dagger through;—
> See what a rent the envious Cafca made.——
> Through this the well-beloved Brutus ftabb'd;
> And as he pluck'd his curfed fteel away,
> Mark how the blood of Cæfar follow'd it!
> As rufhing out of doors, to be refolv'd,
> If Brutus fo unkindly knock'd, or no:
> For Brutus, as you know, was Cæfar's angel.
>   Judge,

Judge, oh you gods! how dearly Cæfar lov'd him;
This, this, was the unkindeft cut of all;
For when the noble Cæfar faw him ftab,
Ingratitude, more ftrong than traitors' arms,
Quite vanquifh'd him; then burft his mighty heart:
And, in his mantle muffling up his face,
Which all the while ran blood, great Cæfar fell,
Even at the bafe of Pompey's ftatue.
O what a fall was there, my countrymen!
Then I and you, and all of us fell down,
Whilft bloody treafon flourifh'd over us.
O, now you weep; and I perceive you feel
The dint of pity; thefe are gracious drops.
Kind fouls! what, weep you when you but be-
            hold
Our Cæfar's vefture wounded? look you here!
Here is himfelf, marr'd, as you fee, by traitors.
                        Julius Cæfar, act 3. *fc.* 6.

Had Antony directed upon the confpirators the thoughts of his audience, without
paving the way by raifing their grief, his
fpeech perhaps might have failed of fuccefs.

Hatred and other diffocial paffions, produce effects directly oppofite to thofe above
mentioned. If I hate a man, his children,
his relations, nay his property, become to
                                    me

me objects of averfion. His enemies, on the other hand, I am difpofed to efteem.

The more flight and tranfitory connec-tions, have generally no power to pro-duce a communicated paffion. Anger, when fudden and violent, is one exception; for if the perfon who did the injury be re-moved out of reach, this paffion will vent itfelf upon any related object, how-ever flight the relation be. Another ex-ception makes a greater figure. A group of beings or things, becomes often the object of a communicated paffion, even where the relation of the individuals to the principal object is but faint. Thus though I put no value upon a fingle man for living in the fame town with myfelf; my townfmen however, confidered in a body, are preferred before others. This is ftill more remarkable with refpect to my countrymen in general. The grandeur of the complex object, fwells the paffion of felf-love by the relation I have to my native country; and every paf-fion, when it fwells beyond its ordinary bounds, hath, in that circumftance, a pe-culiar tendency to expand itfelf along rela-

ted

ted objects. In fact, instances are not rare, of persons, who, upon all occasions, are willing to sacrifice their lives and fortunes for their country. Such influence upon the mind of man, hath a complex object, or, more properly speaking, a general term *.

The sense of order hath, in the communication of passion, an influence not less remarkable than in the communication of emotions. It is a common observation, that a man's affection to his parents is less vigorous than to his children. The order of nature in descending to children, aids the transition of the affection. The ascent to a parent, contrary to this order, makes the transition more difficult. Gratitude to a benefactor is readily extended to his children; but not so readily to his parents. The difference however betwixt the natural and inverted order, is not so considerable, but that it may be balanced by other circumstances. Pliny † gives an account of a woman of rank condemned

* See Essays on morality and natural religion, part 1. ess. 2. ch. 5.

† Lib. 7. cap. 36.

M

to die for a crime; and, to avoid public
fhame, detained in prifon to die of hunger.
Her life being prolonged beyond expectation, it was difcovered, that fhe was nou-
rifhed by fucking milk from the breafts of
her daughter. This inftance of filial piety,
which aided the tranfition and made a-
fcent not lefs eafy than defcent is for ordinary, procured a pardon to the mother,
and a penfion to both. The ftory of Androcles and the lion * may be accounted for
in the fame manner. The admiration, of
which the lion was the caufe, for his kindnefs
and gratitude to Androcles, produced good-
will to Androcles, and pardon of his crime.

And this leads to other obfervations upon
communicated paffions. I love my daughter lefs after fhe is married, and my mother
lefs after a fecond marriage. The marriage
of my fon or my father diminifhes not my affection fo remarkably. The fame obfervation
holds with refpect to friendfhip, gratitude,
and other paffions. The love I bear my
friend, is but faintly extended to his married daughter. The refentment I have

* Aulus Gellius, lib. 5. cap. 14.

against

againſt a man, is readily extended againſt
children who make part of his family: not
ſo readily againſt children who are forisfa-
miliated, eſpecially by marriage.   This
difference is alſo more remarkable in daughters than in ſons.   Theſe are curious facts;
and to evolve the cauſe we muſt examine
minutely, that operation of the mind by
which a paſſion is extended to a related object.   In conſidering two things as related,
the mind is not ſtationary, but paſſeth and
repaſſeth from the one to the other, viewing
the relation from each of them perhaps
oftener than once.   This holds more eſpecially in conſidering a relation betwixt
things of unequal rank, as betwixt the
cauſe and the effect, or betwixt a principal
and an acceſſory.   In contemplating the
relation betwixt a building and its ornaments, the mind is not ſatisfied with a
ſingle tranſition from the former to the
latter.   It muſt alſo view the relation, beginning at the latter, and paſſing from it to
the former.   This vibration of the mind in
paſſing and repaſſing betwixt things that are
related, explains the facts above mentioned.

The

The mind paſſeth eaſily from the father to the daughter; but where the daughter is married, this new relation attracts the mind, and obſtructs, in ſome meaſure, the return from the daughter to the father. Any obſtruction the mind meets with in paſſing and repaſſing betwixt its objects, occaſions a like obſtruction in the communication of paſſion. The marriage of a male obſtructs leſs the eaſineſs of tranſition; becauſe a male is leſs ſunk by the relation of marriage than a female.

The foregoing inſtances, are of paſſion communicated from one object to another. But one paſſion may be generated by another, without change of object. It may in general be obſerved, that a paſſion paves the way to others, ſimilar in their tone, whether directed upon the ſame or upon a different object. For the mind heated by any paſſion, is, in that ſtate, more ſuſceptible of a new impreſſion in a ſimilar tone, than when cool and quieſcent. It is a common obſervation, that pity generally produceth friendſhip for a perſon in diſtreſs.

Pity

Pity interefts us in its object, and recommends all its virtuous qualities. For this reafon, female beauty fhows beft in diftrefs ; and is more apt to infpire love, than upon ordinary occafions. But it is chiefly to be remarked, that pity, warming and melting the fpectator, prepares him for the reception of other tender affections ; and pity is readily improved into love or friendfhip, by a certain tendernefs and concern for the object, which is the tone of both paffions. The aptitude of pity to produce love is beautifully illuftrated by Shakefpear.

Othello.   Her father lov'd me, oft invited me ;
Still queftion'd me the ftory of my life,
From year to year ; the battles, fieges, fortunes,
That I have paft.
I ran it through, e'en from my boyifh days,
To th' very moment that he bad me tell it :
Wherein I fpoke of moft difaft'rous chances,
Of moving accidents by flood and field ;
Of hair-breadth 'fcapes in th' imminent deadly
        breach ;
Of being taken by the infolent foe,
And fold to flavery; of my redemption thence,
And with it, all my travel's hiftory.
——————————— All thefe to hear
                                Would

Would Defdemona ferioufly incline ;
But ftill the houfe-affairs would draw her thence,
Which ever as fhe could with hafte difpatch,
She'd come again, and with a greedy ear
Devour up my difcourfe: which I obferving,
Took once a pliant hour, and found good means
To draw from her a prayer of earneft heart,
That I would all my pilgrimage dilate,
Whereof by parcels fhe had fomething heard,
But not diftinctively. I did confent,
And often did beguile her of her tears,
When I did fpeak of fome diftrefsful ftroke
That my youth fuffer'd. My ftory being done,
She gave me for my pains a world of fighs :
She fwore, in faith, 'twas ftrange, 'twas paffing
    ftrange —
'Twas pitiful, 'twas wondrous pitiful —
She wifh'd fhe had not heard it :— yet fhe wifh'd,
That heav'n had made her fuch a man :— fhe
    thank'd me,
And bad me, if I had a friend that lov'd her,
I fhould but teach him how to tell my ftory,
And that would woo her. On this hint I fpake,
She lov'd me for the dangers I had paft,
And I lov'd her, that fhe did pity them :
This only is the witchcraft I have us'd.

Othello, act 1. *fc.* 8.

In

In this inftance it will be obferved that admiration concurred with pity to produce love.

S E C T.   V.

Caufes of the paffions of fear and anger.

FEar and anger, to anfwer the purpofes of nature, are happily fo contrived as to operate either inftinctively or deliberately. So far as they prompt actions confidered as means leading to a certain end, they fall in with the general fyftem, and require no particular explanation. If any object have a threatening appearance, reafon fuggefts means to avoid the danger. If I am injured, the firft thing I think of, is in what manner I fhall be revenged, and what means I fhall employ. Thefe particulars are not lefs obvious than natural. But as the paffions of fear and anger, fo far as inftinctive, are lefs familiar to us, and their nature generally not underftood; I thought it would not be unacceptable to the reader

to

to have them accurately delineated. He may alſo poſſibly reliſh the opportunity of this ſpecimen, to have the nature of inſtinctive paſſions more fully explained than there was formerly occaſion to do. I begin with fear.

Self-preſervation is to individuals a matter of too great importance to be left entirely under the guardianſhip of ſelf-love, which cannot be put in exerciſe otherwiſe than by the intervention of reaſon and reflection. Nature hath acted here with her uſual precaution and foreſight. Fear and anger are paſſions common to all men; and by operating inſtinctively, they frequently afford ſecurity when the ſlower operations of deliberative reaſon would be too late. We take nouriſhment commonly, not by the direction of reaſon, but by the incitement of hunger and thirſt. In the ſame manner, we avoid danger by the incitement of fear, which often, before there is time for reflection, placeth us in ſafety. This matter then is ordered with conſummate wiſdom. It is not within the reach of fancy, to conceive any thing better fitted

to

to anfwer its purpofe, than this inftinctive paffion of fear, which, upon the firft fur-mife of danger, operates inftantaneoufly without reflection. So little doth the paf-fion, in fuch inftances, depend on reafon, that we often find it exerted even in con-tradiction to reafon, and when we are con-fcious that there is no hazard. A man who is not much upon his guard, cannot avoid fhrinking at a blow, though he knows it to be aimed in fport; nor clofing his eyes at the approach of what may hurt them, though he is confident it will not come their length. Influenced by the fame inftinctive paffion of fear, infants are much affected with a ftern look, a menacing tone, or other expreffion of anger; though, being incapable of reflection, they cannot form the flighteft judge-ment about the import of thefe figns. This is all that is neceffary to be faid in general. The natural connection betwixt fear and the external figns of anger, will be handled in the chapter of the external figns of emotions and paffions.

Fear provides for felf-prefervation by flying from harm; anger, by repelling it. Nothing indeed can be better contrived to repel or prevent injury, than anger or resentment. Destitute of this passion, men, like defence-less lambs, would lie constantly open to mischief *. Deliberate anger caused by a voluntary injury, is too well known to require any explanation. If my desire be in general to resent an affront, I must use means, and these means must be discovered by reflection. Deliberation is here requisite; and in this, which is the ordinary case, the passion seldom exceeds just bounds. But where anger suddenly inflames me to return a blow, the passion is instinctive, and the action ultimate; and it is chiefly in such cases that the passion is rash and un-governable, because it operates blindly, without affording time for reason or delibe-ration.

* Brasidas being surprised by the bite of a mouse he had catched, let it slip out of his fingers. " No creature (says " he) is so contemptible, but what may provide for its own " safety, if it have courage to defend itself."

Plutarch. Apothegmata.

Instinctive

Inftinctive anger is frequently raifed by bodily pain, which, when fudden and exceffive as by a ftroke on a tender part, ruffling the temper and unhinging the mind, is in its tone fimilar to anger. Bodily pain by this means difpofes to anger, which is as fuddenly raifed, provided an object be found to vent it upon. Anger commonly is not provoked otherwife than by a voluntary injury. But when a man is thus beforehand difpofed to anger, he is not nice nor fcrupulous about an object. The man who gave the ftroke, however accidentally, is by an inflammable temper held a proper object, merely becaufe he was the occafion of the pain. It is ftill a ftronger example of the kind, that a ftock or a ftone, by which I am hurt, becomes an object for my refentment. I am violently incited to bray it to atoms. The paffion indeed in this cafe is but momentary. It vanifheth with the firft reflection, being attended with no circumftance that can excufe it in any degree. Nor is this irrational effect confined to bodily pain. Inward diftrefs, when exceffive, may be the occafion of effects equally irrational.

When

When a friend is danger and the event uncertain, the perturbation of mind occafioned thereby, will, in a fiery temper, produce momentary fits of anger againft this very friend, however innocent. Thus Shakefpear, in the *Tempeft*,

Alonzo. —————— Sit down and reft.
Ev'n here I will put off my hope, and keep it
No longer for my flatterer : he is drown'd
Whom thus we ftray to find, and the fea mocks
Our fruftrate fearch on land. Well, let him go.
Act 3. *fc.* 3.

The final words, *Well, let him go*, are an expreffion of impatience and anger at Ferdinand, whofe abfence greatly diftreffed his father, dreading that he was loft in the ftorm. This nice operation of the human mind, is by Shakefpear exhibited upon another occafion, and finely painted. In the tragedy of *Othello*, Iago, by dark hints and fufpicious circumftances, had roufed Othello's jealoufy; which, however, appeared too flightly founded to be vented upon Defdemona, its proper object. The perturbation and diftrefs of mind thereby

by occafioned, produced a momentary refentment againft Iago, confidered as occafioning the jealoufy though innocent.

> *Othello.* Villain, be fure thou prove my love a
> whore ;
> Be fure of it : give me the ocular proof.
> Or by the wrath of man's eternal foul
> Thou hadft been better have been born a dog,
> Than anfwer my wak'd wrath.
> *Iago.* Is't come to this ?
> *Othello.* Make me fee't; or, at the leaft, fo prove
> That the probation bear no hinge or loop   [it,
> To hang a doubt on : or woe upon thy life !
> *Iago.* My Noble Lord ——
> *Othello.* If thou doft flander her and torture me,
> Never pray more ; abandon all remorfe ;
> On horrors head horrors accumulate ;
> Do deeds to make heav'n weep, all earth amaz'd :
> For nothing canft thou to damnation add
> Greater than that.
>
> *Othello*, *act* 3. *fc.* 8.

This blind and abfurd effect of anger, is
more gaily illuftrated by Addifon, in a ftory,
the *dramatis perfonæ* of which are a cardinal,
and a fpy retained in pay for intelligence.
The cardinal is reprefented as minuting
down

down every thing that is told him. The
ſpy begins with a low voice, " Such an one
" the advocate whiſpered to one of his
" friends within my hearing, that your E-
" minence was a very great poltron ;" and
after having given his patron time to take it
down, adds, " That another called him a
" mercenary raſcal in a public converſation."
The cardinal replies, " Very well," and
bids him go on. The ſpy proceeds, and
loads him with reports of the ſame nature,
till the cardinal riſes in great wrath, calls
him an impudent ſcoundrel, and kicks him
out of the room *.

We meet with inſtances every day of reſentment raiſed by loſs at play, and wreak-
ed on the cards or dice. But anger, a furious paſſion, is ſatisfied with a connection
ſtill ſlighter than that of cauſe and effect,
of which Congreve, in the *Mourning Bride*,
gives one beautiful example.

> *Gonſalez.* Have comfort.
> *Almeria.* Curs'd be that tongue that bids me be
> of comfort,

* Spectator, Nº 439.

Curs'd

Curs'd my own tongue that could not move his
       pity,
Curs'd thefe weak hands that could not hold him
       here,
For he is gone to doom Alphonfo's death.

Act 4. *fc.* 8.

I have chofen to exhibit anger in its more
rare appearances, for in thefe we can beft
trace its nature and extent. In the examples
above given, it appears to be an abfurd paffion and altogether irrational. But we ought
to confider, that it is not the intention of
nature to fubject this paffion, in every inftance, to reafon and reflection. It was given us to prevent or to repel injuries; and,
like fear, it often operates blindly and inftinctively, without the leaft view to confequences. The very firft fenfation of harm,
fets it in motion to repel injury by punifhment. Were it more cool and deliberate,
it would lofe its threatening appearance, and
be infufficient to guard us againft violence
and mifchief. When fuch is and ought to
be the nature of the paffion, it is not wonderful to find it exerted irregularly and ca-
pricioufly, as it fometimes is where the mif-
                    chief

chief is fudden and unforefeen. All the harm that can be done by the paffion in this cafe, is inftantaneous; for the fhorteft delay fets all to rights; and circumftances are feldom fo unlucky as to put it in the power of a paffionate man to do much harm in an inftant.

SECT. VI.

Emotions caufed by fiction.

THE attentive reader will obferve, that in accounting for paffions and emotions, no caufe hitherto has been affigned but what hath a real exiftence. Whether it be a being, action, or quality, that moveth us, it is fuppofed to be an object of our knowledge, or at leaft of our belief. This obfervation difcovers to us that the fubject is not yet exhaufted; becaufe our paffions, as all the world know, are moved by fiction as well as by truth. In judging beforehand of man, fo remarkably addicted to truth and reality, one fhould little dream that

that fiction could have any effect upon him. But man's intellectual faculties are too imperfect to dive far even into his own nature. I shall take occasion afterward to show, that this branch of the human constitution, is contrived with admirable wisdom and is subservient to excellent purposes. In the mean time, I must endeavour to unfold, by what means fiction hath such influence on the mind.

That the objects of our senses really exist in the way and manner we perceive, is a branch of intuitive knowledge. When I see a man walking, a tree growing, or cattle grazing, I have a conviction that these things are precisely as they appear. If I be a spectator of any transaction or event, I have a conviction of the real existence of the persons engaged, of their words, and of their actions. Nature determines us to rely on the veracity of our senses. And indeed, if our senses did not convince us of the reality of their objects, they could not in any degree answer their end.

By the power of memory, a thing formerly seen may be recalled to the mind with different degrees of accuracy. We commonly are fatisfied with a flight recollection of the chief circumftances; and, in fuch recollection, the thing is not figured as prefent nor any image formed. I retain the confcioufnefs of my prefent fituation, and barely remember that formerly I was a fpectator. But with refpect to an interefting object or event which made a ftrong impreffion, the mind fometimes, not fatisfied with a curfory review, chufes to revolve every circumftance. In this cafe, I conceive myfelf to be a fpectator as I was originally; and I perceive every particular paffing in my prefence, in the fame manner as when I was in reality a fpectator. For example, I faw yefterday a beautiful woman in tears for the lofs of an only child, and was greatly moved with her diftrefs. Not fatisfied with a flight recollection or bare remembrance, I infift on the melancholy fcene. Conceiving myfelf to be in the place where I was an eye-witnefs, every circumftance appears to me as at firft. I think I fee the woman in tears and hear her moans. Hence it may be juftly faid, that in a complete idea of me-

mory

mory there is no paft nor future.   A thing
recalled to the mind with the accuracy I
have been defcribing, is perceived as in our
view, and confequently as prefently exifting.   Paft time makes a part of an incomplete idea only: I remember or reflect, that
fome years ago I was at Oxford, and faw
the firft ftone laid of the Ratcliff library;
and I remember that at a ftill greater diftance of time, I heard a debate in the
houfe of Commons about a ftanding army.

Lamentable is the imperfection of language, almoft in every particular that falls
not under external fenfe.   I am talking of
a matter exceeding clear in itfelf, and of
which every perfon muft be confcious; and
yet I find no fmall difficulty to exprefs it
clearly in words; for it is not accurate to talk
of incidents long paft as paffing in our fight,
nor of hearing at prefent what we really
heard yefterday or perhaps a year ago.   To
this neceffity I am reduced, by want of proper words to defcribe ideal prefence and to
diftinguifh it from real prefence.   And thus
in the defcription, a plain fubject becomes
obfcure and intricate.   When I recall any

thing

thing in the diftincteft manner, fo as to form an idea or image of it as prefent ; I have not words to defcribe this act, other than that I perceive the thing as a fpectator, and as ex- ifting in my prefence. This means not that I am really a fpectator ; but only that I con- ceive myfelf to be a fpectator, and have a confcioufnefs of prefence fimilar to what a real fpectator hath.

As many rules of criticifm depend on ideal prefence, the reader, it is expected, will take fome pains to form an exact notion of it, as diftinguifhed on the one hand from real prefence, and on the other from a fu- perficial or reflective remembrance. It is diftinguifhed from the former by the follow- ing circumftance. Ideal prefence arifing from an act of memory, may properly be termed *a waking dream* ; becaufe, like a dream, it vanifheth upon the firft reflection of our prefent fituation. Real prefence, on the contrary, vouched by eye-fight, com- mands our belief, not only during the di- rect perception, but in reflecting afterward upon the object. And to diftinguifh ideal prefence from the latter, I give the follow-

ing

ing illuftration.   Two internal acts, both
of them exertions of memory, are clearly
diftinguifhable.   When I think of an event
as paft, without forming any image, it is
barely reflecting or remembering that I was
an eye-witnefs.   But when I recall the
event fo diftinctly as to form a complete
image of it, I perceive it ideally as paffing
in my prefence; and this ideal perception is
an act of intuition, into which reflection enters not more than into an act of fight.

Though ideal prefence be diftinguifhed
from real prefence on the one fide and from
reflective remembrance on the other, it is
however variable without any precife limits;
rifing fometimes toward the former, and often finking toward the latter.   In a vigorous
exertion of memory, ideal prefence is extremely diftinct.   When a man, as in a
reverie, drops himfelf out of his thoughts,
he perceives every thing as paffing before
him, and hath a confcioufnefs of prefence
fimilar to that of a fpectator.   There is no
other difference, but that in the former the
confcioufnefs of prefence is lefs firm and
clear than in the latter.   But this is feldom
the

the cafe. Ideal prefence is often faint, and the image fo obfcure as not to differ widely from reflective remembrance.

Hitherto of an idea of memory. I proceed to confider the idea of a thing I never faw, raifed in me by fpeech, by writing, or by painting. This idea, with refpect to the prefent matter, is of the fame nature with an idea of memory, being either complete or incomplete. An important event, by a lively and accurate defcription, roufes my attention and infenfibly transforms me into a fpectator: I perceive ideally every incident as paffing in my prefence. On the other hand, a flight or fuperficial narrative produceth only a faint and incomplete idea, precifely fimilar to a reflective recollection of memory. Of fuch idea, ideal prefence makes no part. Paft time is a circumftance that enters into this idea, as it doth into a reflective idea of memory. I believe that Scipio exifted about 2000 years ago, and that he overcame Hannibal in the famous battle of Zama. When I revolve in fo curfory a manner that memorable event, I confider it as long paft. But fuppofing me

to

to be warmed with the story, perhaps by a beautiful defcription, I am infenfibly transformed to a fpectator. I perceive thefe two heroes in act to engage; I perceive them brandifhing their fwords, and exhorting their troops; and in this manner I attend them through every circumftance of the battle. This event being prefent to my mind during the whole progrefs of my thoughts, admits not any time but the prefent.

I have had occafion to obferve *, that ideas both of memory and of fpeech, produce emotions of the fame kind with what are produced by an immediate view of the object; only fainter, in proportion as an idea is fainter than an original perception. The infight we have now got, unfolds the means by which this effect is produced. Ideal prefence fupplies the want of real prefence; and in idea we perceive perfons acting and fuffering, precifely as in an original furvey. If our fympathy be engaged by the latter, it muft alfo in fome meafure

* Part 1, fect. 1, of the prefent chapter.

be

be engaged by the former. The distinctness of ideal presence, as above mentioned,
approacheth sometimes to the distinctness
of real presence; and the consciousness of
presence is the same in both. This is the
cause of the pleasure that is felt in a reverie,
where a man, losing sight of himself, is
totally occupied with the objects passing in
his mind, which he conceives to be really existing in his presence. The power of speech
to raise emotions, depends entirely on the
artifice of raising such lively and distinct
images as are here described. The reader's
passions are never sensibly moved, till he be
thrown into a kind of reverie; in which
state, losing the consciousness of self, and
of reading, his present occupation, he conceives every incident as passing in his presence, precisely as if he were an eye-wit-
ness. A general or reflective remembrance
hath not this effect. It may be agreeable
in some slight degree; but the ideas suggested by it, are too faint and obscure to
raise any thing like a sympathetic emotion.
And were they ever so lively, they pass
with too much precipitation to have this
effect.

effect. Our emotions are never inftantaneous: even thofe that come the fooneft to
perfection, have different periods of birth,
growth, and maturity; and to give opportunity for thefe different periods, it is neceffary that the caufe of every emotion be prefent to the mind a due time. The emotion is completed by reiterated impreffions.
We know this to be the cafe of objects of
fight: we are fcarce fenfible of any emotion
in a quick fucceffion even of the moft beautiful objects. And if this hold in the fucceffion of original perceptions, how much
more in the fucceffion of ideas?

Though all this while, I have been only
defcribing what paffeth in the mind of every one and what every one muft be confcious of, it was neceffary to enlarge upon
it; becaufe, however clear in the internal
conception, it is far from being fo when defcribed in words. Ideal prefence, though of
general importance, hath fcarce ever been
touched by any writer; and at any rate
it could not be overlooked in accounting for the effects produced by fiction.
Upon this point, the reader I guefs has
prevented me. It already muft have occur-

red to him, that if, in reading, ideal prefence be the means by which our paffions are moved, it makes no difference whether the fubject be a fable or a reality. When ideal prefence is complete, we perceive every object as in our fight; and the mind, totally occupied with an interefting event, finds no leifure for reflection of any fort. This reafoning, if any one hefitate, is confirmed by conftant and univerfal experience. Let us take under confideration the meeting of Hector and Andromache in the fixth book of the Iliad, or fome of the paffionate fcenes in King Lear. Thefe pictures of human life, when we are fufficiently engaged, give an impreffion of reality not lefs diftinct than that given by the death of Otho in the beautiful defcription of Tacitus. We never once reflect whether the ftory be true or feigned. Reflection comes afterward, when we have the fcene no longer before our eyes. This reafoning will appear in a ftill clearer light, by oppofing ideal prefence to ideas raifed by a curfory narrative; which ideas being faint, obfcure, and imperfect, occupy the mind fo little as to folicit reflection. And accordingly,

cordingly, a curt narrative of feigned incidents is never relifhed. Any flight pleafure
it affords, is more than counterbalanced by
the difguft it infpires for want of truth.

In fupport of the foregoing theory, I add
what I reckon a decifive argument. Upon
examination it will be found, that genuine
hiftory commands our paffions by means of
ideal prefence folely; and therefore that with
refpect to this effect, genuine hiftory ftands
upon the fame footing with fable. To me
it appears clear, that our fympathy muft
vanifh fo foon as we begin to reflect upon
the incidents related in either. The reflection that a ftory is a pure fiction, will indeed prevent our fympathy; but fo will
equally the reflection that the perfons defcribed are no longer exifting. It is prefent
diftrefs only that moves my pity. My concern vanifhes with the diftrefs; for I cannot pity any perfon who at prefent is happy.
According to this theory, founded clearly
on human nature, a man long dead and infenfible now of paft misfortunes, cannot
move our pity more than if he had never
exifted. The misfortunes defcribed in a

P 2   genuine

genuine history command our belief: but then we believe also, that these misfortunes are at an end, and that the persons described are at present under no distress. What effect, for example, can the belief of the rape of Lucretia have to raise our sympathy, when she died above 2000 years ago, and hath at present no painful feeling of the injury done her? The effect of history in point of instruction, depends in some measure upon its veracity. But history cannot reach the heart, while we indulge any reflection upon the facts. Such reflection, if it engage our belief, never fails at the same time to poison our pleasure, by convincing us that our sympathy for those who are dead and gone is absurd. And if reflection be laid aside, history stands upon the same footing with fable. What effect either of them may have to raise our sympathy, depends on the vivacity of the ideas they raise; and with respect to that circumstance, fable is generally more successful than history.

Of all the means for making an impression of ideal presence, theatrical representation is the most powerful. That words inde-

pendent

pendent of action have the fame power in a lefs degree, every one of fenfibility muft have felt: A good tragedy will extort tears in private, though not fo forcibly as upon the ftage. This power belongs alfo to painting. A good hiftorical picture makes a deeper impreffion than can be made by words, though not equal to what is made by theatrical action. And as ideal prefence depends on a lively impreffion, painting feems to poffefs a middle place betwixt reading and acting. In making an impreffion of ideal prefence, it is not lefs fuperior to the former than inferior to the latter.

It muft not however be thought, that our paffions can be raifed by painting to fuch a height as can be done by words. Of all the fucceffive incidents that concur to produce a great event, a picture has the choice but of one, becaufe it is confined to a fingle inftant of time. And though the impreffion it makes, is the deepeft that can be made inftantaneoufly; yet feldom can a paffion be raifed to any height in an inftant, or by a fingle impreffion. It was obferved above, that our paffions, thofe efpecially of

the

the fympathetic kind, require a fucceffion of impreffions; and for that reafon, reading and ftill more acting have greatly the advantage, by the opportunity of reiterating impreffions without end.

Upon the whole, it is by means of ideal prefence that our paffions are excited; and till words produce that charm they avail nothing. Even real events intitled to our belief, muft be conceived prefent and paffing in our fight before they can move us. And this theory ferves to explain feveral phenomena otherwife unaccountable. A misfortune happening to a ftranger, makes a lefs impreffion than happening to a man we know, even where we are no way interefted in him: our acquaintance with this man, however flight, aids the conception of his fuffering in our prefence. For the fame reafon, we are little moved with any diftant event; becaufe we have more difficulty to conceive it prefent, than an event that happened in our neighbourhood.

Every one is fenfible, that defcribing a paft event as prefent, has a fine effect in language. For what other reafon than that

it

it aids the conception of ideal prefence?
Take the following example.

And now with fhouts the fhocking armies clos'd,
To lances lances, fhields to fhields oppos'd;
Hoft againft hoft the fhadowy legions drew,
The founding darts an iron tempeft flew;
Victors and vanquifh'd join promifcuous cries,
Triumphing fhouts and dying groans arife,
With ftreaming blood the flipp'ry field is dy'd,
And flaughter'd heroes fwell the dreadful tide.

In this paffage we may obferve how the
writer inflamed with the fubject, infenfibly
flips from the paft time to the prefent; led
to this form of narration by conceiving every
circumftance as paffing in his own fight.
And this at the fame time has a fine effect
upon the reader, by advancing him to be
as it were a fpectator. But this change
from the paft to the prefent requires fome
preparation; and is not graceful in the fame
fentence where there is no ftop in the fenfe;
witnefs the following paffage.

Thy fate was next, O Phæftus! doom'd to feel
The great Idomeneus' protended fteel;

Whom

Whom Borus fent (his fon and only joy)
From fruitful Tarne to the fields of Troy.
The Cretan jav'lin reach'd him from afar,
And pierc'd his fhoulder as he mounts his car.

Iliad, v. 57.

It is ftill worfe to fall back to the paft in the fame period; for this is an anticlimax in defcription:

Through breaking ranks his furious courfe he
    bends,
And at the goddefs his broad lance extends;
Through her bright veil the daring weapon drove,
Th' ambrofial veil, which all the graces wove:
Her fnowy hand the razing fteel profan'd,
And the tranfparent fkin with crimfon ftain'd.

Iliad, v. 415.

Again, defcribing the fhield of Jupiter,

Here all the terrors of grim War appear,
Here rages Force, here tremble Flight and Fear,
Here ftorm'd Contention, and here Fury frown'd,
And the dire orb portentous Gorgon crown'd.

Iliad, v. 914.

Nor is it pleafant to be carried backward and forward alternately in a rapid fucceffion:

Then

Then dy'd Seamandrius, expert in the chace,
In woods and wilds to wound the favage race;
Diana taught him all her fylvan arts,
To bend the bow and aim unerring darts:
But vainly here Diana's arts he tries,
The fatal lance arrefts him as he flies;
From Menelaus' arm the weapon fent,
Through his broad back and heaving bofom went :
Down finks the warrior with a thund'ring found,
His brazen armor rings againft the ground.

Iliad, v. 65.

It is wonderful to obferve, upon what flender foundations nature, fometimes, erects her moft folid and magnificent works. In appearance at leaft, what can be more flight than ideal prefence of objects? And yet upon it entirely is fuperftructed, that extenfive influence which language hath over the heart; an influence, which, more than any other means, ftrengthens the bond of fociety, and attracts individuals from their private fyftem to exert themfelves in acts of generofity and benevolence. Matters of fact, it is true, and truth in general, may be inculcated without taking advantage of ideal prefence. But without it, the fineft fpeaker or

Vol. I.   Q   writer

writer would in vain attempt to move any of our paſſion : our ſympathy would be confined to objects that are really preſent : and language would loſe entirely that ſignal power it poſſeſſeth, of making us ſympathize with beings removed at the greateſt diſtance of time as well as of place. Nor is the influence of language, by means of this ideal preſence, confined to the heart. It reaches alſo in ſome meaſure the underſtanding, and contributes to belief. When events are related in a lively manner and every circumſtance appears as paſſing before us, it is with difficulty that we ſuffer the truth of the facts to be queſtioned. A hiſtorian accordingly who hath a genius for narration, ſeldom fails to engage our belief. The ſame facts related in a manner cold and indiſtinct, are not ſuffered to paſs without examination. A thing ill deſcribed, is like an object ſeen at a diſtance or through a miſt : we doubt whether it be a reality or a fiction. For this reaſon, a poet who can warm and animate his reader, may employ bolder fictions than ought to be ventured by an inferior genius. The reader, once thoroughly engaged,

engaged, is in that fituation fufceptible of the ftrongeft impreffions:

Veraque conftituunt, quæ bellè tangere poffunt
Aureis, et lepido quæ funt fucata fonore.
                                        Lucretius, *lib*. 1. *l*. 644.

A mafterly painting has the fame effect. Le Brun is no fmall fupport to Quintus Curtius; and among the vulgar in Italy, the belief of fcripture-hiftory is perhaps founded as much upon the authority of Raphael, Michael Angelo, and other celebrated painters, as upon that of the facred writers *.

In eftablifhing the foregoing theory, the reader has had the fatigue of much dry reafoning. But his labour will not be fruitlefs. From this theory are derived many ufeful rules in criticifm, which fhall be mentioned

---

* At quæ Polycleto defuerunt, Phidiæ atque Alcameni dantur. Phidias tamen diis quam hominibus efficiendis melior artifex traditur: in ebore vero longe citra æmulum, vel fi nihil nifi Minervam Athenis, aut Olympium in Elide Jovem feciffet, cujus pulchritudo adjeciffe aliquid etiam receptæ religioni videtur; adeo majeftas operis Deum æquavit.
                        Quintilian, *lib*. 12. *cap*. 10. § 1.

Q 2   in

in their proper places. One specimen, being a fine illustration, I chuse to give at present. In a historical poem representing human actions, it is a rule, that no improbable incident ought to be admitted. A circumstance, an incident, or an event, may be singular, may surprise by being unexpected, and yet be extremely natural. The improbability I talk of, is that of an irregular fact, contrary to the order and course of nature, and therefore unaccountable. A chain of imagined facts linked together according to the order of nature, find easy entrance into the mind; and if described with warmth of fancy, they produce complete images, including ideal presence. But it is with great difficulty that we admit any irregular fact; for an irregular fact always puzzles the judgement. Doubtful of its reality we immediately enter upon reflection, and discovering the cheat, lose all relish and concern. This is an unhappy effect; for thereafter it requires more than an ordinary effort, to restore the waking dream, and to make the reader conceive even the more probable incidents as passing in his presence.

I

I never was an admirer of machinery in an epic poem; and I now find my tafte juftified by reafon; the foregoing argument concluding ftill more ftrongly againft imaginary beings, than againft improbable facts. Fictions of this nature may amufe by their novelty and fingularity: but they never move the fympathetic paffions, becaufe they cannot impofe on the mind any perception of reality. I appeal to the difcerning reader, whether this be not precifely the cafe of the machinery introduced by Taffo and by Voltaire. This machinery is not only in itfelf cold and uninterefting, but is remarkably hurtful, by giving an air of fiction to the whole compofition. A burlefque poem, fuch as the Lutrin or the Difpenfary, may employ machinery with fuccefs; for thefe poems, though they affume the air of hiftory, give entertainment chiefly by their pleafant and ludicrous pictures, to which machinery contributes in a fingular manner. It is not the aim of fuch a poem, to raife our fympathy in any confiderable degree; and for that reafon, a ftrict imitation of nature is not required. A poem profeffedly ludicrous,

ludicrous, may employ machinery to great advantage; and the more extravagant the better. A juft reprefentation of nature, would indeed be incongruous in a compofition intended to give entertainment by the means chiefly of fingularity and furprife.

For accomplifhing the tafk undertaken in the beginning of the prefent fection, what only remains is, to fhow the final caufe of the power that fiction hath over the mind of man. I have already mentioned, that language, by means of fiction, has the command of our fympathy for the good of others. By the fame means, our fympathy may be alfo raifed for our own good. In the third fection it is obferved, that examples both of virtue and of vice raife virtuous emotions ; which becoming ftronger by exercife, tend to make us virtuous by habit as well as by principle. I now further obferve, that examples drawn from real events, are not fo frequent as to contribute much to a habit of virtue. If they be, they are not recorded by hiftorians. It therefore fhows great wifdom, to form us in fuch a manner, as to be fufceptible of the fame improvement

from

from fable that we receive from genuine hiſtory. By this admirable contrivance, examples
to improve us in virtue may be multiplied
without end. No other ſort of diſcipline
contributes more to make virtue habitual;
and no other ſort is ſo agreeable in the application. I add another final cauſe with
thorough ſatisfaction; becauſe it ſhows, that
the author of our nature is not leſs kindly
provident for the happineſs of his creatures,
than for the regularity of their conduct.
The power that fiction hath over the mind
of man, is the ſource of an endleſs variety
of refined amuſement, always ready to employ a vacant hour. Such amuſement is a
fine reſource in ſolitude; and by ſweeten-
ing the temper, improves ſociety.

P A R T   II.

*Emotions and paſſions as pleaſant and painful,
agreeable and diſagreeable. Modifications
of theſe qualities.*

IT will naturally occur at firſt view, that
a diſcourſe upon the paſſions ſhould com-
mence

mence with explaining the qualities now mentioned. But upon trial, I found this could not be done diftinctly, till the difference were afcertained betwixt an emotion and a paffion, and till their caufes were e-volved.

Great obfcurity may be obferved among writers with regard to the prefent point. No care, for example, is taken to diftin-guifh agreeable from pleafant, difagreeable from painful; or rather thefe terms are deemed fynonymous. This is an error not at all venial in the fcience of ethics; as in-ftances can and fhall be given, of painful paffions that are agreeable, and of pleafant paffions that are difagreeable. Thefe terms, it is true, are ufed indifferently in familiar converfations, and in compofition for amufe-ment, where accuracy is not required. But for thofe to ufe them fo who profefs to explain the paffions, is a capital error. In writing upon the critical art, I would avoid every refinement that may feem more cu-rious than ufeful. But the proper meaning of the terms under confideration muft be afcertained, in order to underftand the paf-fions

fions, and fome of their effects that are intimately connected with criticifm.

I fhall endeavour to explain thefe terms by familiar examples. Viewing a fine garden, I perceive it to be beautiful or agreeable; and I confider the beauty or agreeablenefs as belonging to the object, or as one of its qualities. Again, when I turn my thoughts from the garden to what paffes in my mind, I am confcious of a pleafant emotion of which the garden is the caufe. The pleafure here is felt, not as a quality of the garden, but of the emotion produced by it. I give an oppofite example. A rotten carcafs is loathfome and difagreeable, and raifes in the fpectator a painful emotion. The difagreeablenefs is a quality of the object: the pain is a quality of the emotion produced by it. Agreeable and difagreeable, then, are qualities of the objects we perceive: pleafant and painful are qualities of the emotions we feel. The former qualities are perceived as adhering to objects; the latter are felt as exifting within us.

But a paffion or emotion, befide being felt, is frequently made an object of thought

or reflection: we examine it; we inquire
into its nature, its cause, and its effects. In
this view it partakes the nature of other objects: it is either agreeable or disagreeable.
Hence clearly appear the different significa-
tions of the terms under consideration, as
applied to passion.   When a passion is
termed *pleasant* or *painful*, we refer to the
actual feeling: when termed *agreeable* or
disagreeable, it is considered as an object of
thought or reflection.   A passion is pleasant
or painful to the person in whom it exists:
it is agreeable or disagreeable to the person
who makes it a subject of contemplation.

When the terms thus defined are applied
to particular emotions and passions, they do
not always coincide.   And in order to make
this evident, we must endeavour to ascertain,
first, what passions and emotions are pleasant
what painful, and next, what are agreeable
what disagreeable.   With respect to both,
there are general rules, which, so far as I
gather from induction, admit not any exceptions.   The nature of an emotion or passion as pleasant or painful, depends entirely
on its cause.   An agreeable object produceth
always

always a pleasant emotion; and a disagreeable object produceth always a painful emotion *. Thus a lofty oak, a generous action, a valuable discovery in art or science, are agreeable objects that unerringly produce pleasant emotions. A stinking puddle, a treacherous action, an irregular ill-contrived edifice, being disagreeable objects, produce painful emotions. Selfish passions are pleasant; for they arise from self, an agreeable object or cause. A social passion directed upon an agreeable object is always pleasant: directed upon an object in distress, is painful†. Lastly, all dissocial passions, such as envy, resentment, malice, being caused by disagreeable objects, cannot fail to be painful.

It requires a greater compass to evolve the general rule that concerns the agreeableness or disagreeableness of emotions and passions. An action conformable to the common nature of our species, is perceived by us to be

---

* See part 7. of this chapter.
† See the place above cited.

regular

regular and good * ; and confequently every fuch action appears agreeable to us. The
fame obfervation is applicable to paffions and
emotions. Every feeling that is conformable to the common nature of our fpecies,
is perceived by us to be regular and as it
ought to be; and upon that account it muft
appear agreeable. By this general rule we
can afcertain what emotions are agreeable
what difagreeable. Every emotion that is
conformable to the common nature of man,
ought to appear agreeable. And that this
holds true with refpect to pleafant emotions,
will readily be admitted. But why fhould
painful emotions be an exception, when
they are not lefs natural than the other ? The
propofition holds true in both. Thus the
painful emotion raifed by a monftrous birth
or brutal action, is not lefs agreeable upon
reflection, than the pleafant emotion raifed
by a flowing river or a lofty dome. With
refpect to paffions as oppofed to emotions,
it will be obvious from the foregoing propofition, that their agreeablenefs or difagree-

* Effays on the principles of morality and natural religion,
part 1. eff. 2. chap. 1.

ablenefs,

ablenefs, like the actions of which they are
productive, muft be regulated entirely by
the moral fenfe. Every action vicious or
improper is difagreeable to a fpectator, and
fo is the paffion that prompts it. Every action virtuous or proper is agreeable to a fpectator, and fo is the paffion that prompts it.

This deduction may be carried a great
way farther; but to avoid intricacy and obfcurity, I make but one other ftep. A paffion, which, as aforefaid, becomes an object of thought to a fpectator, may have the
effect to produce a paffion or emotion in
him; for it is natural that a focial being
fhould be affected with the paffions of others.
Paffions or emotions thus generated, fubmit, in common with others, to the general law above mentioned, *viz.* that an agreeable object produces a pleafant emotion, and
a difagreeable object a painful emotion.
Thus the paffion of gratitude, being to a
fpectator an agreeable object, produceth in
him the pleafant paffion of love to the grateful perfon. Thus malice, being to a fpectator a difagreeable object, produceth in
him

him the painful paſſion of hatred to the malicious perſon.

We are now prepared for examples of
pleaſant paſſions that are diſagreeable, and
of painful paſſions that are agreeable. Self-
love, ſo long as confined within juſt bounds,
is a paſſion both pleaſant and agreeable. In
exceſs it is diſagreeable, though it continues
to be ſtill pleaſant. Our appetites are preciſely in the ſame condition. Again, vanity,
though pleaſant, is diſagreeable. Reſentment, on the other hand, is, in every ſtage
of the paſſion, painful; but is not diſagreeable
unleſs in exceſs. Pity is always painful,
yet always agreeable. But however diſtinct
theſe qualities are, they coincide, I acknowledge, in one claſs of paſſions. All vicious
paſſions tending to the hurt of others, are
equally painful and diſagreeable.

The foregoing diſtinctions among paſſions and emotions, may ſerve the common
affairs of life, but they are not ſufficient for
the critical art. The qualities of pleaſant
and painful are too familiar to carry us far
into human nature, or to form an accurate
judgement in the fine arts. It is further
                                        neceſſary,

neceffary, that we be made acquainted with the feveral modifications of thefe qualities, with the modifications at leaft that make the greateft figure. Even at firft view every one is fenfible, that the pleafure or pain of one paffion differs from that of another. How diftant the pleafure of revenge from that of love? So diftant, as that we cannot without reluctance admit them to be any way related. That the fame quality of pleafure fhould be fo differently modified in different paffions, will not be furprifing, when we reflect on the boundlefs variety of pleafant founds, taftes, and fmells, daily felt. Our difcernment reaches differences ftill more nice, in objects even of the fame fenfe. We have no difficulty to diftinguifh different fweets, different fours, and different bitters. Honey is fweet, and fo is fugar; and yet they never pafs the one for the other. Our fenfe of fmelling is fufficiently acute, to diftinguifh varieties in fweet-fmelling flowers without end. With refpect to paffions and emotions, their different feelings have no limits; for when we attempt the more delicate modifications,

they

they elude our search, and are scarce discernible. In this matter, however, there is an analogy betwixt our internal and external senses. The latter generally are sufficiently acute for all the useful purposes of life, and so are the former. Some persons indeed, Nature's favourites, have a wonderful acuteness of sense, which to them unfolds many a delightful scene totally hid from vulgar eyes. But if such refined pleasure be refused to the bulk of mankind, it is however wisely ordered that they are not sensible of the defect; and it detracts not from their happiness that others secretly are more happy. With relation to the fine arts only, this qualification seems essential; and there it is termed *delicacy of taste.*

Should an author of such a taste attempt to describe all those differences and shades of pleasant and painful emotions which he himself feels, he would soon meet an invincible obstacle in the poverty of language. No known tongue hitherto has reached such perfection, as to express clearly the more delicate feelings. A people must be thoroughly refined, before their language become

become so comprehensive. We must therefore rest satisfied with an explanation of the more obvious modifications.

In forming a comparison betwixt pleasant passions of different kinds, we conceive some of them to be *gross* some *refined*. Those pleasures of external sense that are felt as at the organ of sense, are conceived to be corporeal or gross*. The pleasures of the eye and ear are felt to be internal; and for that reason are conceived to be more pure and refined.

The social affections are conceived by all to be more refined than the selfish. Sympathy and humanity are reckoned the finest temper of mind; and for that reason, the prevalence of the social affections in the progress of society, is held to be a refinement in our nature. A savage is unqualified for any pleasure but what is thoroughly or nearly selfish: therefore a savage is incapable of comparing selfish and social pleasure. But a man after acquiring a high relish of the latter, loses not thereby a taste for the former. This man can judge, and he

* See the introduction.

will give preference to focial pleafures as more fweet and refined. In fact they maintain that character, not only in the direct feeling, but alfo when we make them the fubject of reflection. The focial paffions are by far more agreeable than the felfifh, and rife much higher in our efteem.

Refined manners and polite behaviour, muft not be deemed altogether artificial. Men accuftomed to the fweets of fociety, who cultivate humanity, find an elegant pleafure in preferring others and making them happy, of which the proud or felfifh fcarce have a conception.

Ridicule, which chiefly arifes from pride, a felfifh paffion, is at beft but a grofs pleafure. A people, it is true, muft have emerged out of barbarity before they can have a tafte for ridicule. But it is too rough an entertainment for thofe who are highly polifhed and refined. Ridicule is banifhed France, and is lofing ground daily in England.

Other modifications of pleafant paffions will be occafionally mentioned hereafter. Particularly the modifications of *high* and *low*

are

are handled in the chapter of grandeur and fublimity; and the modifications of *dignified* and *mean*, in the chapter of dignity and meannefs.

P A R T III.

Interrupted exiftence of emotions and paffions.
——Their growth and decay.

WEre emotions of the fame nature with colour and figure, to continue in their prefent ftate till varied by fome o-perating caufe, the condition of man would be deplorable. It is ordered wifely, that e-motions fhould more refemble another attri-bute of matter, *viz.* motion, which requires the conftant exertion of an operating caufe, and ceafes when the caufe is withdrawn. An emotion may fubfift while its caufe is prefent ; and when its caufe is re-moved, may fubfift by means of an idea, though in a fainter degree. But the mo-ment another thought breaks in and occu-pies the mind, fo as to exclude not only this caufe, but alfo its idea, the emotion

S 2   is

is gone: it is no longer felt. If it return
with its caufe or idea, it again vanifheth with them when other thoughts crowd
in. This obfervation is applicable to emotions and paffions of every kind. And thefe
accordingly are connected with perceptions
and ideas, fo intimately as not to have any
independent exiftence. A ftrong paffion,
it is true, hath a mighty influence to detain
its object in the mind ; but not fo as to detain
it for ever. A fucceffion of perceptions or
ideas is unavoidable * : the object of the
paffion may be often recalled ; but however interefting, it muft by intervals yield
to other objects. For this reafon, a paffion
rarely continues long with an equal degree
of vigour. It is felt ftrong and moderate,
in a pretty quick fucceffion. The fame
object makes not always the fame impreffion ; becaufe the mind, being of a limited
capacity, cannot, at the fame inftant, give
great attention to a plurality of objects.
The ftrength of a paffion depends on the
impreffion made by its caufe ; and a caufe

* See this point explained afterwards, chap. 9.

makes

makes its ſtrongeſt impreſſion, when happening to be the ſingle intereſting object, it
attracts our whole attention *. Its impreſſion is ſlighter when our attention is divided
betwixt it and other objects; and at that
time the paſſion is ſlighter in proportion.

When emotions and paſſions are felt thus
by intervals and have not a continued exiſtence, it may be thought a nice problem,
to aſcertain their identity, and to determine when they are the ſame when different. In a ſtrict philoſophic view, every
ſingle impreſſion made even by the ſame
object, is diſtinguiſhable from what have
gone before, and from what ſucceed. Neither is an emotion raiſed by an idea the
ſame with what is raiſed by a ſight of the
object. But ſuch accuracy is not found in
common apprehenſion, nor is neceſſary in
common language. The emotions raiſed by
a fine landſcape in its ſucceſſive appearances, are not diſtinguiſhed from each other,
nor even from thoſe raiſed by ſucceſſive

* See the appendix, containing definitions and explanation
of terms, ſect. 33.

ideas

ideas of the object: all of them are held to be the fame. A paffion alfo is always reckoned the fame, fo long as it is fixed upon the fame object. Thus love and hatred may continue the fame for life. Nay, fo loofe are we in this way of thinking, that many paffions are reckoned the fame even after a change of object. This is the cafe of all paffions that proceed from fome peculiar propenfity. Envy, for example, is confidered to be the fame paffion, not only while it is directed upon the fame perfon, but even where it comprehends many perfons at once. Pride and malice are in the fame condition. So much was neceffary to be faid upon the identity of a paffion and emotion, in order to prepare for examining their growth and decay.

The growth and decay of paffions and emotions, is a fubject too extenfive to be exhaufted in an undertaking like the prefent. I pretend only to give a curfory view of it, fo far as neceffary for the purpofes of criticifm. Some emotions are produced in their utmoft perfection, and have a very fhort endurance. This is the cafe of furprife,

prife, of wonder, and fometimes of terror. Emotions raifed by infenfible objects, fuch as trees, rivers, buildings, pictures, arrive at perfection almoft inftantaneoufly, and have a long endurance: a fecond view produceth nearly the fame pleafure with the firft. Love, hatred, and fome other paffions, increafe gradually to a certain pitch, and thereafter decay gradually. Envy, malice, pride, fcarce ever decay. Again, fome paffions, fuch as gratitude and revenge, are often exhaufted by a fingle act of gratification. Other paffions, fuch as pride, malice, envy, love, hatred, are not fo exhaufted; but having a long continuance, demand frequent gratification.

In order to explain thefe differences, it would be an endlefs work to examine every emotion and paffion in particular. We muft be fatisfied at prefent with fome general views. And with refpect to emotions, which are quiefcent and not productive of defire, their growth and decay are eafily explained. An emotion caufed by an external object, cannot naturally take longer time to arrive at perfection, than is neceffary for

a

a leifurely furvey. Such emotion alfo muft continue long ftationary, without any fenfible decay; a fecond or third view of the object being nearly as agreeable as the firft. This is the cafe of an emotion produced by a fine profpect, an impetuous river, or a towering hill. While a man remains the fame, fuch objects ought to have the fame effect upon him. Familiarity, however, hath an influence here, as it hath every where. Frequency of view, after fhort intervals efpecially, weans the mind gradually from the object, which at laft lofes all relifh. The nobleft object in the material world, a clear and ferene fky, is quite difregarded, unlefs perhaps after a courfe of bad weather. An emotion raifed by human virtues, qualities, or actions, may grow imperceptibly by reiterated views of the object, till it become fo vigorous as to generate defire. In this condition it muft be handled as a paffion.

As to paffion, I obferve firft, that when nature requires a paffion to be fudden, it is commonly produced in perfection. This is frequently the cafe of fear and of anger. Wonder and furprife are always produced in in perfection. Reiterated impreſſions made by their cauſe, exhauſt theſe paſſions in place of inflaming them. This will be explained afterward *.

In the next place, when a paſſion hath for its foundation an original propenſity peculiar to ſome men, it generally comes ſoon to perfection. The propenſity, upon repreſenting a proper object, is immediately enlivened into a paſſion. This is the caſe of pride, of envy, and of malice.

In the third place, love and hatred have often a ſlow growth. The good qualities or kind offices of a perſon, raiſe in me pleaſant emotions; which, by reiterated views, are ſwelled into a paſſion involving deſire of that perſon's happineſs. This deſire being often put in exerciſe, works gradually a change internally; and at laſt produceth in me a ſettled habit of affection for that perſon, now my friend. Affection thus produced, operates preciſely like an original propenſity. To enliven it into a paſſion, no more is required but the real or ideal pre-

* Chap. 6.

fence of the object. The habit of averfion or hatred is brought on in the fame manner. And here I muft obferve by the way, that love and hatred fignify commonly affection, not paffion. The bulk indeed of our paffions, are thefe affections inflamed into a paffion by different circumftances. The affection of love I bear to my fon, is inflamed into the paffion of fear, when he is in danger; becomes hope, when he hath a profpect of good fortune; becomes admiration, when he performs a laudable action; and fhame, when he commits any wrong. Averfion, again, becomes fear when there is a profpect of good fortune to my enemy; becomes hope when he is in danger; becomes joy when he is in diftrefs; and forrow when a laudable action is performed by him.

Fourthly, the growth of fome paffions depends often on occafional circumftances. Obftacles to gratification never fail to augment and inflame a paffion. A conftant endeavour to remove the obftacle, preferves the object of the paffion ever in view, which fwells the paffion by impreffions frequently reiterated. Thus the reftraint of confcience,

when

when an obftacle to love, agitates the mind
and inflames the paffion :

Quod licet, ingratum eft : quod non licet, acrius
        urit.
Si nunquam Danaën habuiffet ahenea turris,
Non effet Danaë de Jove facta parens.

Ovid. Amor. l. 2.

At the fame time, the mind diftreffed with
the obftacle, is difpofed to indulge its diftrefs by magnifying the pleafure of gratification ; which naturally inflames defire.
Shakefpear expreffes this obfervation finely :

All impediments in fancy's courfe,
Are motives of more fancy.

We need no better example than a lover
who hath many rivals. Even the caprices
of a miftrefs have the effect to inflame love.
Thefe occafioning uncertainty of fuccefs,
tend naturally to make the anxious lover
overvalue the happinefs of fruition.

So much upon the growth of paffions.
Their continuance and decay come next
under confideration. And firft, it is a ge-

T 2   neral

neral law of nature, that things sudden in their growth, are equally sudden in their decay. This is commonly the case of anger; and with respect to wonder and surprise, another reason concurs, that their causes are of short duration. Novelty soon degenerates into familiarity; and the unexpectedness of an object, is soon sunk in the pleasure which the object affords us. Fear, which is a passion of greater importance as tending to self-preservation, is often instantaneous, and yet is of equal duration with its cause. Nay it frequently subsists after the cause is removed.

In the next place, a passion founded on a peculiar propensity, subsists generally for ever. This is the case of pride, envy, and malice. Objects are never wanting, to inflame the propensity into a passion.

Thirdly, it may be laid down as a general law of nature, that every passion ceases upon attaining its ultimate end. To explain this law, we must distinguish betwixt a particular and a general end. I call a particular end what may be accomplished by a single act. A general end, on the contrary,

admits

admits acts without number; becaufe it cannot be faid that a general end is ever fully accomplifhed while the object of the paffion fubfifts. Gratitude and revenge are examples of the firft kind. The ends they aim at may be accomplifhed by a fingle act; and when this act is performed, the paffions are neceffarily at an end. Love and hatred are examples of the other kind. The defire of doing good or of doing mifchief to an individual, is a general end, which admits acts without number, and which feldom is fully accomplifhed. Therefore thefe paffions have frequently the fame duration with their objects.

Laftly, it will afford us another general view, to confider the difference betwixt an original propenfity and an affection produced by cuftom. The former adheres too clofe to the conftitution ever to be eradicated; and for that reafon the paffions to which it gives birth, endure during life with no remarkable diminution of ftrength. The latter, which owes its birth and increment to time, owes its decay to the fame caufe. Affection decays gradually as it grew. Hence

long

ong abfence extinguifheth hatred as well as love. Affection wears out more gradually betwixt perfons, who, living together, are objects to each other of mutual good-will and kindnefs. But here habit comes in luckily, to fupply decayed affection. It makes thefe perfons neceffary to the happinefs of each other, by the pain of feparation *. Affection to children hath a long endurance, longer perhaps than any other affection. Its growth keeps pace with that of its objects. They difplay new beauties and qualifications daily, to feed and augment the affection. But whenever the affection becomes ftationary, it muft begin to decay; with a flow pace indeed, in proportion to its increment. In fhort, man with refpect to this life, is a temporary being. He grows, becomes ftationary, decays; and fo muft all his powers and paffions.

* See chap. 14.

PART

PART IV.

Coexiftent emotions and paffions.

TO have a thorough knowledge of the human paffions and emotions, it is not fufficient that they be examined fingly and feparately. As a plurality of them are fometimes felt at the fame inftant, the manner of their coexiftence, and the effects thereby produced, ought alfo to be examined. This fubject is extenfive, and it will be difficult to evolve all the laws that govern its endlefs variety of cafes. Such an undertaking may be brought to perfection, but it muft be by degrees. The following hints may fuffice for a firft attempt.

We begin with emotions raifed by different founds, as the fimpleft cafe. Two founds that mix, and are, as it were, incorporated before they reach the ear, are faid to be concordant. That each found produceth an emotion of its own, muft be admitted. But then thefe emotions, like the founds

that

that produce them, mix so intimately, as to be rather one complex emotion than two emotions in conjunction. Two sounds, again, that refuse incorporation or mixture, are said to be discordant. Being however heard at the same instant, the emotions produced by them are conjoined; and in that condition are unpleasant, even where separately they are each of them pleasant.

Similar to the emotion raised by mixed sounds, is the emotion that an object of sight raises by means of its several qualities. A tree, for example, with its qualities of colour, figure, size, &c. is perceived to be one object; and the emotion it raises is one, not different emotions combined. But though the emotion be one, it is however not simple. The perception of the tree is complex, and the emotion raised by it must also be complex.

With respect to coexistent emotions produced by different causes or objects, it must be observed, that there cannot be a concordance among objects of sight like what is perceived in sounds. Objects of sight are never mixed or incorporated in the act of vision.

vision. Each object is perceived as it exists, separately from others; and each raiseth its own emotion, which is felt distinctly however intimately connected the objects may be. This doctrine holds in all the causes of emotion or passion, sounds only excepted.

To explain the manner in which such emotions coexist, similar emotions must be distinguished from those that are dissimilar. Two emotions are said to be similar, when they tend each of them to produce the same tone of mind. Chearful emotions, however different their causes may be, are similar; and so are those which are melancholy. Dissimilar emotions are easily explained by their opposition to what are similar. Grandeur and littleness, gaiety and gloominess, are dissimilar emotions.

Emotions perfectly similar, readily combine and unite *, so as in a manner to be-

---

* It is easier to conceive the manner of coexistence of similar emotions, than to describe it. They cannot be said to mix or incorporate like concordant sounds. Their union is rather of agreement or concord; and therefore I have chosen the words in the text, not as sufficient to express clearly the manner of their coexistence, but only as less liable to exception than any other I can find.

U come

come one complex emotion; witnefs the
emotions produced by a number of flowers
in a parterre, or of trees in a wood. Emotions again that are oppofite or extremely
diffimilar, never combine nor unite. The
mind cannot fimultaneoufly take on oppofite
tones: it cannot at the fame inftant be both
joyful and fad, angry and fatisfied, proud
and humble. Diffimilar emotions may fucceed each other with rapidity, but they cannot exift fimultaneoufly.

Betwixt thefe two extremes, emotions
will unite more or lefs, in proportion to
the degree of their refemblance and the
greater or lefs connection of their caufes.
The beauty of a landfcape and the finging
of birds, produce emotions that are fimilar
in a confiderable degree; and thefe emotions
therefore, though proceeding from very
different caufes, readily combine and unite.
On the other hand, when the caufes are intimately connected, the emotions, though
but flightly refembling each other, are forced into a fort of union. I give for an example a miftrefs in diftrefs. When I confider her beauty, I feel a pleafant emotion;
and

and a painful emotion when I confider her diftrefs. Thefe two emotions, proceeding from different views of the object, have very little refemblance to each other : and yet their caufes are fo intimately connected, as to force them into a fort of complex emotion, partly pleafant partly painful. This clearly explains fome expreffions common in poetry, *a fweet diftrefs, a pleafant pain.*

We proceed to the effects produced by means of the different manners of coexiftence above defcribed ; firft, the effects produced within the mind, and next, thofe that appear externally. I difcover two mental effects clearly diftinguifhable from each other. The one may be reprefented by addition and fubtraction in numbers, and the other by harmony in founds. Two pleafant emotions that are fimilar, readily unite when they are coexiftent ; and the pleafure felt in the union, is the fum of the two pleafures. The combined emotions are like multiplied effects from the co-operation of different powers. The fame emotions in fucceffion, are far from making the fame figure ; becaufe the mind at no

U 2 inftant

inftant of the fucceffion is confcious of
more than a fingle emotion. This doctrine
may aptly be illuftrated by a landfcape comprehending hills, vallies, plains, rivers,
trees, &c. The emotions produced by
thefe feveral objects, being fimilar in a high
degree as falling in eafily and fweetly with
the fame tone of mind, are in conjunction
extremely pleafant. And this multiplied
effect is felt from objects even of different
fenfes; as where a landfcape is conjoined
with the mufic of birds and odor of flowers.
Such multiplied effect, as above hinted, depends partly on the refemblance of the e-
motions and partly on the connection of
their caufes; whence it follows, that the
effect muft be the greateft, where the caufes
are intimately connected and the emotions
perfectly fimilar.

The other pleafure arifing from coexiftent
emotions, which may be termed *the pleafure of concord or harmony*, is afcertained by
a different rule. It is directly in proportion
to the degree of refemblance betwixt the
emotions, and inverfely in proportion to
the degree of connection betwixt the caufes.

fes. To feel this pleasure in perfection, the resemblance cannot be too strong, nor the connection too slight. Where the causes are intimately connected, the similar emotions they produce are felt like one complex emotion. But the pleasure of harmony, is not felt from one emotion single or complex. It is felt from various similar emotions, distinct from each other, and yet sweetly combining in the mind; and the less connection the causes have, the more entire is the emotion of harmony. This matter cannot be better illustrated, than by the foregoing example of a landscape, where the sight, hearing, and smelling, are employed. The accumulated pleasure of so many different similar emotions, is not what delights us the most in this combination of objects. The sense of harmony from these emotions sweetly uniting in the mind, is still more delightful. We feel this harmony in the different emotions proceeding from the visible objects; but we feel it still more sensibly in the emotions proceeding from the objects of different senses. This emotion of concord or harmony, will

be

be more fully illuſtrated, when the emotions produced by the ſound of words and their meaning are taken under conſideration *.

This emotion of concord from conjoined emotions, is felt even where the emotions are not perfectly ſimilar. Love is a pleaſant paſſion; but then its ſweetneſs and tenderneſs make it reſemble in a conſiderable degree the painful paſſion of pity or grief; and for that reaſon, love accords better with theſe paſſions than with what are gay and ſprightly. I give the following example from Catullus, where the concord betwixt love and grief, has a fine effect even in ſo ſlight a ſubject as the death of a ſparrow.

Lugete, ô Veneres, Cupidineſque,
Et quantum eſt hominum venuſtiorum!
Paſſer mortuus eſt meæ puellæ,
Quem plus illa oculis ſuis amabat.
Nam mellitus erat, ſuamque norat
Ipſam tam bene, quam puella matrem:
Nec ſeſe a gremio illius movebat;
Sed circumſiliens modo huc, modo illuc,

* Chap. 18. ſect. 3.

Ad

Ad folam dominam ufque pipilabat.
Qui nunc it per iter tenebricofum,
Illuc, unde negant redire quemquam.
At vobis male fit, malæ tenebræ
Orci, quæ omnia bella devoratis;
Tam bellum mihi pafferem abftuliftis.
O factum male, ô mifelle paffer,
Tua nunc opera, meæ puellæ
Flendo turgiduli rubent ocelli.

To complete this branch of the fubject, I proceed to confider the effects of diffimilar emotions. Thefe effects obvioufly muft be oppofite to what are above defcribed; and in order to explain them with accuracy, diffimilar emotions proceeding from connected caufes, muft be diftinguifhed from what proceed from caufes that are unconnected. Diffimilar emotions of the former kind, being forced into a fort of unnatural union, produce a feeling of difcord inftead of harmony. It holds alfo that in computing their force, fubtraction muft be ufed in place of addition, which will be evident from what follows. Diffimilar emotions forced into union, are felt obfcurely and imperfectly;

perfectly; for each tends to vary the tone of mind that is suited to the other; and the mind thus diſtracted betwixt two objects, is at no inſtant in a condition to receive a full impreſſion from either. Diſſimilar e-motions proceeding from unconnected cauſes, are in a very different condition. Diſſi-milar emotions in general are averſe to u-nion; and as there is nothing to force them into union when their cauſes are uncon-nected, emotions of this kind are never felt but in ſucceſſion. By that means, they are not felt to be diſcordant, and each hath an opportunity to make a full impreſſion.

This curious theory muſt be illuſtrated by examples. In reading the deſcription of the diſmal waſte, book 1. of *Paradiſe Loſt*, we are ſenſible of a confuſed feeling, ari-ſing from diſſimilar emotions forced into union, *viz*. the beauty of the deſcription and the horror of the object deſcribed.

Seeſt thou yon dreary plain, forlorn and wild,
The ſeat of deſolation, void of light,
Save what the glimmering of theſe livid flames
Caſts pale and dreadful?

                                        Many

Many other paffages in this juftly celebrated
poem produce the fame effect; and we always obferve, that if the difagreeablenefs
of the fubject be obfcured by the beautiful
defcription, this beauty is not lefs obfcured
by its difcordant union with the difagreeablenefs of the fubject. For the fame reafon, afcending fmoke in a calm morning is
improper in a picture full of violent action.
The emotion of ftillnefs and tranquillity infpired by the former, accords not with the
lively and animated emotion infpired by the
latter. A parterre, partly ornamented
partly in diforder, produces a mixt feeling
of the fame fort. Two great armies in act
to engage, mix the diffimilar emotions of
grandeur and of terror.

Sembra d'alberi denfi alta forefta
L' un campo, e l' altro; di tant' afte abbonda.
Son tefi gli archi, e fon le lance in refta:
Vibranfi i dardi, e rotafi ogni fionda.
Ogni cavallo in guerra anco s' apprefta :
Gli odii, e'l furor del fuo fignor feconda:
Rafpa, batte, nitrifce, e fi raggira,
Gonfia le nari; e fumo, e fuoco fpira.

Bello in sì bella viſta anco è l' orrore :
E di mezzo la tema eſce il diletto.
Ne men le trombe orribili, e canore
Sono a gli orecchi lieto, e fero oggetto.
Pur il campo fedel, benchè minore,
Par di ſuon più mirabile, e d' aſpetto.
E canta in più guerriero, e chiaro carme
Ogni ſua tromba, e maggior luce han l' arme.
                Geruſalemme liberata, cant. 20. *ſt.* 29. & 30.

A virtuous man has drawn on himſelf a
great misfortune, by a fault incident to human nature, and therefore venial. The
remorſe he feels aggravates his diſtreſs, and
conſequently raiſes our pity to a high pitch.
We indeed blame the man ; and the indignation raiſed by the fault he has committed, is diſſimilar to pity. Theſe two
paſſions however proceeding from different
views of the ſame object, are forced into a
ſort of union. But the indignation is ſo
ſlight as ſcarce to be felt in the mixture
with pity. Subjects of this kind, are of all
the fitteſt for tragedy. But of this afterward *.

* Chap. of epic and dramatic compoſitions.

Oppoſite

Oppofite emotions are fo diffimilar as not to admit any fort of union, even where they proceed from caufes the moft intimately connected. Love to a miftrefs, and refentment for her infidelity, are of this nature. They cannot exift otherwife than in fucceffion, which by the connection of their caufes is commonly rapid. And thefe emotions will govern alternately, till one of them obtain the afcendent, or both be obliterated. A fucceffion opens to me by the death of a worthy man, who was my friend as well as my kinfman. When I think of my friend I am grieved; but the fucceffion gives me joy. Thefe two caufes are intimately connected, for the fucceffion is the direct confequence of my friend's death. The emotions however being oppofite, do not mix: they prevail alternately, perhaps for a courfe of time, till grief for my friend's death be banifhed by the pleafures of opulence. A virtuous man fuffering unjuftly, is an example of the fame kind. I pity him, and I have great indignation at the author of the wrong. Thefe emotions proceed from caufes nearly connected; but being directed upon different objects, they

X 2   are

are not forced into union. The oppofition preferves them diftinct; and accordingly they are found to govern alternately, the one fometimes prevailing and fometimes the other.

Next of diffimilar emotions arifing from unconnected caufes. Good and bad news of equal importance arriving at the fame inftant from different quarters, produce oppofite emotions, the difcordance of which is not felt becaufe they are not forced into union. They govern alternately, commonly in a quick fucceffion, till their force be fpent. In the fame manner, good news arriving to a man labouring under diftrefs, occafions a vibration in his mind from the one to the other.

> *Ofmyn.* By heav'n thou'ft rous'd me from my
> lethargy.
> The fpirit which was deaf to my own wrongs,
> And the loud cries of my dead father's blood,
> Deaf to revenge — nay, which refus'd to hear
> The piercing fighs and murmurs of my love
> Yet unenjoy'd; what not Almeria could
> Revive, or raife, my people's voice has waken'd.
> O my Antonio, I am all on fire,

My

My foul is up in arms, ready to charge
And bear amidſt the foe with conqu'ring troops.
I hear 'em call to lead 'em on to liberty,
To victory ; their ſhouts and clamours rend
My ears, and reach the heav'ns : where is the
          king?
Where is Alphonſo? ha! where! where indeed?
O I could tear and burſt the ſtrings of life,
To break theſe chains. Off, off, ye ſtains of
          royalty!
Off, ſlavery! O curſe, that I alone
Can beat and flutter in my cage, when I
Would ſoar and ſtoop at victory beneath!

              Mourning Bride, act 3. ſc. 2.

If the emotions be unequal in force, the
ſtronger after a conflict will extinguiſh the
weaker. Thus the loſs of a houſe by fire
or of a ſum of money by bankruptcy, will
make no figure in oppoſition to the birth of
a long-expected ſon, who is to inherit an
opulent fortune. After ſome ſlight vibra-
tions, the mind ſettles in joy, and the loſs is
forgot.

    The foregoing obſervations, will be found
of great uſe in the fine arts. Many practical rules are derived from them, which I
                  ſhall

shall have occasion afterward to mention.
For instant satisfaction in part, I propose to
show the use of these observations in music,
a theme I insist upon at present, not being
certain of another opportunity more favourable. It will be admitted, that no combination of sounds but what is agreeable to
the ear, is intitled to the name of music.
Melody and harmony are separately agreeable and in union delightful. The agreeableness of vocal music differs from that of
instrumental. The former being intended
to accompany words, ought to be expressive
of the sentiment that is conveyed by the
words. But the latter having no connection with words, may be agreeable without
expressing any sentiment. Harmony properly so called, though delightful when in
perfection, is not expressive of sentiment;
and we often find good melody without the
least tincture of it.

These preliminaries being established, I
proceed directly to the point. In vocal music, the intimate connection of sense and
sound rejects dissimilar emotions, those especially that are opposite. Similar emotions
produced

produced by the fenfe and found go naturally into union; and at the fame time are
felt to be concordant or harmonious. Diffimilar emotions, on the other hand, forced
into union by caufes intimately connected,
not only obfcure each other, but are alfo
unpleafant by difcordance. From thefe
principles it is eafy to fay what fort of poetical compofitions are fitted for mufic. It is
evident that no poem expreffing the fentiments of any difagreeable paffion is proper.
The pain a man feels who is actuated with
malice or unjuft revenge, difqualifies him
for relifhing mufic or any thing that is entertaining. And fuppofing him difpofed,
againft nature, to vent his fentiments in
mufic, the mixture would be unpleafant; for thefe paffions raife difguft and
averfion in the audience *, a tone of mind
oppofite to every emotion that mufic can infpire. A man feized with remorfe cannot
bear mufic, becaufe every fort of it muft be
difcordant with his tone of mind; and when
thefe by an unfkilful artift are forced into

* See part 2. of the prefent chapter, toward the clofe.

union,

union, the mixture is unpleasant to the audience.

In general, music never can have a good effect in conjunction with any composition expressive of malice, envy, peevishness, or any other dissocial passion. The pleasure of music, on the other hand, is similar to all pleasant emotions; and music is finely qualified for every song where such emotions are expressed. Music particularly in a chearful tone, is concordant in the highest degree with every emotion in the same tone; and hence our taste for chearful airs expressive of mirth and jollity. Music is peculiarly well qualified for accompanying every sympathetic emotion. Sympathetic joy associates finely with chearful music, and sympathetic pain not less finely with music that is tender and melancholy. All the different emotions of love, *viz.* tenderness, concern, anxiety, pain of absence, hope, fear, *&c.* accord delightfully with music. A person in love, even when unkindly treated, is soothed by music. The tenderness of love still prevailing, accords with a melancholy strain. This

is

is finely exemplified by Shakefpear in the fourth act of *Othello*, where Defdemona calls for a fong expreffive of her diftrefs. Wonderful is the delicacy of that writer's tafte, which fails him not even in the moft refined emotions of human nature. Melancholy mufic again is fuitable to flight grief, which requires or admits confolation. But deep grief, which refufes all confolation, rejects for that reafon even melancholy mufic. For a different reafon, mufic is improper for accompanying pleafant emotions of the more important kind. Thefe totally ingrofs the mind, and leave no place for mufic or any fort of amufement. In a perilous enterprife to dethrone a tyrant, mufic would be impertinent, even where hope prevails, and the profpect of fuccefs is great. Alexander attacking the Indian town and mounting the wall, had certainly no impulfe to exert his prowefs in a fong. It is true, that not the leaft regard is paid to thefe rules either in the French or Italian opera; and the attachment we have to thefe compofitions, may at firft fight be confidered as a proof that the foregoing doctrine cannot be founded on human nature. But the gene-

ral taſte for operas is at bottom no authority againſt me. In our operas the paſſions
are ſo imperfectly expreſſed, as to leave the
mind free for reliſhing muſic of any ſort indifferently. It cannot be diſguiſed, that
the pleaſure of an opera is derived chiefly
from the muſic, and ſcarce at all from the
ſentiments. A happy coincidence of emotions raiſed by the ſong and by the muſic, is
extremely rare; and I venture to affirm,
that there is no example of it unleſs where
the emotion raiſed by the former is pleaſant
as well as that raiſed by the latter.

The ſubject we have run through, appears not a little entertaining. It is extremely curious to obſerve, in many inſtances, a plurality of cauſes producing in conjunction a great pleaſure : in other inſtances,
not leſs frequent, no conjunction, but each
cauſe acting in oppoſition. To enter blunt-
ly upon a ſubject of ſuch intricacy, might
gravel an acute philoſopher; and yet by
taking matters in a train, the intricacy
vaniſheth.

Next in order, according to the method
propoſed, come external effects. And this
leads to paſſions in particular, which involving

ving defire are the caufes of action. Two
coexiftent paffions that have the fame tendency, muft be fimilar. They accordingly
readily unite, and in conjunction have double force; which muft hold whether the
two paffions have the fame or different caufes. This is verified by experience; from
which we learn, that different paffions having the fame end in view, impel the mind
to action with united force. The mind receives not impulfes alternately from thefe
paffions, but one ftrong impulfe from the
whole in conjunction. And indeed it is not
eafy to conceive what fhould bar the union
of paffions that have all of them the fame
tendency.

Two paffions having oppofite tendencies,
may proceed from the fame object or caufe
confidered in different lights. Thus a miftrefs may at once be the object both of love
and refentment. Her beauty inflames the
paffion of love: her cruelty or inconftancy
caufes refentment. When two fuch paffions
coexift in the fame breaft, the oppofition of
their aim prevents any fort of union. They
are not felt otherwife than in fucceffion.

Y 2   And

And the confequence muft be one of two
things : the paffions will balance each other,
and prevent external action ; or one of them
will prevail, and accomplifh its end. Guari-
ni, in his *Paftor Fido*, defcribes beautifully
the ftruggle betwixt love and refentment
directed upon the fame object.

> *Corifca.* Chi vide mai, chi mai udi più ftrana
> E più folle, e più fera, e più importuna
> Paffione amorofa ? amore, ed odio
> Con sì mirabil tempre in un cor mifti,
> Che l'un per l'altro (e non fo ben dir come)
> E fi ftrugge, e s'avanza, e nafce, e more.
> S' i' miro alle bellezze di Mirtillo
> Dal piè leggiadro al graziofo volto,
> Il vago portamento, il bel fembiante.
> Gli atti, i coftumi, e le parole, e 'l guardo ;
> M'affale Amore con sì poffente foco
> Ch'i' ardo tutta, e par, ch' ogn' altro affetto
> Da quefto fol fia fuperato, e vinto :
> Ma fe poi penfo all' oftinato amore,
> Ch' ei porta ad altra donna, e che per lei
> Di me non cura, e fprezza (il vo' pur dire)
> La mia famofa, e da mill' alme, e mille
> Inchinata beltà, bramata grazia ;
> L'odio così, così l'aborro, e fchivo,
> Che impoffibil mi par, ch'unqua per lui

Mi

Mi s'accendeſſe al cor fiamma amoroſa.
Tallor meco ragiono : o s'io poteſſi
Gioir del mio dolciſſimo Mirtillo,
Sicche foſſe mio tutto, e ch' altra mai
Poſſeder no 'l poteſſe, o pi d' ogn' altra
Beata, e feliciſſima Coriſca!
Ed in quel punto in me ſorge un talento
Verſo di lui sì dolce, e sì gentile,
Che di ſ.guirlo, e di pregarlo ancora,
E di ſcoprirgli il cor prendo conſiglio.
Che più? così mi ſtimola il deſio,
Che ſe poteſſi allor l'adorerei.
Dall' altra parte i' mi riſento, e dico,
Un ritroſo? uno ſchifo? un che non degna?
Un, che può d'altra donna eſſer amante?
Un, ch' ardiſce mirarmi, e non m'adora?
E dal mio volto ſi difende in guiſa,
Che per amor non more? ed io, che lui
Dovrei veder, come molti altri i' veggio
Supplice, e lagrimoſa a' piedi miei,
Supplice, e lagrimoſo a' piedi ſuoi
Soſterro di cadere? ah non fia mai.
Ed in queſto penſier tant' ira accoglio
Contra di lui, contra di me, che volſi
A ſeguirlo il penſier, gli occhi a mirarlo,
Che 'l nome di Mirtillo, e l'amor mio
Odio più che la morte; e lui vorrei
Veder il più dolente, il più infelice

Paſtor,

Paftor, che viva; e fe poteffi allora,
Con le mie proprie man l'anciderei.
Così fdegno, defire, odio, ed amore
Mi fanno guerra, ed io, che ftata fono
Sempre fin qui di mille cor la fiamma,
Di mill' alme il tormento, ardo, e languifco:
E provo nel mio mal le pene altrui.

Aĕt 1. *fc.* 3.

Ovid paints in lively colours the vibration of mind betwixt two oppofite paffions directed upon the fame object. Althea had two brothers much beloved, who were unjuftly put to death by her fon Meleager in a fit of paffion. She was ftrongly impelled to revenge; but the criminal was her own fon. This ought to have with-held her hand. But the ftory makes a better figure and is more interefting, by the violence of the ftruggle betwixt refentment and maternal love.

Dona Deûm templis nato victore ferebat;
Cum videt extinctos fratres Althæa referri.
Quæ plangore dato, mœftis ululatibus urbem
Implet; et auratis mutavit veftibus atras.
At fimul eft auctor necis editus; excidit omnis
Luctus: et a lacrymis in pœnæ verfus amorem eft.

Stipes

Stipes erat, quem, cum partus enixa jaceret
Theftias, in flammam triplices pofuêre forores;
Staminaque impreffo fatalia pollice nentes,
Tempora, dixerunt, eadem lignoque, tibique,
O modo nate, damus. Quo poftquam carmine
    dicto
Exceffere deæ; flagrantem mater ab igne
Erripuit torrem: fparfitque liquentibus undis.
Ille diu fuerat penetralibus abditus imis;
Servatufque, tuos, juvenis, fervaverat annos.
Protulit hunc genitrix, tædafque in fragmina poni
Imperat; et pofitis inimicos admovet ignes.
Tum conata quater flammis imponere ramum
Cœpta quater tenuit. Pugnat materque, fororque,
Et diverfa trahunt unum duo nomina pectus.
Sæpe metu fceleris pallebant ora futuri:
Sæpe fuum fervens oculis dabat ira ruborem,
Et modo nefcio quid fimilis crudele minanti
Vultus erat; modo quem mifereri credere poffes:
Cumque ferus lacrymas animi ficcaverat ardor;
Inveniebantur lacrymæ tamen. Utque carina,
Quam ventus, ventoque contrarius æftus,
Vim geminam fentit, paretque incerta duobus:
Theftias haud aliter dubiis affectibus errat,
Inque vices ponit, pofitamque refufcitat iram.
Incipit effe tamen melior germana parente;
Et, confanguineas ut fanguine leniat umbras,
Impietate pia eft. Nam poftquam peftifer ignis .
                          Convaluit:

Convaluit : Rogus iste cremet mea viscera, dixit.

Utque manu dirâ lignum fatale tenebat;

Ante sepulchrales infelix adstitit aras.

Poenarumque deæ triplices furialibus, inquit,

Eumenides, sacris vultus advertite vestros.

Ulciscor, facioque nefas. Mors morte pianda est;

In scelus addendum scelus est, in funera funus :

Per coacervatos pereat domus impia luctus.

An felix Oeneus nato victore fruetur;

Thestius orbus erit? melius lugebitis ambo.

Vos modo, fraterni manes, animæque recentes,

Officium sentite meum; magnoque paratas

Accipite inferias, uteri mala pignora nostri.

Hei mihi! quo rapior? fratres ignoscite matri.

Deficiunt ad coepta manus. Meruisse fatemur

Illum, cur pereat : mortis mihi displicet auctor.

Ergo impune feret; vivusque, et victor, et ipso

Successu tumidus regnum Calydonis habebit?

Vos cinis exiguus, gelidæque jacebitis umbræ?

Haud equidem patiar. Pereat sceleratus; et ille

Spemque patris, regnique trahat, patriæque ruinam.

Mens ubi materna est; ubi sunt pia jura parentum?

Et, quos sustinui, bis mensûm quinque labores?

O utinam primis arsisses ignibus infans;

Idque ego passa forem! vixisti munere nostro:

Nunc merite moriere tuo. Cape præmia facti;

Bisque datam, primum partu, mox stipite rapto,

Redde animam; vel me fraternis adde sepulchris.

Et

Et cupio, et nequeo. Quid agam? modo vulnera
    fratrum
Ante oculos mihi funt, et tantæ cædis imago ;
Nunc animum pietas, maternaque nomina fran -
    gunt.
Me miferam! male vincetis, fed vincite, fratres:
Dummodo, quæ dedero vobis folatia, vofque
Ipfa fequar, dixit: dextraque averfa trementi
Funereum torrem medios conjecit in ignes.
Aut dedit, aut vifus gemitus eft ille dediffe,
Stipes ; et invitis correptus ab ignibus arfit.

Metamorph. lib. 8. *l.* 445.

In cafes of this kind, one circumftance always augments the fluctuation. A refolu-
tion to prefer one action before another after balancing betwixt them, is an inchoated
gratification of the prevailing paffion, which
foftens it in fome degree. This circumftance tends to give a fuperiority to the oppofite paffion. And another circumftance
alfo concurs, that this oppofite paffion has
by reftraint acquired in the interim fome
additional force.

Love and jealoufy connected by a common object, occupy the mind alternately.
When the object is confidered as beautiful,

VOL. I.   Z   love

love prevails: when confidered as poffibly unfaithful, jealoufy prevails. A fituation of this kind, affords great fcope for fluctuation of paffion, which is painted to the life by feveral mafterly hands in words as well as in colours. Shakefpear handles the fame fubject, but in a manner uncommon and peculiar to himfelf. In Othello's foliloquy before putting his wife to death, love and jealoufy are reprefented, each exerting its whole force, but without any ftruggle. Othello was naturally inflexible; and the tenderest love could not divert him from a purpofe he approved as right, not even for a moment. But every thing confiftent with fuch a character is done to reconcile the two oppofite paffions. He is refolved to put her to death, but he will not fhed her blood, nor fo much as ruffle her fkin.

Othello. It is the caufe, it is the caufe, my foul;—
Let me not name it to you, you chafte ftars!
It is the caufe.———Yet I'll not fhed her blood,
Nor fcar that whiter fkin of hers than fnow,
And fmooth as monumental alabafter.

    [*Lays down the fword.*
Yet fhe muft die; elfe fhe'll betray more men.
Put out the light, and then—Put out the light?—

             If

If I quench thee, thou flaming minister,
I can again thy former light restore,
Should I repent: but once put out *thy* light,
Thou cunning'st pattern of excelling nature,
I know not where is that Promethean heat
That can thy light relumine.—[*Sets down the taper.*
When I have pluck'd thy rose,
I cannot give it vital growth again;
It needs must wither.— I'll smell thee on the tree;
[*Kissing her.*
Oh balmy breath, that dost almost persuade
Justice to break her sword!—— One more; one
more;
Be thus when thou art dead, and I will kill thee,
And love thee after.——One more, that's the last;
So sweet was ne'er so fatal! I must weep,
But they are cruel tears? this sorrow's heav'nly;
It strikes where it doth love.—— She wakes——
Act 5. *sc.* 6.

In Otway's *Orphan*, we have an illustrious
example of the address employed to gratify
opposite passions directed upon the same object. Castalio and Polydore, brothers and
rivals, had sworn mutual confidence. Castalio broke his faith by a private marriage.
By this concealment, Polydore was unwa-
rily betrayed into a dismal deed, that of
polluting

polluting his brother's bed. Thus he had injured his brother, and was injured by him. Juſtice prompted him to make full atonement by his own death: reſentment againſt his brother required a full atonement to be made to himſelf. In coexiſtent paſſions ſo contradictory, one of them commonly prevails after a ſtruggle. But here happily an expedient occurred to gratify both; which was, that Polydore ſhould provoke his brother to put him to death. Polydore's crime in his own opinion merited this puniſhment; and juſtice was ſatisfied when he fell by the hands of the man he had injured. He wanted at the ſame time to puniſh his brother for breach of faith; and he could not do this more effectually than by betraying his brother to be his executioner.

If difference of aim prevent the union of two paſſions though having the ſame object, much more will it prevent their union when their objects are alſo different. In both caſes there is a fluctuation; but in the latter the fluctuation is ſlower than in the former. A beautiful ſituation of this kind is exhibited in the *Cid* of Corneille.

Don

Don Diegue, an old foldier worn out with age, having received a mortal affront from the Count father to Chimene, employs his fon Don Rodrigue, Chimene's lover, to demand fatisfaction. This fituation occafions in the breaft of Don Rodrigue a cruel ftruggle. It is a conteft betwixt love and honour, one of which muft be facrificed. The fcene is finely conducted, chiefly by making love in fome degree take part with honour, Don Rodrigue reflecting, that if he loft his honour he could not deferve his miftrefs. Honour triumphs. The Count, provoked to a fingle combat, falls by the hand of Don Rodrigue.

This produceth another beautiful fituation refpecting Chimene, which for the fake of connection is placed here, though it properly belongs to the foregoing head. It became the duty of that lady to demand juftice againft her lover, for whofe prefervation, in other circumftances, fhe chearfully would have facrificed her own life. The ftruggle betwixt thefe oppofite paffions directed upon the fame object, is finely expreffed in the third fcene of the third act.

Elvire.

Elvire. Il vous prive d'un pére, et vous l'aimez
    encore!

  Chimene C'eſt peu de dire aimer, Elvire, je
    l'adore;

Ma paſſion s'oppoſe à mon reſſentiment,

Dedans mon ennemi je trouve mon amant,

Et je ſens qu'en depit de toute ma colére,

Rodrigue dans mon cœur combat encore mon pére.

Il l'attaque, il le preſſe, il céde, il ſe défend,

Tantôt fort, tantôt foible, et tantôt triomphant;

Mais en ce dur combat de colére et de flame,

Il déchire mon cœur ſans partager mon ame,

Et quoique mon amour ait ſur moi de pouvoir,

Je ne conſulte point pour ſuivre mon devoir.

Je cours ſans balancer où mon honneur m'oblige;

Rodrigue m'eſt bien cher, ſon interêt m'afflige,

Mon cœur prend ſon parti; mais malgré ſon effort,

Je ſai ce que je ſuis, et que mon pére eſt mort.

Not leſs when the objects are different
than when the ſame, are means ſometimes
afforded to gratify both paſſions; and ſuch
means are greedily embraced. In Taſſo's
Geruſalem, Edward and Gildippe, huſband
and wife, are introduced fighting gallantly
againſt the Saracens. Gildippe receives a
mortal wound by the hand of Soliman. Edward inflamed with revenge as well as con-
                              cern

cern for Gildippe, is agitated betwixt the two different objects. The poet * describes him endeavouring to gratify both at once, applying his right hand against Soliman the object of his resentment, and his left hand to support his wife the object of his love.

PART V.

The power of passion to adjust our opinions and belief to its gratification.

THere is such a connection among the perceptions passions and actions of the same person, that it would be wonderful if they should have no mutual influence. That our actions are too much directed by passion, is a sad truth. It is not less certain, though not so commonly observed, that passion hath an irregular influence upon our opinions and belief. The opinions we form of men and things, are generally directed by affection. An advice given by a man of figure, hath great weight; the

* Canto 20. st. 97.

same

same advice from one in a low condition, is utterly neglected. A man of courage under-rates danger; and to the indolent, the slightest obstacle appears unsurmountable. Our opinions indeed, the result commonly of various and often opposite views, are so slight and wavering, as readily to be susceptible of a bias from passion and prejudice.

This subject is of great use in logic; and of still greater use in criticism, being intimately connected with many principles of the fine arts that will be unfolded in the course of this work. Being too extensive to be treated here at large, some cursory illustrations must suffice; leaving the subject to be prosecuted more particularly afterward when occasion shall offer.

Two principles that make an eminent figure in human nature, concur to give passion an undue influence upon our opinions and belief. The first and most extensive, is a strong tendency in the mind to fit objects for the gratification of its passions. We are prone to such opinions of men and things as correspond to our wishes. Where the object, in dignity or importance, corresponds

responds to the paffion beftowed on it, the
gratification is complete and there is no occafion for artifice. But where the object is
too mean for the paffion fo as not to afford
a complete gratification, it is wonderful how
apt the mind is to impofe upon itfelf, and
how difpofed to proportion the object to its
paffion. The other principle is a ftrong
tendency in our nature to juftify our paffions
as well as our actions, not to others only,
but even to ourfelves. This tendency is extremely remarkable with refpect to difagreeable paffions. By its influence, objects are
magnified or leffened, circumftances fuppli-
ed or fuppreffed, every thing coloured and
difguifed, to anfwer the end of juftification.
Hence the foundation of felf-deceit, where
a man impofes upon himfelf innocently, and
even without fufpicion of a bias.

Befide the influence of the foregoing principles to make us form opinions contrary to
truth, the paffions themfelves, by fubordi-
nate means, contribute to the fame effect.
Of thefe means I fhall mention two which
feem to be capital. Firft, There was occa-

fion formerly to obferve *, that though ideas feldom ftart up in the mind without connection, yet that ideas which correfpond to the prefent tone of the mind are readily fuggefted by any flight connection. By this means, the arguments for a favourite opinion are always at hand, while we often fearch in vain for thofe that crofs our inclination. Second, The mind taking delight in agreeable circumftances or arguments, is ftrongly impreffed with them ; while thofe that are difagreeable are hurried over fo as fcarce to make any impreffion. The felf-fame argument, accordingly as it is relifhed or not relifhed, weighs fo differently, as in truth to make conviction depend more on paffion than on reafoning. This obfervation is fully juftified by experience. To confine myfelf to a fingle inftance, the numberlefs abfurd religious tenets that at different times have peftered the world, would be altogether unaccountable but for this irregular bias of paffion.

We proceed to a more pleafant tafk,

* Chap. 1.

which

which is, to illuftrate the foregoing obfervations by proper examples. Gratitude when warm, is often exerted upon
the children of the benefactor; efpecially
where he is removed out of reach by
death or abfence *. Gratitude in this cafe
being exerted for the fake of the benefactor, requires no peculiar excellence in
his children. To find however thefe children worthy of the benefits intended them,
contributes undoubtedly to the more entire
gratification of the paffion. And accordingly, the mind, prone to gratify its paffions, is
apt to conceive a better opinion of thefe children than poffibly they deferve. By this
means, ftrong connections of affection are
often formed among individuals, upon the
flight foundation now mentioned.

Envy is a paffion, which, being altogether unjuftifiable, is always difguifed under
fome more plaufible name. But no paffion
is more eager than envy, to give its object
fuch an appearance as to anfwer a complete
gratification. It magnifies every bad quali-

* See part 1. fect. 1. of the prefent chapter.

ty,

ty, and fixes on the moſt humbling circumſtances.

   Caſſius. I cannot tell what you and other men
Think of this life; but for my ſingle ſelf,
I had as lief not be, as live to be
In awe of ſuch a thing as I myſelf.
I was born free as Cæſar, ſo were you;
We both have fed as well; and we can both
Endure the winter's cold as well as he.
For once, upon a raw and guſty day,
The troubled Tyber chafing with his ſhores,
Cæſar ſays to me, Dar'ſt thou, Caſſius, now
Leap in with me into this angry flood,
And ſwim to yonder point? — Upon the word,
Accoutred as I was, I plunged in,
And bid him follow; ſo indeed he did.
The torrent roar'd, and we did buffet it
With luſty ſinews; throwing it aſide,
And ſtemming it with hearts of controverſy.
But ere we could arrive the point propos'd,
Cæſar cry'd, Help me, Caſſius, or I ſink.
I, as Æneas, our great anceſtor,
Did from the flames of Troy upon his ſhoulder
The old Anchiſes bear; ſo from the waves of
       Tyber
Did I the tired Cæſar: and this man
Is now become a god, and Caſſius is

                  A

A wretched creature; and muſt bend his body,
If Cæſar careleſsly but nod on him.
He had a fever when he was in Spain,
And when the fit was on him, I did mark
How he did ſhake. 'Tis true, this god did ſhake;
His coward lips did from their colour fly,
And that ſame eye whoſe bend doth awe the world,
Did loſe its luſtre; I did hear him grone:
Ay, and that tongue of his, that bade the Romans
Mark him, and write his ſpeeches in their books,
Alas! it cry'd ―― Give me ſome drink, Titi-
            nius ――
As a ſick girl.   Ye gods, it doth amaze me,
A man of ſuch a feeble temper ſhould
So get the ſtart of the majeſtic world,
And bear the palm alone.

                    Julius Cæſar, *act* 1. *ſc.* 3.

Glo'ſter inflamed with reſentment againſt
his ſon Edgar, could even work himſelf into a momentary conviction that they were
not related.

O ſtrange faſten'd villain!
Would he deny his letter?―I never got him.

                    King Lear, *act* 2. *ſc.* 3.

When by a great ſenſibility of heart or
                                    other

other means, grief swells beyond what the
cause can justify, the mind is prone to magnify the cause, in order to gratify the passion. And if the real cause admit not of
being magnified, the mind seeks a cause
for its grief in imagined future events.

Bushy. Madam, your Majesty is much too sad:
You promis'd, when you parted with the King,
To lay aside self-harming heaviness,
And entertain a chearful disposition.
   Queen. To please the King, I did; to please
     myself,
I cannot do it. Yet I know no cause
Why I should welcome such a guest as grief;
Save bidding farewell to so sweet a guest
As my sweet Richard: yet again, methinks,
Some unborn sorrow, ripe in Fortune's womb,
Is coming tow'rd me; and my inward soul
With something trembles, yet at nothing grieves,
More than with parting from my Lord the King.
                Richard II. *act.* 2. *sc.* 5.

The foregoing examples depend on the
first principle. In the following, both principles concur. Resentment at first is wreak-
ed on the relations of the offender, in order

der to punish him.   But as refentment when fo outrageous is contrary to confcience, the mind, to juftify its paffion as well as to gratify it, is difpofed to paint thefe relations in the blackeft colours ; and it actually comes to be convinced, that they ought to be punifhed for their own demerits.

Anger raifed by an accidental ftroke upon a tender part, which gives great and fudden pain, is fometimes vented upon the undefigning caufe.   But as the paffion in this cafe is abfurd, and as there can be no folid gratification in punifhing the innocent; the mind, prone to juftify as well as to gratify its paffion, deludes itfelf inftantly into a conviction of the action's being voluntary. This conviction however is but momentary : the firft reflection fhows it to be erroneous; and the paffion vanifheth almoft inftantaneoufly with the conviction.   But anger, the moft violent of all paffions, has ftill greater influence.   It fometimes forces the mind to perfonify a ftock or a ftone when it occafions bodily pain, in order to be a proper object of refentment.   A conception

ception is formed of it as a voluntary agent. And that we have really a momentary conviction of its being a voluntary agent, muſt be evident from conſidering, that without ſuch conviction, the paſſion can neither be juſtified nor gratified. The imagination can give no aid. A ſtock or a ſtone may be imagined ſenſible; but a notion of this kind cannot be the foundation of puniſhment, ſo long as the mind is conſcious that it is an imagination merely without any reality. Of ſuch perſonification, involving a conviction of reality, there is one illuſtrious inſtance. When the firſt bridge of boats over the Helleſpont was deſtroyed by a ſtorm, Xerxes fell into a tranſport of rage, ſo exceſſive, that he commanded the ſea to be puniſhed with 300 ſtripes; and a pair of fetters to be thrown into it, enjoining the following words to be pronounced. " O thou ſalt and bitter water! thy maſter " hath condemned thee to this puniſhment " for offending him without cauſe; and is " reſolved to paſs over thee in deſpite of thy " inſolence. With reaſon all men neglect " to

" to facrifice to thee, becaufe thou art
" both difagreeable and treacherous *."

Shakefpear exhibits beautiful examples of
the irregular influence of paffion in making
us conceive things to be otherwife than they
are. King Lear, in his diftrefs, perfonifies
the rain, wind, and thunder; and in order
to juftify his refentment, conceives them to
be taking part with his daughters.

> *Lear.* Rumble thy belly-full, fpit fire, fpout
>   rain!
> Nor rain, wind, thunder, fire, are my daughters.
> I tax not you, you elements, with unkindnefs;
> I never gave you kingdom, call'd you children;
> You owe me no fubfcription. Then let fall
> Your horrible pleafure.——Here I ftand, your
>   brave;
> A poor, infirm, weak, and defpis'd old man!
> But yet I call you fervile minifters,
> That have with two pernicious daughters join'd
> Your high engender'd battles, 'gainft a head
> So old and white as this. Oh! oh! 'tis foul.
>   *Act 3. fc. 2.*

King Kichard, full of indignation againft

* Herodotus, book 7.

his favourite horſe for ſuffering Bolingbroke to ride him, conceives for a moment the horſe to be rational.

> *Groom.* O, how it yearn'd my heart, when I be-
> held,
> In London ſtreets, that coronation-day;
> When Bolingbroke rode on Roan Barbary,
> That horſe that thou ſo often haſt beſtrid,
> That horſe that I ſo carefully have dreſs'd.
>   *K. Rich.* Rode he on Barbary? tell me, gentle
>   friend,
> How went he under him?
>   *Groom.* So proudly as he had diſdain'd the
>   ground.
>   *K. Rich.* So proud that Bolingbroke was on his
>   back!
> That jade had eat bread from my royal hand.
> This hand hath made him proud with clapping him.
> Would he not ſtumble? would he not fall down,
> (Since pride muſt have a fall), and break the neck
> Of that proud man that did uſurp his back?
>   *Richard* II. *act* 5. *ſc.* 11.

Hamlet, ſwelled with indignation at his mother's ſecond marriage, is ſtrongly in-clined to leſſen the time of her widowhood; becauſe this circumſtance gratified his paſſion;

fion; and he deludes himfelf by degrees into the opinion of an interval fhorter than the real one.

Hamlet. ————That it fhould come to this!
But two months dead! nay, not fo much; not
    two;—
So excellent a King, that was, to this,
Hyperion to a fatire: fo loving to my mother,
That he permitted not the wind of heav'n
Vifit her face too roughly. Heav'n and earth!
Muft I remember — why, fhe would hang on him,
As if increafe of appetite had grown
By what it fed on; yet, within a month,——
Let me not think— Frailty, thy name is *Woman!*
A little month! or ere thofe fhoes were old,
With which fhe follow'd my poor father's body,
Like Niobe, all tears——Why, fhe, ev'n fhe —
(O heav'n! a beaft that wants difcourfe of reafon,
Would have mourn'd longer—) married with mine
    uncle,
My father's brother; but no more like my father,
Than I to Hercules. Within a month!——
Ere yet the falt of moft unrighteous tears
Had left the flufhing in her gauled eyes,
She married.—— Oh, moft wicked fpeed, to poft
With fuch dexterity to inceftuous fheets!

It

It is not, nor it cannot come to good.
But break, my heart, for I muſt hold my tongue.

Act 1. *ſc.* 3.

The power of paſſion to falſify the computation of time, is the more remarkable,
that time, which hath an accurate meaſure,
is leſs obſequious to our deſires and wiſhes,
than objects which have no preciſe ſtandard
of leſs or more.

Even belief, though partly an act of the
judgment, may be influenced by paſſion.
Good news are greedily ſwallowed upon
very ſlender evidence. Our wiſhes magnify the probability of the event as well as
the veracity of the relater ; and we believe
as certain what at beſt is doubtful.

Quel, che l' huom vede, amor li fa inviſibile
E l' inviſibil fa veder amore.
Queſto creduto fu, che'l miſer ſuole
Dar facile credenza a' quel, che vuole.

Orland. Furioſ. cant. 1. *ſt.* 56.

For the ſame reaſon, bad news gain alſo
credit upon the ſlighteſt evidence. Fear,
if once alarmed, has the ſame effect with
hope

hope to magnify every circumftance that tends to conviction. Shakefpear, who fhows more knowledge of human nature than any of our philofophers, hath in his *Cymbeline* * reprefented this bias of the mind: for he makes the perfon who alone was affected with the bad news, yield to evidence that did not convince any of his companions. And Othello † is convinced of his wife's infidelity from circumftances too flight to move an indifferent perfon.

If the news intereft us in fo low a degree as to give place to reafon, the effect will not be quite the fame. Judging of the probability or improbability of the ftory, the mind fettles in a rational conviction either that it is true or not. But even in this cafe, it is obfervable, that the mind is not allowed to reft in that degree of conviction which is produced by rational evidence. If the news be in any degree favourable, our belief is augmented by hope beyond its true pitch; and if unfavourable, by fear.

* Act 2. fc. 6.
† Act 3. fc. 8.

The

The obfervation holds equally with re-fpeét to future events. If a future event be either much wifhed or dreaded, the mind, to gratify its paffion, never fails to augment the probability beyond truth.

The credit which in all ages has been given to wonders and prodigies, even the moft abfurd and ridiculous, is a ftrange phenomenon. Nothing can be more evi-dent than the following propofition, That the more fingular any event is, the more evidence is required. A familiar event daily occurring, being in itfelf extremely pro-bable, finds ready credit, and therefore is vouched by the flighteft evidence. But a ftrange and rare event, contrary to the courfe of nature, ought not to be eafily be-lieved. It ftarts up without conneétion, and without caufe, fo far as we can difcover; and to overcome the improbability of fuch an event, the very ftrongeft evidence is re-quired. It is certain, however, that won-ders and prodigies are fwallowed by the vulgar, upon evidence that would not be fufficient to afcertain the moft familiar oc-currence. It has been reckoned difficult to explain

explain this irregular bias of the mind. We are now no longer at a lofs about its caufe. The pronenefs we have to gratify our paffions, which difplays itfelf upon fo many occafions, produces this irrational belief. A ftory of ghofts or fairies, told with an air of gravity and truth, raifeth an emotion of wonder, and perhaps of dread. Thefe emotions tending ftrongly to their own gratification, impofe upon a weak mind, and imprefs upon it a thorough conviction contrary to all fenfe and reafon.

Opinion and belief are influenced by propenfity as well as by paffion; for the mind is difpofed to gratify both. A natural propenfity is all we have to convince us, that the operations of nature are uniform. Influenced by this propenfity, we often rafhly conceive, that good or bad weather will never have an end; and in natural philofophy, writers, influenced by the fame propenfity, ftretch commonly their analogical reafonings beyond juft bounds.

Opinion and belief are influenced by affection as well as by propenfity. The noted

ted ſtory of a fine lady and a curate viewing the moon through a teleſcope is a pleaſant illuſtration. I perceive, ſays the lady,
two ſhadows inclining to each other, they
are certainly two happy lovers. Not at all,
replies the curate, they are two ſteeples of
a cathedral.

APPENDIX to Part V.

*Concerning the methods which nature hath
afforded for computing time and ſpace.*

I Introduce here the ſubject propoſed, becauſe it affords ſeveral curious examples
of the power of paſſion to adjuſt objects to
its gratification; a leſſon that cannot be too
much inculcated, as there is not perhaps
another bias in human nature that hath an
influence ſo univerſal, and that is ſo apt to
make us wander from truth as well as from
juſtice.

I begin with time; and the queſtion
ſhortly is, What was the meaſure of time
before artificial meaſures were invented?
and,

and, What is the meafure at prefent when thefe are not at hand? I fpeak not of months and days, which we compute by the moon and fun; but of hours, or in general of the time that runs betwixt any two occurrences when there is not accefs to the fun. The only natural meafure we have, is the train of our thoughts; and we always judge the time to be long or fhort, in proportion to the number of perceptions that have paffed through the mind during that interval. This is indeed a very imperfect meafure; becaufe in the different conditions of a quick or flow fucceffion, the computation is different. But however imperfect, it is the only meafure by which a perfon naturally calculates time; and this meafure is applied on all occafions, without regard to any occafional variation in the rate of fucceffion.

This natural meafure of time, imperfect as it is, would however be tolerable, did it labour under no other imperfection than the ordinary variations that happen in the motion of our perceptions. But in many particular circumftances, it is much more fallacious;

Vol. I.   C c   and

and in order to explain thefe diftinctly, I
muft analize the fubject. Time is generally
computed at two different periods; one while
time is paffing, another after it is paft. I fhall
confider thefe feparately, with the errors to
which each of them is liable. It will be
found that thefe errors often produce very
different computations of the fame period of
time. The computation of time while it is
paffing, comes firft in order. It is a common and trite obfervation, That to lovers abfence appears immeafurably long, every minute an hour, and every hour a day. The
fame computation is made in every cafe
where we long for a diftant event; as where
one is in expectation of good news, or where
a profligate heir watches for the death of an
old man who keeps him from a great eftate.
Oppofite to thefe are inftances not fewer in
number. To a criminal the interval betwixt
fentence and execution appears miferably
fhort; and the fame holds in every cafe
where one dreads an approaching event. Of
this even a fchoolboy can bear witnefs: the
hour allowed him for play, moves, in his
apprehenfion, with a very fwift pace: before

fore he is thoroughly engaged, the hour is gone. A reckoning founded on the number of ideas, will never produce computations so regularly opposite to each other; for a slow succession of ideas is not connected with our wishes, nor a quick succession with our fears. What is it then, that, in the cases mentioned, moves nature to desert her common measure for one very different? I know not that this question ever has been resolved. The false reckonings I have suggested are so common and familiar, that no writer has thought of inquiring for their cause. And indeed, to enter upon this matter at short hand, without preparation, might occasion some difficulty. But to encounter the difficulty, we luckily are prepared by what is said above about the power of passion to fit objects for its gratification. Among the other circumstances that terrify a condemned criminal, the short time he has to live is one. Terror, like our other passions, prone to its gratification, adjusts every one of these circumstances to its own tone. It magnifies in particular the shortness of the interval betwixt the present time

and

and that of the execution; and forces upon the criminal a conviction that the hour of his death approaches with a swift pace. In the same manner, among the other distresses of an absent lover, the time of separation is a capital circumstance, which for that reason is greatly magnified by his anxiety and impatience. He imagines that the time of meeting comes on very slow, or rather that it will never come. Every minute is thought of an intolerable length. Here is a fair and I hope satisfactory account, why we reckon time to be tedious when we long for a future event, and not less fleet when we dread the event. This account is confirmed by other instances. Bodily pain fixt to one part, produceth a slow train of perceptions, which, according to the common measure of time, ought to make it appear short. Yet we know, that in such a state time has the opposite appearance. Bodily pain is always attended with a degree of impatience and an anxiety to be rid of it, which make us judge every minute to be an hour. The same holds where the pain shifts from place to place; but not so remarkably, because such a pain is not attended with the same degree of impatience. The impatience a man hath in travelling through a barren country or in bad roads, makes him imagine, during the journey, that time goes on with a very flow pace. We fhall fhow afterward that he makes a very different computation when his journey is at an end.

How ought it to ftand with a man who apprehends bad news? It will probably be thought, that the cafe of this man refembles that of a criminal, who, in reckoning the fhort time he has to live, imagines every hour to be but a minute, and that time flies fwift away. Yet the computation here is directly oppofite. Reflecting upon this difficulty, there appears one capital circumftance in which the two cafes differ. The fate of the criminal is determined: in the cafe under confideration, the man is ftill in fufpenfe. Every one knows how diftrefsful fufpenfe is to the bulk of mankind. Such diftrefs we wifh to get rid of at any rate, even at the expence of bad news. This cafe therefore, upon a more narrow infpection, refembles that of bodily pain.

The

The prefent diftrefs in both cafes, makes the time appear extremely tedious.

The reader probably will not be difpleafed, to have this branch of the fubject illuftrated in a pleafant manner, by an author acquainted with every maze of the human heart, and who beftows ineffable grace and ornament upon every fubject he handles.

Rofalinda. I pray you, what is't a clock?

Orlando. You fhould afk me, what time o' day; there's no clock in the foreft.

Rof. Then there is no true lover in the foreft; elfe, fighing every minute, and groaning every hour, would detect the lazy foot of Time, as well as a clock.

Orla. Why not the fwift foot of Time? Had not that been as proper?

Rof. By no means, Sir. Time travels in diverfe paces with diverfe perfons. I'll tell you who Time ambles withal, who Time trots withal, who Time gallops withal, and who he ftands ftill withal.

Orla. I pr'y thee whom doth he trot withal?

Rof. Marry, he trots hard with a young maid, between the contract of her marriage, and the day it is folemnized: if the interim be but a fe'ennight,

night, Time's pace is fo hard that it feems the length of feven years.

Orla. Who ambles Time withal?

Rof. With a prieft that lacks Latin, and a rich man that hath not the gout: for the one fleeps eafily, becaufe he cannot ftudy; and the other lives merrily, becaufe he feels no pain: the one lacking the burden of lean and wafteful learning; the other knowing no burthen of heavy tedious penury. Thefe Time ambles withal.

Orla. Whom doth he gallop withal?

Rof. With a thief to the gallows: for though he go as foftly as foot can fall, he thinks himfelf too foon there.

Orla. Whom ftays it ftill withall?

Rof. With lawyers in the vacation; for they fleep between term and term, and then they perceive not how Time moves.

As you like it, act 3. fc. 8.

Reflecting upon the natural method of computing prefent time, it fhows how far from truth we may be led by the irregular power of paffion. Nor are our eyes immediately opened when the fcene is paft: the deception continues while there remain any traces of the paffion. But looking back upon paft time when the joy or diftrefs is no longer

longer remembered, the computation we make is very different. In this situation, passion being out of the question, we apply the ordinary measure, *viz.* the course of our perceptions; and I shall now proceed to the errors that this measure is subjected to. In order to have an accurate notion of this matter, we must distinguish betwixt a train of perceptions, and a train of ideas. Real objects make a strong impression, and are faithfully remembered. Ideas, on the contrary, however entertaining at the time, are apt to escape an after recollection. Hence it is, that in retrospection, the time that was employed upon real objects, appears longer than the time that was employed upon ideas. The former are more accurately recollected than the latter; and we measure the time by the number that is recollected. I proceed to particulars. After finishing a journey through a populous country, the frequency of agreeable objects distinctly recollected by the traveller, makes the time spent in the journey appear to him longer than it was in reality. This is chiefly remarkable in a first journey, where every object

object is new and makes a strong impression. On the other hand, after finishing a
journey through a barren country thinly
peopled, the time appears short, being mea-
sured by the number of objects, which were
few and far from interesting. Here in both
instances a reckoning is brought out, directly opposite to that made during the journey. And this, by the way, serves to account for a thing which may appear singular, that in a barren country the computed
miles are always longer, than near the capital, where the country is rich and populous.
The traveller has no natural measure of the
space gone through, other than the time
bestowed upon it; nor any natural measure
of the time, other than the number of his perceptions. These being proportioned to the
number of visible objects, he imagines that
he hath consumed more time on his day's
journey, and accomplished a greater number
of miles, in a populous than in a waste
country. By this method of calculation, e-
very computed mile in the former must in
reality be shorter than in the latter.

Again, the travelling with an agreeable

companion produceth a short computation both of the road and of time; especially if there be few objects that demand attention, or if the objects be familiar. The case is the same of young people at a ball, or of a joyous company over a bottle. The ideas with which they have been entertained, being transitory, escape the memory. After all is over, they reflect that they have been much diverted, but scarce can say about what.

When one is totally occupied in any a-greeable work that admits not many objects, time runs on without observation; and upon an after recollection must appear short, in proportion to the paucity of objects. This is still more remarkable in close contemplation and in deep thinking, where the train, composed wholly of ideas, proceeds with an extreme slow pace. Not only are the ideas few in number, but are apt to escape an after-reckoning. The like false reckoning of time may proceed from an opposite state of mind. In a reverie, where ideas float at random without making any impression, time goes on unheeded and the

reckoning

reckoning is loft. A reverie may be so profound as to prevent the recollection of any one idea: that the mind was busied in a train of thinking, will in general be remembered; but what was the subject, has quite escaped the memory. In such a case, we are altogether at a loss about the time: we have no *data* for making a computation. No cause produceth so false a reckoning of time, as immoderate grief. The mind, in this state, is violently attached to a single object, and admits not a different thought. Any other object breaking in, is instantly banished, so as scarce to give an appearance of succession. In a reverie, we are uncertain of the time that is past: but in the example now given, there is an appearance of certainty, so far as the natural measure of time can be trusted, that the time must have been short, when the perceptions are so few in number.

The natural measure of space appears more obscure than that of time. I venture however to enter upon it, leaving it to be further prosecuted, if it be thought of any importance.

D d 2   The

The fpace marked out for a houfe, appears confiderably larger after it is divided into its proper parts. A piece of ground appears larger after it is furrounded with a fence; and ftill larger when it is made a garden and divided into different copartments.

On the contrary, a large plain looks lefs after it is divided into parts. The fea muft be excepted, which looks lefs from that very circumftance of not being divided into parts.

A room of a moderate fize appears larger when properly furnifhed. But when a very large room is furnifhed, I doubt whether it be not leffened in appearance.

A room of a moderate fize, looks lefs by having a ceiling lower than in proportion. The fame low ceiling makes a very large room look larger than it is in reality.

Thefe experiments are by far too fmall a ftock for a general theory. But they are all that occur at prefent; and without attempting any regular fyftem, I fhall fatisfy myfelf with a few conjectures.

The largeft angle of vifion feems to me
the

the natural meafure of fpace. The eye is
the only judge; and in examining with it
the fize of any plain, or the length of any
line, the moft accurate method that can be
taken is, to run over the object in parts.
The largeft part that can be taken in at one
ftedfaft look, determines the largeft angle
of vifion; and when that angle is given,
one may inftitute a calculation by trying
with the eye how many of thefe parts are in
the whole.

Whether this angle be the fame in all
men, I know not. The fmalleft angle of
vifion is afcertained; and to afcertain the
largeft angle, would not be lefs curious.

But fuppofing it known, it would be a very imperfect meafure; perhaps more fo than
the natural meafure of time. It requires
great fteadinefs of eye to meafure a line with
any accuracy, by applying to it the largeft
angle of diftinct vifion. And fuppofe this fteadinefs to be acquired by practice, the meafure
will be imperfect from other circumftances.
The fpace comprehended under this angle,
will be different according to the diftance,
and alfo according to the fituation of the object.

ject. Of a perpendicular this angle will comprehend the fmalleft fpace. The fpace will be larger in looking upon an inclined plain ; and will be larger or lefs in proportion to the degree of inclination.

This meafure of fpace, like the meafure of time, is liable to fome extraordinary errors from certain operations of the mind, which will account for fome of the erroneous judgements above mentioned. The fpace marked out for a dwelling-houfe, where the eye is at any reafonable diftance, is feldom greater than can be feen at once without moving the head. Divide this fpace into two or three equal parts, and none of thefe parts will appear much lefs than what can be comprehended at one diftinct look ; confequently each of them will appear equal, or nearly equal, to what the whole did before the divifion. If, on the other hand, the whole be very fmall, fo as fcarce to fill the eye at one look, its divifions into parts will, I conjecture, make it appear ftill lefs. The minutenefs of the parts is, by an eafy tranfition of ideas, transferred to the whole. Each part hath a diminutive appearance, and by the

the intimate connection of these parts with the whole, we pass the same judgement upon all.

The space marked out for a small garden, is surveyed almost at one view; and requires a motion of the eye so slight, as to pass for an object that can be comprehended under the largest angle of distinct vision. If not divided into too many parts, we are apt to form the same judgement of each part; and consequently to magnify the garden in proportion to the number of its parts.

A very large plain without protuberances, is an object not less rare than beautiful; and in those who see it for the first time, it must produce an emotion of wonder. This emotion, however slight, tending to its own gratification, imposes upon the mind, and makes it judge that the plain is larger than it is in reality. Divide this plain into parts, and our wonder ceases. It is no longer considered as one great plain, but as so many different fields or inclosures.

The first time one beholds the sea, it appears to be large beyond all bounds. When

it

it becomes familiar, and raifes our wonder in no degree, it appears lefs than it is in reality. In a ftorm it appears larger, being diftinguifhable by the rolling waves into a number of great parts. Iflands fcattered at confiderable diftances, add in appearance to its fize. Each intercepted part looks extremely large, and we filently apply arithmetic to increafe the appearance of the whole. Many iflands fcattered at hand, give a diminutive appearance to the fea, by its connection with its diminutive parts. The Lomond lake would undoubtedly look larger without its iflands.

Furniture increafeth in appearance the fize of a fmall room, for the fame reafon that divifions increafe in appearance the fize of a garden. The emotion of wonder which is raifed by a very large room without furniture, makes it look larger than it is in reality. If completely furnifhed, we view it in parts, and our wonder is not raifed.

A low ceiling hath a diminutive appearance, which, by an eafy tranfition of ideas, is communicated to the length and breadth, provided they bear any fort of proportion to the

the height. If they be out of all proportion, the oppofition feizes the mind, and
raifes fome degree of wonder, which makes
the difference appear greater than it really is.

P A R T   VI.

*Of the refemblance emotions bear to their
caufes.*

THat many emotions bear a certain refemblance to their caufes, is a truth
that can be made clear by induction; though,
fo far as I know, the obfervation has not
been made by any writer. Motion, in its
different circumftances, is productive of
feelings that refemble it. Sluggifh motion,
for example, caufeth a languid unpleafant
feeling; flow uniform motion, a feeling
calm and pleafant; and brifk motion, a
lively feeling that roufes the fpirits and pro-
motes activity. A fall of water through
rocks, raifes in the mind a tumultuous con-
fufed agitation, extremely fimilar to its

caufe. When force is exerted with any effort, the fpectator feels a fimilar effort as of
force exerted within his mind. A large
object fwells the heart. An elevated object
makes the fpectator ftand erect.

Sounds alfo produce emotions that refemble them. A found in a low key, brings
down the mind. Such a found in a full tone,
hath a certain folemnity, which it commu-
nicates to the emotion produced by it. A
found in a high key, chears the mind by
raifing it. Such a found in a full tone,
both elevates and fwells the mind.

Again, a wall or pillar that declines from
the perpendicular, produceth a painful emotion, as of a tottering and falling within the
mind. An emotion fomewhat fimilar is
produced by a tall pillar that ftands fo tick-
lifh as to look like falling. For this reafon,
a column upon a bafe looks better than upon the naked ground. The bafe, which
makes a part of the column, infpires a feeling of firmnefs and ftability. The ground
fupporting a naked column, is too large to
be confidered as its bafe. And for the fame
reafon, a cube as a bafe, is preferred before

a

a cylinder, though the latter is a more beautiful figure. The angles of a cube, being extended to a greater diſtance from the centre than the circumference of a cylinder, give the column a greater appearance of ſtability. This excludes not a different reaſon, that the baſe, ſhaft, and capital, of a pillar, ought, for the ſake of variety, to differ from each other. If the ſhaft be round, the baſe and capital ought to be ſquare.

A conſtrained poſture, uneaſy to the man himſelf, is diſagreeable to the ſpectator; which makes it a rule in painting, that the drapery ought not to adhere to the body, but hang looſe, that the figures may appear eaſy and free in their movements. Hence the diſagreeable figure of a French dancing-maſter is one of Hogarth's pieces. It is alſo ridiculous, becauſe the conſtraint is aſſumed and not forced.

The foregoing obſervation is not confined to emotions raiſed by ſtill life. It holds alſo in thoſe which are raiſed by the qualities, actions, and paſſions, of a ſenſible being. Love inſpired by a fine woman, aſſumes her qualities. It is ſublime, ſoft, tender,

E e 2   der,

der, fevere, or gay, according to its caufe.
This is ftill more remarkable in emotions
raifed by human actions. It hath already
been remarked *, that any fignal inftance
of gratitude, befide procuring efteem for
the author, raifeth in the fpectator a vague
emotion of gratitude, which difpofeth him
to be grateful. I now further remark, that
this vague emotion, being of the fame kind
with what produced the grateful action,
hath a ftrong refemblance to its caufe.
Courage exerted infpires the reader as well
as the fpectator with a like emotion of courage. A juft action fortifies our love to
juftice, and a generous action roufes our
generofity. In fhort, with refpect to all virtuous actions, it will be found by induction,
that they lead us to imitation by infpiring
emotions refembling the paffions that produced thefe actions. And hence the benefit of dealing in choice books and in
choice company.

Grief as well as joy are infectious: the
emotions they raife in a fpectator refemble

* Part 1. of this chapter, fect. 3.

them

them perfectly. Fear is equally infectious : and, hence in an army, fear, even from the slightest cause, making an impression on a few, spreads generally through all, and becomes an univerfal panic. Pity is fimilar to its caufe. A parting fcene betwixt lovers or friends, produceth in the fpectator a fort of pity, which is tender like the diftrefs. The anguifh of remorfe, produceth pity of a harfh kind ; and if the remorfe be extreme, the pity hath a mixture of horror. Anger I think is fingular ; for even where it is moderate and caufeth no difguft, it difpofes not the fpectator to anger in any degree *. Covetoufnefs, cruelty, treachery, and other vicious paffions, are fo far from raifing any emotion fimilar to themfelves, to incite a fpectator to imitation, that they have an oppofite effect. They raife abhorrence, and fortify the fpectator in his averfion to fuch actions. When anger is immoderate, it cannot fail to produce the fame effect.

* Ariftotle, poet. cap. 18. § 3. fays, that anger raifeth in the fpectator a fimilar emotion of anger.

PART

PART   VII.

*Final causes of the more frequent emotions
and paſſions.*

IT is a law in our nature, that we never
act but by the impulſe of deſire; which
in other words is ſaying, that it is paſſion,
by the deſire included in it, which determines the will.   Hence in the conduct of
life, it is of the utmoſt importance, that
our paſſions be directed upon proper objects, tend to juſt and rational ends, and
with relation to each other be duly balanced.   The beauty of contrivance, ſo
conſpicuous in the human frame, is not
confined to the rational part of our nature,
but is viſible over the whole.   Concerning
the paſſions in particular, however irregular,
headſtrong, and perverſe, in an overly
view, they may appear, I propoſe to ſhow,
that they are by nature adjuſted and tem-
pered with admirable wiſdom, for the good
of ſociety as well as for private good.
                                   This

This ſubject is extenſive : but as the nature
of the preſent undertaking will not admit a
complete diſcuſſion, it ſhall ſuffice to give
a few obſervations in general upon the ſenſitive part of our nature, without regarding
that ſtrange irregularity of paſſion diſcovered in ſome individuals. Such topical irregularities, if I may uſe the term, cannot
fairly be held an objection to the preſent
theory. We are frequently, it is true,
miſled by inordinate paſſion : but we are
alſo, and perhaps not leſs frequently, miſled
by wrong judgement.

In order to a diſtinct apprehenſion of the
preſent ſubject, it muſt be premiſed, that
an agreeable object produceth always a
pleaſant emotion, and a diſagreeable object
one that is painful. This is a general law
of nature, which admits not a ſingle exception. Agreeableneſs in the object or cauſe is
indeed ſo eſſentially connected with pleaſure
in the emotion its effect, that an agreeable
object cannot be better defined, than by its
power of producing a pleaſant emotion.
Diſagreeableneſs in the object or cauſe, has
the

the fame neceffary connection with pain in the emotion produced by it.

From this preliminary it appears, that to inquire for what end an emotion is made pleafant or painful, refolves into an inquiry for what end its caufe is made agreeable or difagreeable. And from the moft accurate induction it will be difcovered, that no caufe of an emotion is made agreeable or difagreeable arbitrarily; but that thefe qualities are fo diftributed as to anfwer wife and good purpofes. It is an invincible proof of the benignity of the Deity, that we are furrounded with things generally agreeable, which contribute remarkably to our entertainment and to our happinefs. Some things are made difagreeable, fuch as a rotten carcafs, becaufe they are noxious. Others, a dirty marfh, for example, or a barren heath, are made difagreeable in order to excite our induftry. And with refpect to the few things that are neither agreeable nor difagreeable; it will be made evident, that their being left indifferent is not a work of chance but of wifdom. Of fuch I fhall have occafion to give feveral inftances.

Having

Having attempted to affign the final caufes of emotions and paffions confidered as
pleafant or painful, we proceed to the final
caufes of the defires involved in them.
This feems a work of fome difficulty; for
the defires that accompany different paffions have very different aims, and feldom
or never demand precifely the fame gratification. One paffion moves us to cling to
its object, one to fly from it; one paffion
impels to action for our own good, and
one for the good of others; one paffion
prompts us to do good to ourfelves or o-
thers, and one to do mifchief, frequently
to others, and fometimes even to ourfelves. Deliberating upon this intricate
fubject, and finding an intimate correfpondence betwixt our defires and their
objects, it is natural to think that the former
muft be regulated in fome meafure by the
latter. In this view, I begin with defire
directed upon an inanimate object.

Any pleafure we have in an agreeable
object of this kind, is enjoyed by the continuance of the pleafant impreffion it makes upon us; and accordingly the defire involved in

the pleasant emotion tends to that end, and is gratified by dwelling upon the agreeable object. Hence such an object may be properly termed *attractive*. Thus a flowing river, a towering hill, a fine garden, are attractive objects. They fix the attention of the spectator, by inspiring pleasant emotions, which are gratified by adhering to these objects and enjoying them. On the other hand, a disagreeable object of the same kind, raises in us a painful emotion including a desire to turn from the object, which relieves us of course from the pain ; and hence such an object may be properly termed *repulsive*. A monstrous birth, for example, a rotten carcass, a confusion of jarring sounds, are repulsive. They repel the mind, by inspiring painful or unpleasant emotions, which are gratified by flying from such objects. Thus in general, with regard to inanimate objects, the desire included in every pleasant passion tends to prolong the pleasure, and the desire included in every painful passion tends to put an end to the pain. Here the final cause is evident. Our desires, so far, are modelled

in

in such a manner as to correspond precisely to the sensitive part of our nature, prone to happiness and averse to misery. These operations of adhering to an agreeable inanimate object, and flying from one that is disagreeable, are performed in the beginning of life by means of desire impelling us, without the intervention of reason or reflection. Reason and reflection directing self-love, become afterward motives that unite their force with desire; because experience informs us, that the adhering to agreeable objects and the flying from those that are disagreeable, contribute to our happiness.

Sensible Beings considered as objects of passion, lead us into a more complex theory. A sensible being that is agreeable by its attributes, inspires us with a pleasant emotion; and the desire included in this emotion has evidently different means of gratification. A man regarding himself only, may be satisfied with viewing and contemplating this being, precisely as if it were inanimate; or he may desire the more generous gratification of making it happy. Were man altogether

selfish,

selfish, it would be conformable to his nature, that he should indulge the pleasant
emotion without making any acknowledge-
ment to the person who gives him pleasure,
more than to a pure air or temperate clime
when he enjoys these benefits. But as man
is endued with a principle of benevolence
as well as of selfishness, he is prompted by
his nature to desire the good of every sensible being that gives him pleasure. And
the final cause of desire so directed, is illustrious. It contributes to a man's own happiness, by affording him more means of
gratification than he can have when his desire terminates upon himself alone ; and at
the same time it tends eminently to improve the happiness of those with whom he
is connected. The directing our desires
in this manner, occasions a beautiful coa-
lition of self-love with benevolence ; for
both are equally promoted by the same internal impulse, and by the same external
conduct. And this consideration, by the
way, ought to silence those minute philosophers, who, ignorant of human nature,
teach a most disgustful doctrine, That to

serve

ferve others unlefs with a view to our own good, is weaknefs and folly; as if felf-love only contributed to happinefs and not benevolence. The hand of God is too vifible in the human frame, to permit us to think ferioufly, that there ever can be any jarring or inconfiftency among natural principles, thofe efpecially of felf-love and benevolence, which regulate the bulk of our actions.

Next in order come fenfible Beings that are in afflidion or pain. It is difagreeable to behold a perfon in diftrefs; and therefore this objedt muft raife in the fpedtator an uneafy emotion. Were man purely a felfifh being, he would be prompted by his nature to turn from every objedt, animate or inanimate, that gives him uneafinefs. But the principle of benevolence gives an oppofite diredtion to his defire. It impels him to afford relief; and by relieving the perfon from diftrefs, his defire is fully gratified. Our benevolence to a perfon in diftrefs is inflamed into an emotion of fympathy, fignifying in Greek the painful emotion that is raifed in us by that perfon.
Thus

Thus sympathy, though a painful emotion, is in its nature attractive. And with respect to its final cause, we can be at no loss. It not only tends to relieve a fellow-creature from pain, but in its gratification is greatly more pleasant than if it were repulsive.

We in the last place bring under consideration persons hateful by vice or wickedness. Imagine a wretch who has lately perpetrated some horrid crime. He is disagreeable to every spectator; and consequently raises in every spectator a painful emotion. What is the natural gratification of the desire that accompanies this painful emotion? I must here again observe, that supposing man to be entirely a selfish being, he would be prompted by his nature to relieve himself from the pain by averting his eye, and banishing the criminal from his thoughts. But man is not so constituted. He is composed of many principles, which, though seemingly contradictory, are perfectly concordant. The principle of benevolence influences his conduct, not less remarkably than that of selfishness. And in order to

answer

anfwer the foregoing queftion, I muft introduce a third principle, not lefs remarkable in its influence than either of thofe mentioned. It is that principle common to all, which prompts us to punifh thofe who do wrong. An envious, malicious, or cruel action, is difagreeable to me even where I have no connection with the fufferer, and raifes in me the painful emotion of refentment. The gratification of this emotion, when accompanied with defire, is directed by the principle now unfolded. Being prompted by my nature to punifh guilt as well as to reward virtue, my defire is not gratified but by inflicting punifhment. I muft chaftife the wretch by indignation at leaft and hatred, if not more feverely. Here the final caufe is felf-evident.

An injury done to myfelf, touching me more than when done to others, raifes my refentment in a higher degree. The defire accordingly included in this paffion, is not fatisfied with fo flight a punifhment as indignation or hatred. It is not fully gratified without retaliation; and the author muft by my hand fuffer mifchief, as great at leaft

as

as he has done me. Neither can we be at any lofs about the final caufe of this higher degree of refentment. The whole vigor of this paffion is required to fecure individuals from the injuftice and oppreffion of others *.

A wicked or difgraceful action, is difagreeable not only to others, but even to the delinquent himfelf. It raifes in him as well as in others a painful emotion including a defire of punifhment. The painful emotion which the delinquent feels, is diftinguifhed by the name of *remorfe*; and in this cafe the defire he has to punifh is directed againft himfelf. There cannot be imagined a better contrivance to deter us from vice; for remorfe is the fevereft of all punifhments. This paffion and the defire of felf-punifhment derived from it, are touched delicately by Terence.

Menedemus. Ubi comperi ex iis, qui ei fuere confcii,
Domum revortor mœftus, atque animo fere
Perturbato, atque incerto præ ægritudine:
Adfido, adcurrunt fervi, foccos detrahunt:
Video alios feftinare, lectos fternere,

* See Hiftorical law-tracts, tract 1.

Cœnam

Cœnam adparare: pro se quisque sedulo
Faciebat, quo illam mihi lenirent miseriam.
Ubi video hæc, cœpi cogitare: Hem! tot mea
Solius solliciti sint causa, ut me unum expleant?
Ancillæ tot me vestiant? sumptus domi
Tantos ego solus faciam? sed gnatum unicum,
Quem pariter uti his decuit, aut etiam amplius,
Quod illa ætas magis ad hæc utenda idonea 'st,
Eum ego hinc ejeci miserum injustitia mea.
Malo quidem me dignum quovis deputem,
Si id faciam. nam usque dum ille vitam illam colet
Inopem, carens patria ob meas injurias,
Interea usque illi de me supplicium dabo:
Laborans, quærens, parcens, illi serviens,
Ita facio prorsus: nihil relinquo in ædibus,
Nec vas, nec vestimentum: conrasi omnia,
Ancillas, servos, nisi eos, qui opere rustico
Faciundo facile sumptum exercerent suum:
Omnes produxi ac vendidi: inscripsi ilico
Ædeis mercede: quasi talenta ad quindecim
Coëgi: agrum hunc mercatus sum: hic me exer-
   ceo.
Decrevi tantisper me minus injuriæ,
Chreme, meo gnato facere, dum fiam miser:
Nec fas esse ulla me voluptate hic frui,
Nisi ubi ille huc salvos redierit meus particeps.

     Heautontimorumenos, act I. *sc.* I.

Otway reaches the fame fentiment :

> *Monimia.* Let mifchiefs multiply! let ev'ry hour
> Of my loath'd life yield me increafe of horror!
> Oh let the fun to thefe unhappy eyes
> Ne'er fhine again, but be eclips'd for ever!
> May every thing I look on feem a prodigy,
> To fill my foul with terror, till I quite
> Forget I ever had humanity,
> And grow a curfer of the works of nature!
>
> *Orphan,* act 4.

The cafes mentioned are, where benevolence alone or where defire of punifhment alone, governs without a rival. And it was neceffary to handle thefe cafes feparately, in order to elucidate a fubject which by writers is left in great obfcurity. But neither of thefe principles operates always without rivalfhip. Cafes may be figured, and cafes actually exift, where the fame perfon is an object both of fympathy and of defire to punifh. Thus the fight of a profligate in the venereal difeafe, over-run with botches and fores, actuates both principles. While his diftrefs fixes my attention, fympathy exerts itfelf;

itfelf; but fo foon as I think of his profliga-
cy, hatred prevails, and a defire to punifh.
This in general is the cafe of diftrefs occafioned by immoral actions that are not highly criminal. And if the diftrefs and the immoral action be in any proportion, fympathy
and hatred counterbalancing each other will
not fuffer me either to afford relief or to in-
flict punifhment. What then will be the
refult of the whole? The principle of felf-
love folves the queftion. Abhorring an object fo loathfome, I naturally avert my eye,
and walk off as faft as I can, in order to be
relieved from the pain.

The prefent fubject gives birth to feveral
other obfervations, for which I could not
find room above, without relaxing more
from the ftrictnefs of order and connection,
than with fafety could be indulged in dif-
courfing upon a matter that with difficulty
is made perfpicuous, even with all the advantages of order and connection. Thefe
obfervations I fhall throw out loofely as they
occur, without giving myfelf any further
trouble about method.

No action good or bad is altogether indif-

ferent

ferent even to a mere fpectator. If good, it
infpires efteem; and indignation, if wicked.
But it is remarkable, that thefe emotions feldom are accompanied with defire. The abi-
lities of man are limited, and he finds fufficient employment, in relieving the diftreffed, in requiting his benefactors, and in punifhing thofe who wrong him, without moving out of his own fphere for the benefit or
chaftifement of thofe with whom he has no
connection.

If the good qualities of others excite my
benevolence, the fame qualities in myfelf
muft produce a fimilar effect in a fuperior
degree, upon account of the natural partia-
lity every man hath for himfelf. This increafes felf-love. If thefe qualities be of a
high rank, they produce a feeling of fuperiority, which naturally leads me to affume
fome fort of government over others. Mean
qualities, on the other hand, produce in me
a feeling of inferiority, which naturally leads
me to fubmit to others. Unlefs fuch feelings were diftributed among individuals in
fociety by meafure and proportion, there
could be no natural fubordination of fome

to

to others, which is the principal foundation of government.

No other branch of the human conftitution fhows more vifibly our deftination for fociety, nor tends more to our improvement, than appetite for fame or efteem. The whole conveniencies of life being derived from mutual aid and fupport in fociety, it ought to be a capital aim, to form connections with others fo ftrict and fo extenfive as to produce a firm reliance on many for fuccour in time of need. Reafon dictates this leffon. But reafon folely is not relied on in a matter of fuch confequence. We are moved by a natural appetite, to be folicitous about efteem and refpect as we are about food when hungry. This appetite, at the fame time, is finely adjufted to the moral branch of our conftitution, by promoting all the moral virtues. For what infallible means are there to attract love and efteem, other than a virtuous courfe of life? If a man be juft and beneficent, if he be temperate modeft and prudent, he will infallibly gain the efteem and love of all who know him.

The communication of paffion to related objects,

objects, is an illuftrious inftance of the care of Providence, to extend focial connections as far as the limited nature of man can admit. This communication of paffion is fo far unhappy as to fpread the malevolent paffions beyond their natural bounds. But let it be remarked, that this unhappy effect regards favages only, who give way to malevolent paffions. Under the difcipline of fociety, thefe paffions are fubdued, and in a good meafure eradicated. In their place fucceed the kindly affections, which, meeting with all encouragement, take poffeffion of the mind and govern our whole actions. In this condition, the progrefs of paffion along related objects, by fpreading the kindly affections through a multitude of individuals, hath a glorious effect.

Nothing can be more entertaining to a rational mind, than the œconomy of the human paffions, of which I have attempted to give fome faint notion. It muft however be confeffed, that our paffions, when they happen to fwell beyond their proper limits, take on a lefs regular appearance. Reafon may proclaim our duty, but the will influen-

ced

ced by paſſion, makes gratification always
welcome. Hence the power of paſſion,
which, when in exceſs, cannot be reſiſted
but by the utmoſt fortitude of mind. It is
bent upon gratification ; and where proper
objects are wanting, it clings to any object at
hand without diſtinction. Thus joy inſpired by a fortunate event, is diffuſed upon
every perſon around by acts of benevolence ;
and reſentment for an atrocious injury done
by one out of reach, ſeizes the firſt object
that occurs to vent itſelf upon. Thoſe who
believe in prophecies, even wiſh the accom-
pliſhment ; and a weak mind is diſpoſed vo-
luntarily to fulfil a prophecy, in order to
gratify its wiſh. Shakeſpear, whom no
particle of human nature hath eſcaped, however remote from common obſervation, de-
ſcribes this weakneſs :

K. Henry. Doth any name particular belong
Unto that lodging where I firſt did ſwoon ?
 Warwick. 'Tis call'd *Jeruſalem,* my Noble
   Lord.
 K. Henry. Laud be to God! even there my life
   muſt end.
It hath been propheſy'd to me many years,

        I

I fhould not die but in Jerufalem,
Which vainly I fuppos'd the holy land.
But bear me to that chamber, there I'll lie:
In that Jerufalem fhall Henry die.

Second part, Henry IV. act 4. fc. laft.

I could not deny myfelf the amufement of the foregoing obfervation, though it doth not properly come under my plan. The irregularities of paffion proceeding from peculiar weakneffes and biaffes, I do not undertake to juftify; and of thefe we have had many examples *. It is fufficient that paffions common to all and as generally exerted, are made fubfervient to beneficial purpofes. I fhall only obferve, that in a polifhed fociety inftances of irregular paffions are rare, and that their mifchief doth not extend far.

* Part 5. of the prefent chapter.

C H A P.

CHAP. III.

BEAUTY.

HAVING difcourfed in general of e-
motions and paffions, I proceed to
a more narrow infpection of fome
particulars that ferve to unfold the principles
of the fine arts. It is the province of a writer upon ethics, to give a full enumeration
of all the paffions; and of each feparately
to affign the nature, the caufe, the gratification, and the effects. But a treatife of
ethics is not my province. I carry my view
no farther than to the elements of criticifm,
in order to fhow that the fine arts are a fubject of reafoning as well as of tafte. An
extenfive work would be ill fuited to a defign fo limited; and to keep within moderate bounds, the following plan may contribute. It has already been obferved, that
things are the caufes of emotions, by means
of their properties and attributes *. This

* Chap. 2. part. 1. fect. 1. firft note.

Vol. I.　　　H h　　　furnifheth

furnisheth a hint for diftribution. Inftead of a painful and tedious examination of the feveral paffions and emotions, I propofe to confine my inquiries to fuch attributes, relations, and circumftances, as in the fine arts are chiefly employed to raife agreeable emotions. Attributes of fingle objects, as the moft fimple, fhall take the lead ; to be followed with particulars that depend on the relations of objects, and are not found in any one object fingly confidered. Difpatching next fome coincident matters, I approach nearer to practice, by applying the principles unfolded in the foregoing parts of the work. This is a general view of the intended method ; referving however a privilege to vary it in particular inftances, where a different method may be more commodious. I begin with beauty, the moft noted of all the qualities that belong to fingle objects.

The term *beauty*, in its native fignification, is appropriated to objects of fight. Objects of the other fenfes may be agreeable, fuch as the founds of mufical inftruments, the fmoothnefs and foftnefs of fome

surfaces :

furfaces : but the agreeablenefs denominated *beauty* belongs to objects of fight.

Of all the objects of the external fenfes,
an object of fight is the moft complex. In
the very fimpleft, colour is perceived, figure, and length breadth and thicknefs.
A tree is compofed of a trunk, branches,
and leaves. It has colour, figure, fize,
and fometimes motion. By means of each
of thefe particulars, feparately confidered,
it appears beautiful : how much more fo,
when they enter all into one complex perception ? The beauty of the human figure
is extraordinary, being a compofition of
numberlefs beauties arifing from the parts
and qualities of the object, various colours,
various motions, figure, fize, &c.; all u-
niting in one complex perception, and ftriking the eye with combined force. Hence
it is, that beauty, a quality fo remarkable
in vifible objects, lends its name to exprefs
every thing that is eminently agreeable.
Thus, by a figure of fpeech, we fay a beautiful found, a beautiful thought or expreffion, a beautiful theorem, a beautiful e-
vent, a beautiful difcovery in art or fcience.

But as figurative expreſſion is not our preſent theme, this chapter is confined to beauty in its genuine ſignification.

It is natural to ſuppoſe, that a perception ſo various as that of beauty, comprehending ſometimes many particulars, ſometimes few, ſhould occaſion emotions equally various. And yet all the various emotions of beauty maintain one general character of ſweetneſs and gaiety.

Conſidering attentively the beauty of viſible objects, we diſcover two kinds. One may be termed *intrinſic* beauty, becauſe it is diſcovered in a ſingle object viewed apart without relation to any other object. The examples above given, are of that kind. The other may be termed *relative* beauty, being founded on the relation of objects. The former is a perception of ſenſe merely; for to perceive the beauty of a ſpreading oak or of a flowing river, no more is required but ſingly an act of viſion. The latter is accompanied with an act of underſtanding and reflection; for of a fine inſtrument or engine, we perceive not the relative beauty, until we be made acquainted with its uſe and deſtination.

deftination.   In a word, intrinfic beauty is
ultimate : relative beauty is that of means
relating to fome good end or purpofe. Thefe
different beauties agree in one capital circumftance, that both are equally perceived
as fpread upon the object.   This will be
readily admitted with refpect to intrinfic
beauty ; but is not fo obvious with refpect
to the other. The utility of the plough, for
example, may make it an object of admiration or of defire ; but why fhould utility
make it appear beautiful ? A principle mentioned above *, will explain this doubt.
The beauty of the effect, by an eafy tranfition of ideas, is transferred to the caufe,
and is perceived as one of the qualities of
the caufe. Thus a fubject void of intrinfic
beauty, appears beautiful from its utility.
An old Gothic tower that has no beauty in
itfelf, appears beautiful, confidered as proper to defend againft an enemy.   A dwelling-houfe void of all regularity, is however
beautiful in the view of convenience ; and
the want of form or fymmetry in a tree,

* Chap. 2. part 1. fect. 4.

will

will not prevent its appearing beautiful, if it be known to produce good fruit.

When thefe two beauties concur in any object, it appears delightful. Every member of the human body poffeffes both in a high degree. The flender make of a horfe deftined for running, pleafes every tafte; partly from fymmetry, and partly from utility.

The beauty of utility, being proportioned accurately to the degree of utility, requires no illuftration. But intrinfic beauty, fo complex as I have faid, cannot be handled diftinctly without being analized into its conftituent parts. If a tree be beautiful by means of its colour, its figure, its fize, its motion, it is in reality poffeffed of fo many different beauties, which ought to be examined feparately, in order to have a clear notion of the whole. The beauty of colour is too familiar to need explanation. The beauty of figure requires an accurate difcuffion, for in it many circumftances are involved. When any portion of matter is viewed as a whole, the beauty of its figure arifes from regularity and fimplicity. Viewing

ing the parts with relation to each other, uniformity, proportion, and order, contribute to its beauty. The beauty of motion deserves a chapter by itself; and another chapter is destined for grandeur, being distinguishable from beauty in a strict sense. For the definitions of regularity, uniformity, proportion, and order, if thought necessary, I remit my reader to the appendix at the end of the book. Upon simplicity I must make a few cursory observations, such as may be of use in examining the beauty of single objects.

A multitude of objects crowding into the mind at once, disturb the attention, and pass without making any impression, or any lasting impression. In a group, no single object makes the figure it would do apart, when it occupies the whole attention *. For the same reason, even a single object, when it divides the attention by the multiplicity of its parts, equals not, in strength of impression, a more simple object com-

---

* See the appendix, containing definitions and explanation of terms.

prehended

prehended in a single view. Parts extremely complex muſt be conſidered in portions ſucceſſively; and a number of impreſſions in ſucceſſion, which cannot unite becauſe not ſimultaneous, never touch the mind like one entire impreſſion made as it were at one ſtroke. This juſtifies ſimplicity in works of art, as oppoſed to complicated circumſtances and crowded ornaments. There is an additional reaſon for ſimplicity, in works that make an impreſſion of dignity or elevation. The mind attached to beauties of a high rank, cannot deſcend to inferior beauties. And yet, notwithſtanding theſe reaſons, we find profuſe decoration prevailing in works of art. But this is no argument againſt ſimplicity. For authors and architects who cannot reach the higher beauties, endeavour to ſupply their want of genius by dealing in thoſe that are inferior. In all ages, the beſt writers and artiſts have been governed by a taſte for ſimplicity.

Theſe things premiſed, I proceed to examine the beauty of figure, as ariſing from the above-mentioned particulars, *viz.* regularity,

gularity, uniformity, proportion, order,
and fimplicity. To exhauft this fubject,
would of itfelf require a large volume. I li-
mit myfelf to a few curfory remarks, as
matter for future difquifition. To inquire
why an object, by means of the particulars
mentioned, appears beautiful, would I am
afraid be a vain attempt. It feems the moft
probable opinion, that the nature of man
was originally framed with a relifh for them,
in order to anfwer wife and good purpofes.
The final caufes have not hitherto been afcertained, though they are not probably
beyond our reach. One thing is clear, that
regularity, uniformity, order, and fimplicity, contribute each of them to readinefs of
apprehenfion; and enable us to form more
diftinct images of objects, than can be done
with the utmoft attention where thefe particulars are not found. This final caufe is,
I acknowledge, too flight, to account fa-
tisfactorily for a tafte that makes a figure fo
illuftrious in the nature of man. That this
branch of our conftitution hath a purpofe
ftill more important, we have great reafon
to believe. With refpect to proportion, I

am ftill lefs fuccefsful. In feveral inftances, accurate proportion is connected with utility. This in particular is the cafe of animals; for thofe that are the beft proportioned, are the ftrongeft and moft active. But inftances are ftill more numerous, where the proportions we relifh the moft, have no connection, fo far as we fee, with utility. Writers on architecture infift much upon the proportions of a column; and affign different proportions to the Doric, Ionic, and Corinthian. But no architect will maintain, that the moft accurate proportions contribute more to ufe, than feveral that are lefs accurate and lefs agreeable. Neither will it be maintained, that the proportions affigned for the length breadth and height of rooms, tend to make them the more commodious. It appears then, fo far as we can difcover, that we have a tafte for proportion independent altogether of utility. One thing indeed is certain, that any external object proportioned to our tafte, is delightful. This furnifhes a hint. May it not be thought a good final caufe of proportion, that it contributes to our entertainment? The author of our

nature

nature has given many fignal proofs, that this end is not below his care. And if fo, why fhould we hefitate in affigning this as an additional final caufe of regularity, and the other particulars above mentioned? We may be confirmed in this thought, by reflecting, that our tafte, with refpect to thefe, is not occafional or accidental, but uniform and univerfal, making an original branch of human nature.

One might fill a volume with the effects that are produced by the endlefs combinations of the principles of beauty. I have room only for a flight fpecimen, confined to the fimpleft figures. A circle and a fquare are each of them perfectly regular, being equally confined to a precife form, and admitting not the flighteft variation. A fquare however is lefs beautiful than a circle, becaufe it is lefs fimple. A circle has parts as well as a fquare; but its parts not being diftinct like thofe of a fquare, it makes one entire impreffion; whereas the attention is divided among the fides and angles of a fquare. The effect of fimplicity may be illuftrated by another example. A fquare, though not more regular than a hexagon or octagon, is more beautiful than either; for what other reason, than that a square is more simple, and the attention less divided? This reasoning will appear still more solid when we consider any regular polygon of very many sides; for of such figure the mind can never have any distinct perception. Simplicity thus contributes to beauty.

A square is more beautiful than a parallelogram. The former exceeds the latter in regularity and in uniformity of parts. But this holds with respect to intrinsic beauty only; for in many instances, utility comes in to cast the balance on the side of the parallelogram. This figure for the doors and windows of a dwelling-house, is preferred because of utility; and here we find the beauty of utility prevailing over that of regularity and uniformity.

A parallelogram again depends, for its beauty, on the proportion of its sides. The beauty is lost by a great inequality of sides. It is also lost, on the other hand, by the approximation toward equality. Proportion in this circumstance degenerates into imperfect

fect uniformity; and the figure upon the whole appears an unfuccefsful attempt toward a fquare.

An equilateral triangle yields not to a fquare in regularity nor in uniformity of parts, and it is more fimple. But an equilateral triangle is lefs beautiful than a fquare, which muft be owing to inferiority of order in the pofition of its parts. The fides of an equilateral triangle incline to each other in the fame angle, which is the moft perfect order they are fufceptible of. But this order is obfcure, and far from being fo perfect as the parallelifm of the fides of a fquare. Thus order contributes to the beauty of vifible objects, not lefs than fimplicity and regularity.

A parallelogram exceeds an equilateral triangle in the orderly difpofition of its parts; but being inferior in uniformity and fimplicity, it is lefs beautiful.

Uniformity is fingular in one capital circumftance, that it is apt to difguft by excefs. A number of things contrived for the fame ufe, fuch as chairs fpoons, &c. cannot be too uniform. But a fcrupulous uniformity

formity of parts in a large garden or field, is far from being agreeable. Uniformity among connected objects, belongs not to the present subject. It is handled in the chapter of uniformity and variety.

In all the works of nature, simplicity makes an illustrious figure. The works of the best artists are directed by it. Profuse ornament in painting, gardening, or architecture, as well as in dress and language, shows a mean or corrupted taste.

Poets, like painters, thus unskill'd to trace
The naked nature and the living grace,
With gold and jewels cover ev'ry part,
And hide with ornaments their want of art.
Pope's Essay on criticism.

No one property recommends a machine more than its simplicity; not singly for better answering its purpose, but by appearing in itself more beautiful. Simplicity hath a capital effect in behaviour and manners; no other particular contributing more to gain esteem and love. The artificial and intricate manners of modern times, have little of dignity

dignity in them. General theorems, abſ-
tracting from their importance, are delightful by their ſimplicity, and by the eaſineſs of
their application to a variety of caſes. We
take equal delight in the laws of motion,
which, with the greateſt ſimplicity, are
boundleſs in their influence.

A gradual progreſs from ſimplicity to complex forms and profuſe ornament, ſeems to
be the fate of all the fine arts; reſembling
behaviour, which from original candor and
ſimplicity has degenerated into artificial re-
finements. At preſent, written productions
are crowded with words, epithets, figures,
&c. In muſic, ſentiment is neglected, for
the luxury of harmony, and for difficult
movement which ſurpriſes in its execution.
In *taſte* properly ſo called, poignant ſauces
with complicated mixtures of different ſa-
vours, prevail among people of condition.
The French, accuſtomed to the artificial red
on their women's cheeks, think the modeſt
colouring of nature diſplayed on a fine face
altogether inſipid.

The ſame tendency appears in the progreſs of the arts among the ancients. Of
this

this we have traces ftill remaining in architecture. Some veftiges of the oldeft Gre-
cian buildings prove them to be of the Doric
order. The Ionic fucceeded, and feems to
have been the favourite order, while architecture was in its height of glory. The
Corinthian came next in vogue: and in
Greece, the buildings of that order appear
moftly to have been erected after the Romans got footing there. At laft came the
Compofite with all its extravagancies, where
proportion is facrificed to finery and crowded
ornament.

But what tafte is to prevail next? for fafhion is in a continual flux, and tafte muft
vary with it. After rich and profufe ornaments become familiar, fimplicity appears
by contraft lifelefs and infipid. This would
be an unfurmountable obftruction, fhould
any man of genius and tafte endeavour to
reftore ancient fimplicity.

In reviewing what is faid above, I am
under fome apprehenfion of an objection,
which, as it may poffibly occur to the reader, ought to be obviated. A mountain, it
will be obferved, is an agreeable object,
without

without fo much as the appearance of regularity ; and a chain of mountains ftill more
agreeable, without being arranged in any
order.   But thefe facts confidered in a proper light, afford not an objection.   Regularity, order, and uniformity, are intimately
connected with beauty ; and in this view
only, have I treated them.   Every regular
object, for example, muft in refpect of its regularity be beautiful.   But I have not faid,
that regularity, order, and uniformity, are
effential to beauty, fo as that it cannot exift
without them.   The contrary appears in the
beauty of colour.   Far lefs have I faid, that
an object cannot be agreeable in any refpect
independent of thefe qualities.   Grandeur,
as diftinguifhed from beauty, requires very
little regularity.   This will appear more fully when that article is handled.   In the
mean time, to fhow the difference betwixt
beauty and grandeur with refpect to regularity, I fhall give a few examples.   Imagine
a fmall body, let it be a globe, in a continual flux of figure, from the moft perfect
regularity till there remain no appearance of
that quality.   The beauty of this globe,

VOL. I.   K k   depending

depending on its regular figure, will gradually wear away with its regularity; and
when it is no longer regular, it no longer
will appear beautiful. The next example
shall be of the same globe, gradually enlarging its size, but retaining its figure. In
this body, we at first perceive the beauty of
regularity only. But so soon as it begins to
swell into a great size, it appears agreeable
by its greatness, which joins with the beauty of regularity to make it a delightful object.
In the last place, let it be imagined, that
the figure as well as the quantity of matter
are in a continual flux ; and that the body,
while it increases in size, becomes less and
less regular, till it lose altogether the appearance of that quality. In this case, the beauty
of regularity wearing off gradually, gives place
to an agreeableness of a different sort, *viz.*
that of greatness : and at last the emotion arising from greatness will be in perfection, when
the beauty of regularity is gone. Hence it
is, that in a large object the want of regularity is not much regarded by the spectator
who is struck with its grandeur. A swelling
eminence is agreeable, though not strictly
regular.

regular.   A towering hill is delightful, if it
have but any diftant refemblance of a cone.
A fmall furface ought to be fmooth; but in
a wide-extended plain, confiderable inequa-
lities are overlooked.   This obfervation
holds equally in works of art.   The flighteft irregularity in a houfe of a moderate fize
hurts the eye; while the mind, ftruck with
the grandeur of a fuperb edifice, which occupies it totally, cannot bear to defcend to
its irregularities unlefs extremely grofs.   In a
large volume we pardon many defects that
would make an epigram intolerable.   In
fhort, the obfervation holds in general, that
beauty is connected with regularity in great
objects as well as in fmall; but with a remarkable difference, that in paffing from
fmall to great, regularity is lefs and lefs required.

The diftinction betwixt primary and fecondary qualities in matter, feems now fully eftablifhed.   Heat and cold, though
feeming to exift in bodies, are difcovered to
be effects caufed by thefe bodies in a fenfitive being.   Colour, which the eye reprefents as fpread upon a fubftance, has no ex-

iftence

istence but in the mind of the spectator. Perceptions of this kind, which, by a delusion of sense, are attributed to external subjects, are termed *secondary qualities*, in contradistinction to figure, extension, solidity, which are primary qualities, and which are not separable, even in imagination, from the subjects they belong to. This suggests a curious inquiry, Whether beauty be a primary or only a secondary quality of objects? The question is easily determined with respect to the beauty of colour; for if colour be a secondary quality existing no where but in the mind of the spectator, its beauty must be of the same kind. This conclusion must also hold with respect to the beauty of utility, which is plainly a conception of the mind, arising not merely from sight, but from reflecting that the thing is fitted for some good end or purpose. The question is more intricate with respect to the beauty of regularity. If regularity be a primary quality, why not also its beauty? That this is not a good consequence, will appear from considering, that beauty, in its very conception, refers to a percipient; for

an

an object is said to be beautiful, for no
other reason but that it appears so to a
spectator. The same piece of matter which
to man appears beautiful, may possibly to another being appear ugly. Beauty therefore,
which for its existence depends upon the
percipient as much as upon the object perceived, cannot be an inherent property of either.
What else then can it be, but a perception
in the mind occasioned by certain objects?
The same reasoning is applicable to the
beauty of order, of uniformity, of grandeur. Accordingly, it may be pronounced
in general, that beauty in no case whatever
is a real quality of matter. And hence it
is wittily observed by the poet, that beauty
is not in the countenance, but in the lover's
eye. This reasoning is undoubtedly solid:
and the only cause of doubt or hesitation is,
that we are taught a different lesson by
sense. By a singular determination of nature, we perceive both beauty and colour as
belonging to the object; and, like figure or
extension, as inherent properties. This
mechanism is uncommon; and when nature, to fulfil her intention, chuseth any
singular

singular method of operation, we may be
certain of some final cause that cannot be
reached by ordinary means. It appears to
me, that a perception of beauty in external
objects, is requisite to attach us to them.
Doth not this mechanism, in the first
place, greatly promote industry, by
prompting a desire to possess things that are
beautiful? Doth it not further join with
utility, in prompting us to embellish our
houses and enrich our fields? These however are but slight effects, compared with
the connections which are formed among
individuals in society by means of this singular mechanism. The qualifications of
the head and heart, are undoubtedly the
most solid and most permanent foundations
of such connections. But as external beauty
lies more in view, and is more obvious to
the bulk of mankind than the qualities now
mentioned, the sense of beauty possesses the
more universal influence in forming these
connections. At any rate, it concurs in an
eminent degree with mental qualifications,
to produce social intercourse, mutual good-
will,

will, and confequently mutual aid and fupport, which are the life of fociety.

It muft not however be overlooked, that this fenfe doth not tend to advance the interefts of fociety, but when in a due mean with refpect to ftrength. Love in particular arifing from a fenfe of beauty, lofes, when exceffive, its fociable character *. The appetite for gratification, prevailing over affection for the beloved object, is ungovernable; and tends violently to its end, regardlefs of the mifery that muft follow. Love in this ftate is no longer a fweet agreeable paffion. It becomes painful like hunger or thirft; and produceth no happinefs but in the inftant of fruition. This difcovery fuggefts a moft important leffon, that moderation in our defires and appetites, which fits us for doing our duty, contributes at the fame time the moft to happinefs. Even focial paffions, when moderate, are more pleafant than when they fwell beyond proper bounds.

* See chap. 2. part 1. fect. 1.

CHAP.

C H A P. IV.

Grandeur and Sublimity.

NATURE hath not more remarkably diſtinguiſhed us from the other a-nimals by an erect poſture, than by a capacious and aſpiring mind, inclining us to every thing great and elevated. The ocean, the ſky, or any large object, ſeizes the attention, and makes a ſtrong impreſ-ſion *. Robes of ſtate are made large and full to draw reſpect. We admire elephants and whales for their magnitude, notwith-ſtanding their unwieldineſs.

The elevation of an object affects us not leſs than its magnitude. A high place is choſen for the ſtatue of a deity or hero.

---

* Longinus obſerves, that nature inclines us to admire, not a ſmall rivulet, however clear and tranſparent, but the Nile, the Iſter, the Rhine, or ſtill more the ocean. The ſight of a ſmall fire produceth no emotion; but we are ſtruck with the boiling furnaces of Ætna, pouring out whole rivers of liquid flame. *Treatiſe of the Sublime,* chap. 29.

A

A tree growing upon the brink of a preci-
pice viewed from the plain below, affords
by that circumftance an additional pleafure.
A throne is erected for the chief magiftrate,
and a chair with a high feat for the prefi-
dent of a court.

In fome objects, greatnefs and elevation
concur to make a complicated impreffion.
The Alps and the pike of Teneriff are proper examples; with the following difference, that in the former greatnefs feems to
prevail, elevation in the latter.

The emotions raifed by great and by e-
levated objects, are clearly diftinguifhable,
not only in the internal feeling, but even in
their external expreffions. A great object
dilates the breaft, and makes the fpectator
endeavour to enlarge his bulk. This
is remarkable in perfons, who, neglecting
delicacy in behaviour, give way to nature
without referve. In defcribing a great object, they naturally expand themfelves by
drawing in air with all their force. An e-
levated object produces a different expreffion. It makes the fpectator ftretch upward and ftand a tiptoe.

Great and elevated objects confidered with relation to the emotions produced by them, are termed *grand* and *fublime*. Grandeur and fublimity have a double fignification. They generally fignify the quality or circumftance in the objects by which the emotions are produced; fometimes the emotions themfelves.

Whether magnitude fingly in an object of fight, have the effect to produce an emotion diftinguifhable from the beauty or deformity of that object; or whether it be only a circumftance modifying the beauty or deformity, is an intricate queftion. If magnitude produce an emotion of its own diftinguifhable from others, this emotion muft either be pleafant or painful. But this feems to be contradicted by experience; for magnitude, as it would appear, contributes in fome inftances to beauty, in fome to deformity. A hill, for inftance, is agreeable, and a great mountain ftill more fo. But an ugly monfter, the larger, the more horrid. Greatnefs in an enemy, great power, great courage, ferve but to augment our terror. Hath not this

this an appearance as if grandeur were not
an emotion diftinct from all others, but only
a circumftance that qualifies beauty and deformity?

I am notwithftanding fatisfied, that grandeur is an emotion, not only diftinct from
all others, but in every circumftance pleafant. Thefe propofitions muft be examined feparately. I begin with the former,
and fhall endeavour to prove, that magnitude produceth a peculiar emotion diftinguifhable from all others. Magnitude is
undoubtedly a real property of bodies, not
lefs than figure, and more than colour.
Figure and colour, even in the fame body,
produce feparate emotions, which are never mifapprehended one for the other. Why
fhould not magnitude produce an emotion
different from both? That it has this effect,
will be evident from a plain experiment of
two bodies, one great and one little, which
produce different emotions, though they be
precifely the fame as to figure and colour. There is indeed an obfcurity in this
matter, occafioned by the following circumftance, that the grandeur and beauty of the

fame

same object mix so intimately as scarce to
be distinguished. But the beauty of colour
comes in happily to enable us to make the
distinction. For the emotion of colour u-
nites with that of figure, not less intimately
than grandeur does with either. Yet the
emotion of colour is distinguishable from
that of figure; and so is grandeur, attentively considered : though when these three
emotions are blended together, they are
scarce felt as different emotions.

Next, that grandeur is an emotion in e-
very circumstance pleasant, appears from
the following considerations. Magnitude or
greatness, abstracted from all other circumstances, swells the heart and dilates the
mind. We feel this to be a pleasant effect;
and we feel no such effect in contracting
the mind upon little objects. This may be
illustrated by considering grandeur in an e-
nemy. Beauty is an agreeable quality,
whether in a friend or enemy; and when
the emotion it raiseth is mixed with resentment against an enemy, it must have the
effect to moderate our resentment. In the
same manner, grandeur in an enemy, undoubtedly

doubtedly foftens and blunts our refentment.
Grandeur indeed may indirectly and by reflection produce an unpleafant effect. Grandeur in an enemy, like courage, may increafe our fear, when we confider the advantage he hath over us by this quality. But
the fame indirect effect may be produced
by many other agreeable qualities, fuch as
beauty or wifdom.

The magnitude of an ugly object, ferves,
it is true, to augment our horror or averfion. But this proceeds not from magnitude feparately confidered. It proceeds
from the following circumftance, that in a
large object a great quantity of ugly parts
are prefented to view.

The fame chain of reafoning is fo obvioufly applicable to fublimity, that it would
be lofing time to fhow the application.
Grandeur therefore and fublimity fhall
hereafter be confidered both of them as
pleafant emotions.

The pleafant emotion raifed by large objects, has not efcaped the poets :

——————He doth beftride the narrow world
         Like

Like a Coloſſus; and we petty men
Walk under his huge legs.

Julius Cæſar, act 1. ſc. 3.

    Cleopatra. I dreamt there was an Emp'ror An-
tony;
Oh ſuch another ſleep, that I might ſee
But ſuch another man!
His face was as the heav'ns: and therein ſtuck
A ſun and moon, which kept their courſe and
lighted
The little O o' th' earth.
His legs beſtrid the ocean, his rear'd arm
Creſted the world.

Antony and Cleopatra, act 5. ſc. 3.

—————————————— Majeſty
Dies not alone, but, like a gulf, doth draw
What's near it with it.   It's a maſſy wheel
Fixt on the ſummit of the higheſt mount;
To whoſe huge ſpokes, ten thouſand leſſer things
Are mortis'd and adjoin'd; which when it falls,
Each ſmall annexment, petty conſequence,
Attends the boiſt'rous ruin.

Hamlet, act 3. ſc. 8.

    The poets have alſo made good uſe of
the

the emotion produced by the elevated fituation of an object.

Quod fi me lyricis vatibus inferes,
Sublimi feriam fidera vertice.

Horace, Carm. l. 1. ode 1.

Oh thou! the earthly author of my blood,
Whofe youthful fpirit, in me regenerate,
Doth with a twofold vigour lift me up,
To reach at victory above my head.

Richard II. act 1. fc. 4.

Northumberland, thou ladder wherewithal
The mounting Bolingbroke afcends my throne.

Richard II. act 5. fc. 2.

Anthony. Why was I rais'd the meteor of the
world,
Hung in the fkies and blazing as I travell'd,
Till all my fires were fpent; and then caft down-
ward
To be trod out by Cæfar?

Dryden, All for love, act 1.

Though the quality of magnitude produceth a pleafant emotion, we muft not conclude that the oppofite quality of littlenefs
produceth a painful emotion. It would be
unhappy

unhappy for man, were an object difagreeable from its being of a fmall fize merely,
when he is furrounded with fo many objects of that kind. The fame obfervation is
applicable to elevation of place. A body
placed high is agreeable; but the fame body
placed low, is not by that circumftance
rendered difagreeable. Littlenefs, and lownefs of place, are precifely fimilar in the following particular, that they neither give
pleafure nor pain. And in this may vifibly
be difcovered peculiar attention in fitting
the internal conftitution of man to his external circumftances. Were littlenefs, and
lownefs of place agreeable, greatnefs and
elevation could not be fo. Were littlenefs,
and lownefs of place difagreeable, they would
occafion uninterrupted uneafinefs.

The difference betwixt great and little
with refpect to agreeablenefs, is remarkably
felt in a feries when we pafs gradually from
the one extreme to the other. A mental
progrefs from the capital to the kingdom,
from that to Europe—to the whole earth
—to the planetary fyftem—to the univerfe,
is extremely pleafant: the heart fwells and
the

the mind is dilated, at every ftep. The returning in an oppofite direction is not pofitively painful, though our pleafure leffens at
every ftep, till it vanifh into indifference.
Such a progrefs may fometimes produce a
pleafure of a different fort, which arifes from
taking a narrower and narrower infpection.
The fame obfervation is applicable to a progrefs upward and downward. Afcent is
pleafant becaufe it elevates us. But defcent
is never painful: it is for the moft part pleafant from a different caufe, that it is according to the order of nature. The fall of a
ftone from anyheight, is extremely agreeable
by its accelerated motion. I feel it pleafant
to defcend from a mountain: the defcent
is natural and eafy. Neither is looking
downward painful. On the contrary, to
look down upon objects, makes part of the
pleafure of elevation. Looking down becomes then only painful when the object is
fo far below as to create dizzinefs: and even
when that is the cafe, we feel a fort of pleafure mixt with the pain. Witnefs Shakefpear's defcription of Dover cliffs:

    VOL. I.   M m   ——How

———————————————— How fearful
And dizzy 'tis, to caſt one's eyes ſo low!
The crows and choughs, that wing the midway-air,
Shew ſcarce ſo groſs as beetles.   Half-way down
Hangs one, that gathers ſamphire; dreadful trade!
Methinks he ſeems no bigger than his head.
The fiſhermen that walk upon the beach,
Appear like mice; and yon tall anchoring bark
Diminiſh'd to her cock; her cock, a buoy
Almoſt too ſmall for ſight   The murmuring ſurge,
That on th' unnumber'd idle pebbles chafes,
Cannot be heard ſo high.   I'll look no more,
Leſt my brain turn, and the deficient ſight
Topple down headlong.

King Lear, *act* 4. *ſc.* 6.

An obſervation is made above, that the
emotions of grandeur and ſublimity are
nearly allied.   Hence it is, that the one
term is frequently put for the other.   I give
an example.   An increaſing ſeries of numbers produceth an emotion ſimilar to that of
mounting upward, and for that reaſon is
commonly termed *an aſcending ſeries*.   A
ſeries of numbers gradually decreaſing, produceth an emotion ſimilar to that of going
downward, and for that reaſon is commonly
ly

ly termed *a descending series*. We talk familiarly of going up to the capital, and of going down to the country. From a lesser kingdom we talk of going up to a greater, whence the *anabasis* in the Greek language when one travels from Greece to Persia. We discover the same way of speaking in the language even of Japan*; and its universality proves it the offspring of a natural feeling.

The foregoing observation leads us naturally to consider grandeur and sublimity in a figurative sense, and as applicable to the fine arts. Hitherto I have considered these terms in their proper meaning, as applicable to objects of sight only: and I thought it of importance, to bestow some pains upon that article; because, generally speaking, the figurative sense of a word is derived from its proper sense; which will be found to hold in the present subject. Beauty in its original signification, is confined to objects of sight. But as many other objects, intellectual as well as moral, raise emotions resembling that

* Kempfer's history of Japan, b. 5. ch. 2.

of

of beauty, the refemblance of the effects prompts us naturally to extend the term *beauty* to thefe objects. This equally accounts for the terms *grandeur* and *fublimity* taken in a figurative fenfe. Every emotion, from whatever caufe proceeding, that refembles an emotion of grandeur or elevation, is called by the fame name. Thus generofity is faid to be an elevated emotion, as well as great courage; and that firmnefs of foul which is fuperior to misfortunes, obtains the peculiar name of *magnanimity*. On the other hand, every emotion that contracts the mind and fixeth it upon things trivial or of no importance, is termed *low*, by its refemblance to an emotion produced by a little or low object of fight. Thus an appetite for trifling amufements, is called *a low tafte*. The fame terms are applied to characters and actions. We talk familiarly of an elevated genius, of a great man, and equally fo of littlenefs of mind. Some actions are great and elevated, others are low and groveling. Sentiments and even expreffions are characterifed in the fame manner. An expreffion or fentiment that raifes

fes

fes the mind, is denominated *great* or *elevated*; and hence the fublime * in poetry. In fuch figurative terms, the diftinction is loft that is made betwixt *great* and *elevated* in their proper fenfe; for the refemblance is not fo entire, as to preferve thefe terms diftinct in their figurative application. We carry this figure ftill farther. Elevation in its proper fenfe, includes fuperiority of place; and lownefs, inferiority of place. Hence a man of fuperior talents, of fuperior rank, of inferior parts, of inferior tafte, and fuch like. The veneration we have for our anceftors and for the ancients in general, being fimi-

* Longinus gives a pretty good defcription of the fublime, though not entirely juft in every one of the circumftances, " That the mind is elevated by it, and fo fenfibly affected as " to fwell in tranfport and inward pride, as if what is only " heard or read, were its own invention." But he adheres not to this defcription. In his 6th chapter he juftly obferves, that many paffions have nothing of the grand, fuch as grief, fear, pity, which deprefs the mind inftead of raifing it. And yet in chapter 8th, he mentions Sappho's ode upon love as fublime. Beautiful it is undoubtedly, but it cannot be fublime, becaufe it really depreffes the mind inftead of raifing it. His tranflator Boileau is not more fuccefsful in his inftances. In his 10th reflection he cites a paffage from Demofthenes and another from Herodotus as fublime, which are not fo.

lar

lar to the emotion produced by an elevated
object of fight, juftifies the figurative expreffion, of the ancients being raifed above us,
or poffeffing a fuperior place. And we may
remark by the way, that as words are intimately connected with ideas, many, by this
form of expreffion, are led to conceive their
anceftors as really above them in place, and
their pofterity below them:

A grandam's name is little lefs in love
Than is the doting title of a mother:
They are as children but one ftep below.

Richard III. *act* 4. *fc.* 5.

The notes of the gamut, proceeding regularly from the blunter or groffer founds to
thofe which are more acute and piercing,
produce in the hearer a feeling fomewhat
fimilar to what is produced by mounting
upward; and this gives occafion to the figurative expreffions, *a high note*, *a low
note*.

Such is the refemblance in feeling betwixt real and figurative grandeur, that
among the nations on the eaft coaft of A-
fric, who are directed purely by nature, the
different

different dignities of the officers of state are marked by the length of the batoon each carries in his hand. And in Japan, princes and great lords shew their rank by the length and size of their sedan-poles *. Again, it is a rule in painting, that figures of a small size are proper for grotesque pieces; but that in an historical subject, which is grand and important, the figures ought to be as great as the life. The resemblance of these feelings is in reality so strong, that elevation in a figurative sense is observed to have the same effect even externally, that real elevation has:

K. Henry. This day is call'd the feast of Crispian.
He that outlives this day, and comes safe home,
Will stand a tiptoe when this day is nam'd,
And rouse him at the name of Crispian.
Henry V. *act* 4. *sc.* 8.

The resemblance in feeling betwixt real and figurative grandeur, is humorously illustrated by Addison in criticising upon the English tragedy. " The ordinary me-

* Kempfer's history of Japan.

" thod

" thod of making an hero, is to clap a huge
" plume of feathers upon his head, which
" rifes fo high, that there is often a greater
" length from his chin to the top of his
" head, than to the fole of his foot. One
" would believe, that we thought a great
" man and a tall man the fame thing. As
" thefe fuperfluous ornaments upon the
" head make a great man, a princefs gene-
" rally receives her grandeur from thofe
" additional incumbrances that fall into her
" tail. I mean the broad fweeping train
" that follows her in all her motions, and
" finds conftant employment for a boy who
" ftands behind her to open and fpread it
" to advantage *." The Scythians, impreffed with the fame of Alexander, were
aftonifhed when they found him a little
man.

A gradual progrefs from fmall to great,
is not lefs remarkable in figurative than in
real grandeur or elevation. Every one muft
have obferved the delightful effect of a
number of thoughts or fentiments, artfully

* Spectator, N° 42.

difpofed

difpofed like an afcending feries, and making impreffions ftronger and ftronger. Such difpofition of members in a period, is diftinguifhed by a proper name, being termed a *climax*.

In order to have a juft conception of grandeur and fublimity, it is neceffary to be obferved, that within certain limits they produce their ftrongeft effects, which leffen by excefs as well as by defect. This is remarkable in grandeur and fublimity taken in their proper fenfe. The ftrongeft emotion of grandeur is raifed by an object that can be taken in at one view. An object fo immenfe as not to be comprehended but in parts, tends rather to diftract than fatisfy the mind *. In like manner, the ftrongeft emotion produced by elevation is where the object is feen diftinctly. A greater elevation leffens in appearance the

---

* It is juftly obferved by Addifon, that perhaps a man would have been more aftonifhed with the majeftic air that appeared in one of Lyfippus's ftatues of Alexander, though no bigger than the life, than he might have been with Mount Athos, had it been cut into the figure of the hero, according to the propofal of Phidias, with a river in one hand and a city in the other. *Spectator*, Nº 415.

object,

object, till it vanish out of fight with its
pleasant emotion. The same is equally remarkable in figurative grandeur and elevation, which shall be handled together, because, as observed above, they are scarce
distinguishable. Sentiments may be so
strained, as to become obscure, or to exceed
the capacity of the human mind. Against
such licence of imagination, every good
writer will be upon his guard. And therefore it is of greater importance to observe,
that even the true sublime may be carried
beyond that pitch which produces the highest entertainment. We are undoubtedly
susceptible of a greater elevation than can be
inspired by human actions the most heroic
and magnanimous; witness what we feel
from Milton's description of superior beings.
Yet every man must be sensible of a more
constant and pleasant elevation, when the
history of his own species is the subject. He
enjoys an elevation equal to that of the
greatest hero, of an Alexander or a Cæsar,
of a Brutus or an Epaminondas. He accompanies these heroes in their sublimest
sentiments and most hazardous exploits,
with

with a magnanimity equal to theirs; and finds it no ftretch to preferve the fame tone of mind for hours together, without finking. The cafe is by no means the fame in defcribing the actions or qualities of fuperior beings. The reader's imagination cannot keep pace with that of the poet; and the mind, unable to fupport itfelf in a ftrained elevation, falls as from a height; and the fall is immoderate like the elevation. Where this effect is not felt, it muft be prevented by fome obfcurity in the conception, which frequently attends the defcription of unknown objects.

On the other hand, objects of fight that are not remarkably great or high, fcarce raife any emotion of grandeur or fublimity; and the fame holds in other objects. The mind is often roufed and animated without being carried to the height of grandeur or fublimity. This difference may be difcerned in many forts of mufic, as well as in fome mufical inftruments. A kettledrum roufes, and a hautboy is animating; but neither of them infpire an emotion of fublimity. Revenge animates the mind in a confiderable

degree;

degree; but I think it never produceth an emotion that can be termed *grand* or *sublime*; and I shall have occasion afterward to observe, that no disagreeable passion ever has this effect. I am willing to put this to the test, by placing before my reader the most spirited picture of revenge ever drawn. It is a speech of Antony wailing over the body of Cæsar.

Wo to the hand that shed this costly blood!
Over thy wounds now do I prophesy,
(Which, like dumb mouths, do ope their ruby lips,
To beg the voice and utterance of my tongue),
A curse shall light upon the kind of men;
Domestic fury, and fierce civil strife,
Shall cumber all the parts of Italy;
Blood and destruction shall be so in use,
And dreadful objects so familiar,
That mothers shall but smile, when they behold
Their infants quarter'd by the hands of war,
All pity choak'd with custom of fell deeds.
And Cæsar's spirit, ranging for revenge,
With *Atè* by his side come hot from hell,
Shall in these confines, with a monarch's voice,
Cry *Havock*, and let slip the dogs of war.
                              Julius Cæsar, act 3. sc. 4.

When

When the fublime is carried to its due height and circumfcribed within proper bounds, it inchants the mind and raifes the moft delightful of all emotions. The reader, ingroffed by a fublime object, feels himfelf raifed as it were to a higher rank. When fuch is the cafe, it is not wonderful that the hiftory of conquerors and heroes fhould be univerfally the favourite entertainment. And this fairly accounts for what I once erroneoufly fufpected to be a wrong bias originally in human nature. The groffeft acts of oppreffion and injuftice, fcarce blemifh the character of a great conqueror. We notwithftanding warmly efpoufe his intereft, accompany him in his exploits, and are anxious for his fuccefs. The fplendor and enthufiafm of the hero transfufed into the readers, elevate their minds far above the rules of juftice, and render them in a great meafure infenfible of the wrong that is done:

For in thofe days might only fhall be admir'd
And valour and heroic virtue call'd;
To overcome in battle, and fubdue
Nations, and bring home fpoils with infinite
Manflaughter,

Manflaughter, fhall be held the higheft pitch
Of human glory, and for glory done
Of triumph, to be ftyl'd great conquerors,
Patrons of mankind, gods, and fons of gods.
Deftroyers rightlier called, and plagues of men.
Thus fame fhall be atchiev'd, renown on earth,
And what moft merits fame in filence hid.

Milton, b. 11.

The attachment we have to things grand
or lofty may be thought to proceed from an
unwearied inclination we have to be exalted. No defire is more univerfal than to be
refpected and honoured. Upon that account chiefly, are we ambitious of power,
riches, titles, fame, which would fuddenly
lofe their relifh, did they not raife us above
others, and command fubmiffion and defe-
rence *. But the preference given to things
grand and fublime muft have a deeper root
in human nature. Many beftow their time

---

* Honeftum per fe effe expetendum indicant pueri, in quibus, ut in fpeculis, natura cernitur. Quanta ftudia decer-
tantium funt! Quanta ipfa certamina! Ut illi efferuntur læti-
tia, cum vicerunt! Ut pudet victos! Ut fe accufari nolunt!
Ut cupiunt laudari! Quos illi labores non perferunt, ut æqua-
lium principes fint! *Cicero de finibus.*

upon

upon low and trifling amufements, without
fhowing any defire to be exalted. Yet thefe
very perfons talk the fame language with
the reft of mankind; and at leaft in their
judgement, if not in their tafte, prefer the
more elevated pleafures. They acknowledge a more refined tafte, and are afhamed
of their own as low and groveling. This
fentiment, conftant and univerfal, muft be
the work of nature; and it plainly indicates
an original attachment in human nature to
every object that elevates the mind. Some
men may have a greater relifh for an object
not of the higheft rank: but they are confcious of the common nature of man, and
that it ought not to be fubjected to their
peculiar tafte.

The irregular influence of grandeur,
reaches alfo to other matters. However
good, honeft, or ufeful, a man may be,
he is not fo much refpected, as one of a
more elevated character is, though of lefs
integrity; nor do the misfortunes of the
former affect us fo much as thofe of the
latter. I add, becaufe it cannot be difguifed, that the remorfe which attends breach

of

of engagement, is in a great meafure proportioned to the figure that the injured perfon makes. The vows and proteftations of
lovers are an illuftrious example of this obfervation; for thefe commonly are little regarded when made to women of inferior
rank.

What I have faid fuggefts a capital rule for
reaching the fublime in fuch works of art as
are fufceptible of it; and that is, to put in
view thofe parts or circumftances only which
make the greateft figure, keeping out of
fight every thing that is low or trivial. Such
judicious felection of capital circumftances,
is by an eminent critic ftyled *grandeur of
manner* *. The mind, from an elevation
infpired by important objects, cannot,
without reluctance, be forced down to beftow any fhare of its attention upon trifles.
In none of the fine arts is there fo great
fcope for this rule as in poetry, which, by
that means, enjoys a remarkable power of
beftowing upon objects and events an air of
grandeur. When we are fpectators, every

* Spectator, N° 415.

minute

minute object prefents itfelf in its order. But in defcribing at fecond hand, thefe are laid afide, and the capital objects are brought clofe together. A judicious tafte in felecting, after this manner, the moft interefting incidents to give them an united force, accounts for a fact which at firft fight may appear furprifing, that we are more moved by a poetical narrative at fecond hand, than when we are fpectators of the event itfelf in all its circumftances.

Longinus exemplifies the foregoing rule by a comparifon of two paffages *. The firft from Ariftæus is thus tranflated.

Ye pow'rs, what madnefs! how on fhips fo frail
(Tremendous thought!) can thoughtlefs mortals
    fail?
For ftormy feas they quit the pleafing plain,
Plant woods in waves and dwell amidft the main.
Far o'er the deep (a tracklefs path) they go,
And wander oceans in purfuit of wo.
No eafe their hearts, no reft their eyes can find,
On heaven their looks, and on the waves their
    mind.

* Chap. 8. of the Sublime.

Sunk are their spirits, while their arms they rear,
And gods are wearied with their fruitless prayer.

The other from Homer I shall give in
Pope's translation.

Bursts as a wave that from the cloud impends,
And swell'd with tempests on the ship descends.
White are the decks with foam : the winds aloud
Howl o'er the masts, and sing through every
  shrowd.
Pale, trembling, tir'd. the sailors freeze with fears,
And instant death on every wave appears.

In the latter passage, the most striking
circumstances are selected to fill the mind
with the grand and terrible. The former
is a collection of minute and low circumstances, which scatter the thought and
make no impression. The passage at the
same time is full of verbal antitheses and low
conceit, extremely improper in a scene of
distress. But this last observation is made
occasionally only, as it belongs not to the
present subject.

The following passage from the twenty-
first book of the Odyssey, deviates widely
       from

from the rule above laid down. It concerns that part of the hiſtory of Penelope
and her ſuitors, in which ſhe is made to
declare in favour of him who ſhould prove
the moſt dexterous in ſhooting with the
bow of Ulyſſes.

Now gently winding up the fair aſcent,
By many an eaſy ſtep, the matron went:
Then o'er the pavement glides with grace divine,
(With poliſh'd oak the level pavements ſhine);
The folding gates a dazling light diſplay'd,
With pomp of various architrave o'erlay'd.
The bolt, obedient to the ſilken ſtring,
Forſakes the ſtaple as ſhe pulls the ring;
The wards reſpondent to the key turn round;
The bars fall back; the flying valves reſound.
Loud as a bull makes hill and valley ring;
So roar'd the lock when it releas'd the ſpring.
She moves majeſtic through the wealthy room
Where treaſur'd garments caſt a rich perfume;
There from the column where aloft it hung,
Reach'd, in its ſplendid caſe, the bow unſtrung.

Virgil ſometimes errs againſt this rule.
In the following paſſages minute circumſtances are brought into full view; and
what is ſtill worſe, they are deſcribed in all

the

the fublimity of poetical defcription. *Æneid,* *L.* 1. *l.* 214. *to* 219. *L.* 6. *l.* 176. *to* 182. *L.* 6. *l.* 212. *to* 231. And the laft, which is a defcription of a funeral, is the lefs ex-cufeable, as it relates to a man who makes no figure in the poem.

The fpeech of Clytemneftra, defcending from her chariot in the Iphigenia of Euri-pides, beginning of act 3. is ftuffed with a number of low, common, and trivial cir-cumftances.

But of all writers Lucan in this article is the moft injudicious. The fea-fight be-twixt the Romans and Maffilians *, is de-fcribed fo much in detail without exhibiting any grand or general view, that the reader is quite fatigued with endlefs circumftances, and never feels any degree of elevation. And yet there are fome fine incidents, thofe for example of the two brothers, and of the old man and his fon, which, feparated from the reft, would affect us greatly. But Lu-can once engaged in a defcription, knows no bounds. See other paffages of the fame

* Lib. 3. beginning at line 567.

kind,

kind, *L.* 4. *l.* 292. *to* 337. *L.* 4. *l.* 750.
to 765. The epifode of the forcerefs E-
ricktho, end of book 6. is intolerably minute and prolix.

To thefe I venture to oppofe a paffage
from an old hiftorical ballad :

> Go, little page, tell Hardiknute
>   That lives on hill fo high *,
> To draw his fword, the dread of faes,
>   And hafte to follow me.
> The little page flew fwift as dart
>   Flung by his mafter's arm.
> Come down, come down, Lord Hardiknute,
>   And rid your king from harm.

This rule is alfo applicable to other fine
arts. In painting it is eftablifhed, that the
principal figure muft be put in the ftrongeft light ; that the beauty of attitude confifts
in placing the nobler parts moft in view,
and in fuppreffing the fmaller parts as much
as poffible ; that the folds of the drapery
muft be few and large ; that forefhortenings
are bad, becaufe they make the parts ap-

---

* *High,* in the old Scotch language, is pronounced *hee.*

pear

pear little ; and that the muſcles ought to be kept as entire as poſſible, without being divided into ſmall ſections.   Every one at preſent is ſenſible of the importance of this rule when applied to gardening, in oppoſition to the antiquated taſte of parterres ſplit into a thouſand ſmall parts in the ſtricteſt regularity of figure.   Thoſe who have ſucceeded beſt in architecture, have governed themſelves by this rule in all their models.

Another rule chiefly regards the ſublime, though it may be applied to every literary performance intended for amuſement ; and that is, to avoid as much as poſſible abſtract and general terms.   Such terms, perfectly well fitted for reaſoning and for conveying inſtruction, ſerve but imperfectly the ends of poetry.   They ſtand upon the ſame footing with mathematical ſigns, contrived to expreſs our thoughts in a conciſe manner. But images, which are the life of poetry, cannot be raiſed in any perfection, otherwiſe than by introducing particular objects.   General terms, that comprehend a number of individuals, muſt be excepted from this rule.   Our kindred, our clan, our country,

and

and words of the like import, though they scarce raise any image, have notwithstanding a wonderful power over our passions. The greatness of the complex object overbalances the obscurity of the image.

What I have further to say upon this subject, shall be comprehended in a few observations. A man is capable of being raised so much above his ordinary pitch by an emotion of grandeur, that it is extremely difficult by a single thought or expression to produce that emotion in perfection. The rise must be gradual and the result of reiterated impressions. The effect of a single expression can be but momentary; and if one feel suddenly somewhat like a swelling or exaltation of mind, the emotion vanisheth as soon as felt. Single expressions, I know, are often justly cited as examples of the sublime. But then their effect is nothing compared with a grand subject displayed in its capital parts. I shall give a few examples, that the reader may judge for himself. In the famous action of Thermopylæ, where Leonidas the Spartan King with his chosen band fighting for their country,

country, were cut off to the laſt man, a
ſaying is reported of Dieneces one of the
band, which, expreſſing chearful and un-
diſturbed bravery, is well intitled to the firſt
place in examples of this kind. Talking of
the number of their enemies, it was obſerved, that the arrows ſhot by ſuch a multitude would intercept the light of the ſun.
So much the better, ſays he; for we ſhall
then fight in the ſhade *.

> *Somerſet.* Ah! Warwick, Warwick, wert thou
> > as we are,
> We might recover all our loſs again.
> The Queen from France hath brought a puiſſant
> > power,
> Ev'n now we heard the news. Ah! couldſt thou
> > fly!
> > *Warwick.* Why, then I would not fly.
> > > *Third part*, *Henry* VI. *act* 5. *ſc.* 3.

Such a ſentiment from a man expiring of
his wounds, is truly heroic, and muſt elevate the mind to the greateſt height that can
be done by a ſingle expreſſion. It will not

* Herodotus, book 7.

ſuffer

suffer in a comparifon with the famous fentiment *Qu'il mourut* in Corneille's Horace.
The latter is a fentiment of indignation
merely, the former of invincible fortitude.

In oppofition to thefe examples, to cite
many a fublime paffage, enriched with the
fineft images, and dreffed in the moft ner-
vous expreffions, would fcarce be fair. I
fhall produce but one inftance from Shakefpear, which fets a few objects before the
eye, without much pomp of language. It
works its effect, by reprefenting thefe objects in a climax, raifing the mind higher
and higher till it feel the emotion of grandeur in perfection.

The cloud-capt tow'rs, the gorgeous palaces,
The folemn temples, the great globe itfelf,
Yea all which it inherit, fhall diffolve, *&c.*

The cloud-capt tow'rs produce an elevating
emotion, heightened by the *gorgeous palaces.*
And the mind is carried ftill higher and
higher by the images that follow. Succef-
five images, making thus ftronger and
ftronger impreffions, muft elevate more than
any fingle image can do.

I proceed to another obfervation. In the chapter of beauty it is remarked, that regularity is required in fmall figures, and order in fmall groups; but that in advancing gradually from fmall to great, regularity and order are lefs and lefs required. This remark ferves to explain the extreme delight we have in viewing the face of nature, when fufficiently enriched and diverfified by objects. The bulk of the objects feen in a natural landfcape are beautiful, and fome of them grand. A flowing river, a fpreading oak, a round hill, an extended plain, are delightful; and even a rugged rock or barren heath, though in themfelves difagreeable, contribute by contraft to the beauty of the whole. Joining to thefe, the verdure of the fields, the mixture of light and fhade, and the fublime canopy fpread over all; it will not appear wonderful, that fo extenfive a group of glorious objects fhould fwell the heart to its utmoft bounds, and raife the ftrongeft emotion of grandeur. The fpectator is confcious of an enthufiafm, which cannot bear confinement nor the ftrictnefs of regularity and order. He loves

to

to range at large; and is so inchanted with
shining objects, as to neglect slight beauties
or defects. Thus it is, that the delightful
emotion of grandeur, depends little on order
and regularity. And when the emotion is
at its height by a survey of the greatest objects, order and regularity are almost totally
disregarded.

The same observation is applicable in
some measure to works of art. In a small
building the slightest irregularity is disagreeable. In a magnificent palace or a large
Gothic church, irregularities are less regarded. In an epic poem we pardon many
negligences, which would be intolerable in
a sonnet or epigram. Notwithstanding such
exceptions, it may be justly laid down for a
rule, That in all works of art, order and
regularity ought to be governing principles.
And hence the observation of Longinus *,
" In works of art we have regard to exact
" proportion; in those of nature, to gran-
" deur and magnificence."

I shall add but one other observation,

* Chap. 30.

P p 2   That

That no means can be more succefsfully employed to fink and deprefs the mind than grandeur or fublimity. By the artful introduction of an humbling object, the fall is great in proportion to the former elevation. Of this doctrine Shakefpear affords us a beautiful illuftration, in a paffage part of which is cited above for another purpofe:

The cloud-capt tow'rs, the gorgeous palaces,
The folemn temples, the great globe itfelf,
Yea all which it inherit, fhall diffolve,
And like the bafelefs fabric of a vifion
Leave not a rack behind——

Tempeft, act 4. fc. 4.

The elevation of the mind in the former part of this beautiful paffage, makes the fall great in proportion when the moft humbling of all images is introduced, that of an utter diffolution of the earth and its inhabitants. A fentiment makes not the fame impreffion in a cool ftate, that it does when the mind is warmed; and a depreffing or melancholy fentiment makes the ftrongeft impreffion, when it brings down the mind from its higheft ftate of elevation or chearfulnefs.

This

This indirect effect of elevation to sink the mind, is sometimes produced without the intervention of any humbling image. There was occasion above to remark, that in describing superior beings, the reader's imagination, unable to support itself in a strained elevation, falls often as from a height, and sinks even below its ordinary tone. The following instance comes luckily in view; for a better illustration cannot be given : " God said, Let there be light, " and there was light." Longinus cites this passage from Moses as a shining example of the sublime; and it is scarce possible in fewer words, to convey so clear an image of the infinite power of the Deity. But then it belongs to the present subject to remark, that the emotion of sublimity raised by this image is but momentary; and that the mind, unable to support itself in an elevation so much above nature, immediately sinks down into humility and veneration for a being so far exalted above us groveling mortals. Every one is acquainted with a dispute about this passage betwixt

two

two French critics *, the one pofitively affirming, the other as pofitively deny- ing, it to be fublime. What I have o- pened, fhows that both of them have reached the truth, but neither of them the whole truth. Every one of tafte muft be fenfible, that the primary effect of this paf- fage is an emotion of grandeur. This fo far juftifies Boileau. But then every one of tafte muft be equally fenfible, that the emo- tion is merely a flafh, which vanifheth in- ftantly, and gives way to the deepeft humi- lity and veneration. This indirect effect of fublimity, juftifies Huet on the other hand, who being a man of true piety, and perhaps of inferior imagination, felt the humbling paffions more fenfibly than his antagonift. And even laying afide any peculiarity of character, Huet's opinion may I think be defended as the more folid; upon the fol- lowing account, that in fuch images, the depreffing emotions are the more fenfibly felt, and have the longer endurance.

The ftraining an elevated fubject beyond

* Boileau and Huet.

due

due bounds and beyond the reach of an ordinary conception, is not a vice fo frequent as to require the correction of criticifm. But falfe fublime is a rock which writers of more fire than judgement generally fplit on. And therefore a collection of examples may be of ufe as a beacon to future adventurers. One fpecies of falfe fublime, known by the name of *bombaft*, is common among writers of a mean genius. It is a ferious endeavour, by ftrained defcription, to raife a low or familiar fubject above its rank; which inftead of being fublime, never fails to be ridiculous. I am extremely fenfible how prone the mind is, in fome animating paffions, to magnify its objects beyond natural bounds. But fuch hyperbolical defcription has its limits. If carried beyond the impulfe of the propenfity, the colouring no longer pleafes: it degenerates into the burlefque. Take the following examples.

Sejanus. ——————— Great and high
The world knows only two, that's Rome and I.
My roof receives me not; 'tis air I tread,

And

And at each ftep I feel my advanc'd head
Knock out a ftar in heav'n.

Sejanus, Ben Johnfon, act 5.

A writer who has no natural elevation of
genius, is extremely apt to deviate into bombaft. He ftrains above his genius; and the
violent effort he makes carries him generally beyond the bounds of propriety. Boileau expreffes this happily :

L'autre à peur de ramper, il fe perd dans la nue *.

The fame author Ben Johnfon abounds
in the bombaft:

——————————— The mother,
Th'expulfed Apicata, finds them there;
Whom when fhe faw lie fpread on the degrees,
After a world of fury on herfelf,
Tearing her hair, defacing of her face,
Beating her breafts and womb, kneeling amaz'd,
Crying to heav'n, then to them; at laft
Her drowned voice got up above her woes :
And with fuch black and bitter execrations,
(As might affright the gods, and force the fun
Run backward to the eaft; nay, make the old

* L'art poet. chant 1. l. 68.

Deformed

Deformed Chaos rise again t' o'erwhelm
Them, us, and all the world) she fills the air,
Upbraids the heavens with their partial dooms,
Defies their tyrannous powers, and demands
What she and those poor innocents have trans-
       gress'd,
That they must suffer such a share in vengeance.
                     Sejanus, act 5. sc. last.

——————————Lentulus, the man,
If all our fire were out, would fetch down new,
Out of the hand of Jove; and rivet him
To Caucasus, should he but frown; and let
His own gaunt eagle fly at him to tire.
                      Catiline, act 3.

Can these, or such, be any aids to us?
Look they as they were built to shake the world,
Or be a moment to our enterprise?
A thousand, such as they are, could not make
One atom of our souls.   They should be men
Worth heaven's fear, that looking up, but thus,
Would make Jove stand upon his guard, and draw
Himself within his thunder; which, amaz'd,
He should discharge in vain, and they unhurt.
Or, if they were, like Capaneus at Thebes,
They should hang dead upon the highest spires,
And ask the second bolt to be thrown down.
Why Lentulus talk you so long?   This time

Had been enough t' have fcatter'd all the ftars,
T' have quench'd the fun and moon, and made the
world
Defpair of day, or any light but ours.

Catiline, act 4.

This is the language of a madman:

Guilford. Give way, and let the gufhing torrent
come,
Behold the tears we bring to fwell the deluge,
Till the flood rife upon the guilty world
And make the ruin common.

Lady Jane Gray, act 4. near the end.

Another fpecies of falfe fublime, is ftill
more faulty than bombaft; and that is, to
force an elevation by introducing imaginary
beings without preferving any propriety in
their actions; as if it were lawful to afcribe
every extravagance and inconfiftence to beings of the poet's creation. No writers are
more licentious in this article than Johnfon
and Dryden.

Methinks I fee Death and the furies waiting
What we will do, and all the heaven at leifure
For the great fpectacle. Draw then your fwords:
And

And if our deſtiny envy our virtue
The honour of the day, yet let us care
To ſell ourſelves at ſuch a price, as may
Undo the world to buy us, and make Fate,
While ſhe tempts ours, to fear her own eſtate.

Catiline, act 5.

—————————The furies ſtood on hills
Circling the place, and trembled to ſee men
Do more than they: whilſt Piety left the field,
Griev'd for that ſide, that in ſo bad a cauſe
They knew not what a crime their valour was.
The Sun ſtood ſtill, and was, behind the cloud
The battle made, ſeen ſweating to drive up
His frighted horſe, whom ſtill the noiſe drove
    backward.

Ibid. act. 5.

Oſmyn. While we indulge our common happi-
        neſs,
He is forgot by whom we all poſſeſs,
The brave Almanzor, to whoſe arms we owe
All that we did, and all that we ſhall do ;
Who like a tempeſt that outrides the wind,
Made a juſt battle ere the bodies join'd.
    Abdalla. His victories we ſcarce could keep in
        view,
Or poliſh 'em ſo faſt as he rough drew.

Q q 2   *Abdemelech.*

Abdemelech. Fate after him below with pain did
move,
And Victory could scarce keep pace above.
Death did at length so many slain forget,
And lost the tale, and took 'em by the great.
Conquest of Granada, act. 2. at beginning.

The gods of Rome fight for ye; loud Fame calls
ye,
Pitch'd on the toplefs Apenine, and blows
To all the under world, all nations,
The seas and unfrequented deferts, where the
snow dwells,
Wakens the ruin'd monuments, and there
Where nothing but eternal death and sleep is,
Informs again the dead bones.
Beaumont and Fletcher, Bonduca, act. 3. fc. 3.

I close with the following observation,
That an actor upon the stage may be guilty
of bombast as well as an author in his
closet. A certain manner of acting, which
is grand when supported by dignity in the
fentiment and force in the expression, is
ridiculous where the fentiment is mean,
and the expression flat.

CHAP.

C H A P. V.

Motion and Force.

THAT motion is agreeable to the eye without relation to purpose or design, may appear from the a-musement it gives to infants. Juvenile exercises are relished chiefly upon that account.

If to see a body in motion be agreeable, one will be apt to conclude, that to see it at rest is disagreeable. But we learn from experience, that this would be a rash conclusion. Rest is one of those circumstances that are neither agreeable nor disagreeable. It is viewed with perfect indifferency. And happy it is for mankind that the matter is so ordered. If rest were agreeable, it would disincline us to motion, by which all things are performed. If it were disagreeable, it would be a source of perpetual uneasiness; for the bulk of the things we see appear to be at rest.

reſt. A ſimilar inſtance of deſigning wiſdom I have had occaſion to explain, in oppoſing grandeur to littleneſs, and elevation to lowneſs of place *. Even in the ſimpleſt matters, the finger of God is conſpicuous. The happy adjuſtment of the internal nature of man to his external circumſtances, diſplayed in the inſtances here given, is indeed admirable.

Motion is certainly agreeable in all its varieties of quickneſs and ſlowneſs. But motion long continued admits ſome exceptions. That degree of continued motion which correſponds to the natural courſe of our perceptions, is the moſt agreeable †. The quickeſt motion is for an inſtant delightful. But it ſoon appears to be too rapid. It becomes painful, by forcibly accelerating the courſe of our perceptions. Slow continued motion becomes diſagreeable for an oppoſite reaſon, that it retards the natural courſe of our perceptions.

There are other varieties in motion, be-

* See chap. 4.
† See chap. 9.

ſide

fide quicknefs and flownefs, that make it
more or lefs agreeable. Regular motion is
preferred before what is irregular, witnefs
the motion of the planets in orbits nearly
circular. The motion of the comets in orbits lefs regular, is lefs agreeable.

Motion uniformly accelerated, refembling an afcending feries of numbers, is
more agreeable than when uniformly retarded. Motion upward is agreeable by
the elevation of the moving body. What
then fhall we fay of downward motion regularly accelerated by the force of gravity,
compared with upward motion regularly
retarded by the fame force? Which of
thefe is the moft agreeable? This queftion
is not eafily folved.

Motion in a ftraight line is no doubt a-
greeable. But we prefer undulating motion, as of waves, of a flame, of a fhip
under fail. Such motion is more free, and
alfo more natural. Hence the beauty of a
ferpentine river.

The eafy and fliding motion of fluids,
from the lubricity and incoherence of their
parts, is agreeable upon that account. But
the

the agreeableneſs chiefly depends upon the following circumſtance, that the motion is perceived, not as of one body, but as of an endleſs number moving together with order and regularity. Poets ſtruck with this beauty, draw more images from fluids than from ſolids.

Force is of two kinds; one quieſcent, and one exerted by motion. The former, dead weight for example, muſt be laid a-ſide; for a body at reſt is not by that cir-cumſtance either agreeable or diſagreeable. Moving force only belongs to the preſent ſubject; and though it is not ſeparable from motion, yet by the power of abſtraction, either of them may be conſidered independ-ent of the other. Both of them are agree-able, becauſe both of them include activity. It is agreeable to ſee a thing move : to ſee it moved, as when it is dragged or puſhed along, is neither agreeable nor diſagree-able, more than when at reſt. It is agree-able to ſee a thing exert force; but it makes not the thing either agreeable or diſagree-able, to ſee force exerted upon it.

Though motion and force are each of them

them agreeable, the impreſſions they make are different. This difference, clearly felt, is not eaſily deſcribed. All we can ſay is, that the emotion raiſed by a moving body, reſembles its cauſe : it feels as if the mind were carried along. The emotion raiſed by force exerted, reſembles alſo its cauſe : it feels as if force were exerted within the mind.

To illuſtrate this difference, I give the following examples. It has been explained why ſmoke aſcending in a calm day, ſup-poſe from a cottage in a wood, is an agree-able objeᵫ *. Landſcape-painters are fond of this objeᵫ, and introduce it upon all occaſions. As the aſcent is natural and without effort, it is delightful in a calm ſtate of mind. It makes an impreſſion of the ſame ſort with that of a gently-flowing river, but more agreeable, becauſe aſcent is more to our taſte than deſcent. A fire-work or a *jet d'eau* rouſes the mind more ; becauſe the beauty of force viſibly exerted, is ſuperadded to that of upward motion.

* Chap. 1.

To a man reclining indolently upon a bank of flowers, afcending fmoke in a ftill morning is delightful. But a fire-work or a *jet d'eau* roufes him from this fupine pofture, and puts him in motion.

A *jet d'eau* makes an impreffion diftinguifhable from that of a water-fall. Downward motion being natural and without effort, tends rather to quiet the mind than to roufe it. Upward motion, on the contrary, overcoming the refiftance of gravity, makes an impreffion of a great effort, and thereby roufes and enlivens the mind.

The public games of the Greeks and Romans, which gave fo much entertainment to the fpectators, confifted chiefly in exerting force, wreftling, leaping, throwing great ftones, and fuch like trials of ftrength. When great force is exerted, the effort felt within the mind produces great life and vivacity. The effort may be fuch, as in fome meafure to overpower the mind. Thus the explofion of gun-powder, the violence of a torrent, the weight of a mountain, and the crufh of an earthquake, create aftonifhment rather than pleafure.

No

No quality nor circumſtance contributes more to grandeur than force, eſpecially as exerted by ſenſible beings. I cannot make this more evident than by the following citations.

——————————Him the almighty power
Hurl'd headlong flaming from th' ethereal ſky,
With hideous ruin and combuſtion, down
To bottomleſs perdition, there to dwell
In adamantine chains and penal fire,
Who durſt defy th' Omnipotent to arms.

Paradiſe Loſt, *book* 1.

——————————Now ſtorming fury roſe,
And clamour ſuch as heard in heaven till now
Was never; arms on armour claſhing bray'd
Horrible diſcord, and the madding wheels
Of brazen chariots rag'd; dire was the noiſe
Of conflict; over head the diſmal hiſs
Of fiery darts in flaming vollies flew,
And flying vaulted either hoſt with fire.
So under fiery cope together ruſh'd
Both battles main, with ruinous aſſault
And inextinguiſhable rage: all heav'n
Reſounded; and had earth been then, all earth
Had to her centre ſhook.

Ibid, *book* 6.

They

They ended parle, and both addrefs'd for fight
Unfpeakable; for who, though with the tongue
Of angels, can relate, or to what things
Liken on earth confpicuous, that may lift
Human imagination to fuch height
Of godlike pow'r? for likeft gods they feem'd,
Stood they or mov'd, in ftature, motion, arms,
Fit to decide the empire of great Heav'n.
Now wav'd their fiery fwords, and in the air
Made horrid circles; two broad funs their fhields
Blaz'd oppofite, while Expectation ftood
In horror: from each hand with fpeed retir'd,
Where erft was thickeft fight, th' angelic throng,
And left large field, unfafe within the wind
Of fuch commotion; fuch as, to fet forth
Great things by fmall, if Nature's concord broke,
Among the conftellations war were fprung,
Two planets, rufhing from afpect malign
Of fierceft oppofition, in mid fky,
Should combat, and their jarring fpheres confound.

Ibid, book 6.

We fhall now confider the effect of motion and force in conjunction. In contemplating the planetary fyftem, what
ftrikes us the moft, is the fpherical figures
of the planets and their regular motions.
The conception we have of their activity
and

and enormous bulk is more obfcure.   The
beauty accordingly of this fyftem, raifes a
more lively emotion than its grandeur.
But if we could imagine ourfelves fpectators
comprehending the whole fyftem at one
view, the activity and irrefiftible force of
thefe immenfe bodies would fill us with a-
mazement.   Nature cannot furnifh another
fcene fo grand.

Motion and force, agreeable in themfelves,   are alfo agreeable by their utility
when employed as means to accomplifh
fome beneficial end.   Hence the fuperior
beauty of fome machines, where force and
motion concur to perform the work of
numberlefs hands.   Hence the beautiful
motions, firm and regular, of a horfe trained for war.   Every fingle ftep is the fitteft
that can be for obtaining the end propofed.
But the grace of motion is vifible chiefly in
man, not only for the reafons mentioned,
but alfo becaufe every gefture is fignificant.
The power however of agreeable motion is
not a common talent.   Every limb of the
human body has a good and a bad, an agreeable and difagreeable action.   Some mo-

tions are extremely graceful, others are plain and vulgar : some express dignity, others meanness. But the pleasure here, arising not singly from the beauty of motion, but from indicating character and sentiment, belongs to a different chapter *.

I should conclude with the final cause of the relish we have for motion and force, were it not so evident as to require no explanation. We are placed here in such circumstances as to make industry essential to our well-being ; for without industry the plainest necessaries of life are not to be obtained. When our situation therefore in this world requires activity and a constant exertion of motion and force, Providence indulgently provides for our welfare in making these agreeable to us. It would be a blunder in our nature, to make things disagreeable that we depend on for existence ; and even to make them indifferent, would tend to make us relax greatly from that degree of activity which is indispensable.

* Chap. 15.

C H A P.

C H A P. VI.

Novelty, and the unexpected appearance of objects.

OF all the particulars that contribute to raise emotions, not excepting beauty, or even greatness, novelty hath the most powerful influence. A new spectacle attracts multitudes. It produceth instantaneously an emotion which totally occupies the mind, and for a time excludes all other objects. The soul seems to meet the strange appearance with a certain elongation of itself; and all is hushed in close contemplation. In some instances, there is perceived a degree of agony, attended with external symptoms extremely expressive. Conversation among the vulgar never is more interesting, than when it runs upon strange objects and extraordinary events. Men tear themselves from their native country in search of things rare and new; and

curiosity

curiofity converts into a pleafure, the fatigues,
and even perils of travelling. To what caufe
fhall we afcribe thefe fingular appearances?
The plain account of the matter follows.
Curiofity is implanted in human nature, for
a purpofe extremely beneficial, that of acquiring knowledge. New and ftrange objects, above all others, excite our curiofity;
and its gratification is the emotion above defcribed, known by the name of *wonder*.
This emotion is diftinguifhed from *admiration*. Novelty where-ever found, whether
in a quality or action, is the caufe of wonder : admiration is directed upon the operator who performs any thing wonderful.

During infancy, every new object is probably the occafion of wonder, in fome degree; becaufe, during infancy, every object at firft is ftrange as well as new. But
as objects are rendered familiar by cuftom,
we ceafe by degrees to wonder at new appearances that have any refemblance to what
we are acquainted with. A thing muft be
fingular as well as new, to excite our curiofity and to raife our wonder. To fave mul-
tiplying words, I would be underftood to
comprehend

comprehend both circumstances when I hereafter talk of novelty.

In an ordinary train of perceptions where one thing introduces another, not a single object makes its appearance unexpectedly *. The mind thus prepared for the reception of its objects, admits them one after another without perturbation. But when a thing breaks in unexpectedly and without the preparation of any connection, it raises a singular emotion known by the name of *surprise*. This emotion may be produced by the most familiar object, as when one accidentally meets a friend who was reported to be dead; or a man in high life, lately a beggar. On the other hand, a new object, however strange, will not produce this emotion if the spectator be prepared for the sight. An elephant in India will not surprise a traveller who goes to see one; and yet its novelty will raise his wonder. An Indian in Britain would be much surprised to stumble upon an elephant feeding at large in the open fields; but the creature

* See chap. 1.

itfelf, to which he was accuftomed, would not raife his wonder.

Surprife thus in feveral refpects differs from wonder. Unexpectednefs is the caufe of the former emotion : novelty is the caufe of the latter. Nor differ they lefs in their nature and circumftances, as will be explained by and by. With relation to one circumftance they perfectly agree, which is the fhortnefs of their duration. The inftantaneous production of thefe emotions in perfection, may contribute to this effect, in conformity to a general law, That things foon decay which foon come to perfection. The violence of the emotions may alfo contribute; for an ardent emotion, which is not fufceptible of increafe, cannot have a long courfe. But their fhort duration is occafioned chiefly by that of their caufes. We are foon reconciled to an object, however unexpected; and novelty foon degenerates into familiarity.

Whether thefe emotions be pleafant or painful, is not a clear point. It may appear ftrange, that our own feelings and their capital qualities fhould afford any matter for a

doubt.

doubt.   But when we are ingroffed by any emotion, there is no place for fpeculation; and when fufficiently calm for fpeculation, it is not eafy to recal the emotion with fuffi- cient accuracy.   New objects are fometimes terrible, fometimes delightful.   The terror which a tyger infpires is greateft at firft, and wears off gradually by familiarity.   On the other hand, even women will acknow- ledge, that it is novelty which pleafes the moft in a new fafhion.   At this rate, it fhould be thought, that wonder is not in itfelf pleafant or painful, but that it affumes either quality according to circumftances. This doctrine, however plaufible, muft not pafs without examination.   And when we reflect upon the principle of curiofity and its operations, a glimpfe of light gives fome faint view of a different theory.   Our cu- riofity is never more thoroughly gratified, than by new and fingular objects.   That very gratification is the emotion of wonder, which therefore, according to the analogy of nature, ought always to be pleafant *.

* See chap. 2. part 1. fect. 2.

And indeed it would be a great defect in
human nature, were the gratification of fo
ufeful a principle unpleafant. But upon a
more ftrict fcrutiny, we fhall not have occafion to mark curiofity as an exception from
the general rule. A new object, it is true,
that hath a threatening appearance, adds to
our terror by its novelty. But from this experiment it doth not follow, that novelty is in
itfelf difagreeable. It is perfectly confiftent,
that we fhould be delighted with an object
in one view, and terrified with it in another.
A river in flood fwelling over its banks, is a
grand and delightful object; and yet it may
produce no fmall degree of fear when we
attempt to crofs it. Courage and magnanimity are agreeable; and yet when we view
thefe qualities in an enemy, they ferve to
increafe our terror *. In the fame manner, novelty has two effects clearly diftinguifhable from each other. A new object,
by gratifying curiofity, muft always be a-
greeable. It may, at the fame time, have
an oppofite effect indirectly, which is, to in-

* See chap. 4.

fpire

spire terror. For when a new object appears in any degree dangerous, our ignorance of its powers and qualities affords ample scope for the imagination to dress it in the most frightful colours *. Thus the first sight of a lion at some distance, may at the same instant produce two opposite feelings, the pleasant emotion of wonder, and the painful passion of terror. The novelty of the object, produces the former directly, and contributes to the latter indirectly. Thus, when the subject is analized, we find, that the power which novelty hath indirectly to inflame terror, is perfectly consistent with its being in every case agreeable. The matter may be put in a still clearer light by varying the scene. If a lion be first seen from a place of safety, the spectacle is altogether agreeable without the least mixture of terror. If again the first sight put us within reach of this dangerous animal, our terror may be so great as quite to exclude any sense of novelty. But this fact proves not

* Essays on the principles of morality and natural religion, part 2. ess. 6.

that

that wonder is painful: it proves only that wonder may be excluded by a more powerful paſſion. And yet it is this fact, which, in ſuperficial thinking, has thrown the ſubject into obſcurity. I preſume we may now boldly affirm, that wonder is in every caſe a pleaſant emotion. This is acknowledged as to all new objects that appear inoffenſive. And even as to objects that appear offenſive, I urge that the ſame muſt hold ſo long as the ſpectator can attend to the novelty.

Whether ſurpriſe be in itſelf pleaſant or painful, is a queſtion not leſs intricate than the former. It is certain, that ſurpriſe inflames our joy when unexpectedly we meet with an old friend: and not leſs our terror, when we ſtumble upon any thing noxious. To clear this point, we muſt trace it ſtep by ſtep. And the firſt thing to be remarked is, that in ſome inſtances an unexpected object overpowers the mind ſo as to produce a momentary ſtupefaction. An unexpected object, not leſs than one that is new, is apt to ſound an alarm and to raiſe terror. Man, naturally a defenceleſs being, is happily ſo conſtituted as to apprehend danger in all
doubtful

doubtful cafes.　Accordingly, where the
object is dangerous, or appears fo, the fudden alarm it gives, without preparation, is
apt totally to unhinge the mind, and for a
moment to fufpend all the faculties, even
thought itfelf *.　In this ftate a man is quite
helplefs; and if he move at all, is as likely
to run upon the danger as from it.　Surprife carried to this height, cannot be either
pleafant or painful; becaufe the mind, during fuch momentary ftupefaction, is in a
good meafure, if not totally, infenfible.

If we then inquire for the character of
this emotion, it muft be where the unexpected object or event produceth lefs violent
effects.　And while the mind remains fenfible of pleafure and pain, is it not natural to
fuppofe, that furprife, like wonder, fhould
have an invariable character?　I am inclined however to think, that furprife has no
invariable character, but affumes that of the
object which raifes it.　Wonder is the gratification of a natural principle, and upon

---

* Hence the Latin names for furprife, *torpor, animi
ftupor.*

that

that account muft be pleafant. There, novelty is the capital circumftance, which, for
a time, is intitled to poffefs the mind entirely in one unvaried tone. The unexpected
appearance of an object, feems not equally
intitled to produce an emotion diftinguifhable from the emotion, pleafant or painful,
that is produced by the object in its ordinary appearance. It ought not naturally to
have any effect, other than to fwell that e-
motion, by making it more pleafant or more
painful than it commonly is. And this conjecture is confirmed by experience, as well
as by language, which is built upon experience. When a man meets a friend unexpectedly, he is faid to be agreeably furprifed; and when he meets an enemy unexpectedly, he is faid to be difagreeably
furprifed. It appears then, that the fole effect of furprife is to fwell the emotion raifed
by the object. And this effect can be clearly explained. A tide of connected perceptions, glides gently into the mind, and produceth no perturbation. An object on the
other hand breaking in unexpectedly, founds
an alarm, roufes the mind out of its calm
                                    ftate,

ftate, and directs its whole attention upon the object, which, if agreeable, becomes doubly fo. Several circumftances concur to produce this effect. On the one hand, the agitation of the mind and its keen attention, prepare it in the moft effectual manner for receiving a deep impreffion. On the other hand, the object by its fudden and unforefeen appearance, makes an impreffion, not gradually as expected objects do, but as at one ftroke with its whole force. The circumftances are precifely fimilar, where the object is in itfelf difagreeable.

The pleafure of novelty is eafily diftinguifhed from that of variety. To produce the latter, a plurality of objects is neceffary. The former arifes from a circumftance found in a fingle object. Again, where objects, whether coexiftent or in fucceffion, are fufficiently diverfified, the pleafure of variety is complete, though every fingle object of the train be familiar. But the pleafure of novelty, directly oppofite to familiarity, requires no diverfification.

There are different degrees of novelty, and its effects are in proportion. The low-

VOL. I.   T t   eft

eft degree is found in objects that are surveyed a second time after a long interval. That
in this case an object takes on some appearance of novelty, is certain from experience.
A large building of many parts variously ad-
orned, or an extensive field embellished
with trees, lakes, temples, statues, and other
ornaments, will appear new oftener than
once. The memory of an object so complex is soon lost; of its parts at least, or of
their arrangement. But experience teaches,
that even without any decay of remembrance,
absence alone will give an air of novelty to
a once familiar object; which is not surpri-
sing, because familiarity wears off gradually
by absence. Thus a person with whom
we have been intimate, returning after a
long interval, appears like a new acquaintance. Distance of place contributes to this
appearance, not less than distance of time.
A friend after a short absence in a remote
country, has the same air of novelty as if he
had returned after a longer interval from a
place nearer home. The mind forms a connection betwixt him and the remote country, and bestows upon him the singularity
of

of the objects he has seen. When two things equally new and singular are presented, the spectator balances betwixt them. But when told that one of them is the product of a distant quarter of the world, he no longer hesitates, but clings to this as the more singular. Hence the preference given to foreign luxuries and to foreign curiosities, which appear rare in proportion to their original distance.

The next degree of novelty, mounting upward, is found in objects of which we have some information at second hand. For description, though it contribute to familiarity, cannot altogether remove the appearance of novelty when the object itself is presented. The first sight of a lion occasions some wonder, after a thorough acquaintance with the correctest pictures or statues of that animal.

A new object that bears some distant resemblance to a known species, is an instance of a third degree of novelty. A strong resemblance among individuals of the same species, prevents almost entirely the effect of novelty; unless distance of

place

place or some other circumstance concur. But where the resemblance is faint, some degree of wonder is felt ; and the emotion rises in proportion to the faintness of the resemblance.

The highest degree of wonder ariseth from unknown objects that have no analogy to any species we are acquainted with. Shakespear in a simile introduces this species of novelty.

As glorious to the sight
As is a winged messenger from heaven
Unto the white upturned wondring eye
Of mortals, that fall back to gaze on him
When he bestrides the lazy-pacing clouds,
And sails upon the bosom of the air.

Romeo and Juliet.

One example of this species of novelty deserves peculiar attention; and that is, when an object altogether new is seen by one person only, and but for once. These circumstances heighten remarkably the emotion. The singularity of the condition of the spectator concurs with the singularity
of

of the object, to inflame wonder to its highest pitch.

In explaining the effects of novelty, the place a being occupies in the scale of existence, is a circumstance that must not be omitted. Novelty in the individuals of a low class, is perceived with indifference, or with a very slight emotion. Thus a pebble, however singular in its appearance, scarce moves our wonder. The emotion rises with the rank of the object; and, other circumstances being equal, is strongest in the highest order of existence. A strange animal affects us more than a strange vegetable; and were we admitted to view superior beings, our wonder would rise proportionably; and accompanying Nature in her amazing works, be completed in the contemplation of the Deity.

However natural the love of novelty may be, it is a matter of experience, that those who relish novelty the most, are careful to conceal its influence. This relish, it is true, prevails in children, in idle people, and in men of a weak mind. And yet, after all, why should one be ashamed for indulging

a

a natural propensity? A distinction will explain this difficulty. No man is ashamed
to own, that he loves to contemplate new
or strange objects. He neither condemns
himself nor is censured by others, for this
appetite. But every man studies to conceal,
that he loves a thing or performs an action,
merely for its novelty. The reason of the
difference will set the matter in a clear
light. Curiosity is a natural principle directed upon new and singular objects, in
the contemplation of which its gratification
consists, without leading to any end other
than knowledge. The man therefore who
prefers any thing merely because it is new,
hath not this principle for his justification;
nor indeed any good principle. Vanity is
at the bottom, which easily prevails upon
those who have no taste, to prefer things
odd, rare, or singular, in order to distinguish themselves from others. And in
fact, the appetite for novelty, as above
mentioned, reigns chiefly among persons
of a mean taste, who are ignorant of refined
and elegant pleasures.

The gratification of curiosity, as mentioned

tioned above, is diſtinguiſhed by a proper name, *viz. wonder*; an honour denied to the gratification of any other principle, e-motion, or paſſion, ſo far as I can recollect. This ſingularity indicates ſome important final cauſe, which I endeavour to unfold. An acquaintance with the various things that may affect us, and with their properties, is eſſential to our well-being. Nor will a ſlight or ſuperficial acquaintance be ſuffi-cient. It ought to be ſo deeply ingraved on the mind, as to be ready for uſe upon every occaſion. Now, in order to a deep impreſſion, it is wiſely contrived, that things ſhould be introduced to our acquaintance, with a certain pomp and ſolemnity produc-tive of a vivid emotion. When the impreſ-ſion is once fairly made, the emotion of novelty, being no longer neceſſary, vaniſh-eth almoſt inſtantaneouſly; never to return, unleſs where the impreſſion happens to be obliterated by length of time or other means; in which caſe the ſecond introduc-tion is nearly as ſolemn as the firſt.

Deſigning wiſdom is no where more le-gible than in this part of the human frame.

If

If new objects did not affect us in a very peculiar manner, their impressions would be so slight as scarce to be of any use in life. On the other hand, did objects continue to affect us as deeply as at first, the mind would be totally ingrossed with them, and have no room left either for action or reflection.

The final cause of surprise is still more evident than of novelty. Self-love makes us vigilantly attentive to self-preservation. But self-love, which operates by means of reason and reflection, and impells not the mind to any particular object or from it, is a principle too cool for a sudden emergency. An object breaking in unexpectedly, affords no time for deliberation; and, in this case, the agitation of surprise is artfully contrived to rouse self-love into action. Surprise gives the alarm, and if there be any appearance of danger, our whole force is instantly summoned up to shun or to prevent it.

CHAP.

C H A P. VII.

Rifible Objects.

SUCH is the nature of man, that his powers and faculties are foon blunted by exercife. The returns of fleep, fufpending all activity, are not alone fufficient to preferve him in vigor. During his waking hours, amufement by intervals is requifite to unbend his mind from ferious occupation. The imagination, of all our faculties the moft active, and not always at reft even in fleep, contributes more than any other caufe to recruit the mind and reftore its vigor, by amufing us with gay and ludicrous images; and when relaxation is neceffary, fuch amufement is much relifhed. But there are other fources of amufement befide the imagination. Many objects, natural as well as artificial, may be diftinguifhed by the epithet of *rifible*, becaufe they raife in us a peculiar emotion ex-

VOL. I. U u preffed

preſſed externally by *laughter*. This is a pleaſant emotion ; and being alſo mirthful, it moſt ſuccefsfully unbends the mind and recruits the ſpirits.

Ludicrous is a general term, ſignifying, as we may conjecture from its derivation, what is playſome, ſportive, or jocular. *Ludicrous* therefore ſeems the genus, of which *riſible* is a ſpecies, limited as above to what makes us laugh.

However eaſy it may be, concerning any particular object, to ſay whether it be riſible or not ; it ſeems difficult, if at all practicable, to eſtabliſh beforehand any general character by which objects of this kind may be diſtinguiſhed from others. Nor is this a ſingular caſe. Upon a review, we find the ſame difficulty in moſt of the articles already handled. There is nothing more eaſy, viewing a particular object, than to pronounce that it is beautiful or ugly, grand or little : but were we to attempt general rules for ranging objects under different claſſes, according to theſe qualities, we ſhould find ourſelves utterly at a loſs. There is a ſeparate cauſe which increaſes the difficulty

culty of diftinguifhing rifible objects by a
general character. All men are not equally
affected by rifible objects; and even the
fame perfon is more difpofed to laugh at
one time than another. In high fpirits a
thing will make us laugh outright, that will
fcarce provoke a fmile when we are in a
grave mood. We muft therefore abandon
the thought of attempting general rules for
diftinguifhing rifible objects from others.
Rifible objects however are circumfcribed
within certain limits, which I fhall fuggeft,
without pretending to any degree of accuracy. And, in the firft place, I obferve,
that no object is rifible but what appears
flight, little, or trifling. For man is fo
conftituted as to be ferioufly affected with
every thing that is of importance to his own
intereft or to that of others. Secondly,
with refpect to the works both of nature
and of art, nothing is rifible but what deviates from the common nature of the fubject : it muft be fome particular out of rule,
fome remarkable defect or excefs, a very
long vifage, for example, or a very fhort
one. Hence nothing juft, proper, decent,

U u 2   beautiful,

beautiful, proportioned, or grand, is rifible.
A real diftrefs raifes pity, and therefore
cannot be rifible.   But a flight or imaginary
diftrefs, which moves not pity, is rifible.
The adventure of the fulling-mills in Don
Quixote is extremely rifible ; fo is the fcene
where Sancho, in a dark night, tumbles into a pit, and attaches himfelf to the fide
by hand and foot, there hanging in terrible
difmay till the morning, when he difcovers
himfelf to be within a foot of the bottom.   A
nofe remarkably long or fhort is rifible ; but
to want the nofe altogether, far from provo-
king laughter, raifes horror in the fpectator.

From what is faid, it will readily be con-
jectured, that the emotion raifed by a rifible
object is of a nature fo fingular as fcarce to
find place while the mind is occupied with
any other paffion or emotion.   And this
conjecture is verified by experience.   We
fcarce ever find this emotion blended with
any other.   One emotion I muft except,
and that is contempt raifed by fome fort of
improprieties.   Every improper act infpires
us with fome degree of contempt for the
author.

author. And if an improper act be at the same time rifible and provoke laughter, of which blunders and abfurdities are noted inftances, the two emotions of contempt and of laughter unite intimately in the mind, and produce externally what is termed *a laugh of derifion* or *of fcorn*. Hence objects that caufe laughter, may be diftinguifhed into two kinds. They are either *rifible* or *ridiculous*. A rifible object is mirthful only; a ridiculous object is both mirthful and contemptible. The firft raifes an emotion of laughter that is altogether pleafant: the emotion of laughter raifed by the other, is qualified with that of contempt; and the mixed emotion, partly pleafant partly painful, is termed *the emotion of ridicule*. I avenge myfelf of the pain a ridiculous object gives me by a laugh of derifion. A rifible object, on the other hand, gives me no pain: it is altogether pleafant by a certain fort of titillation, which is expreffed externally by mirthful laughter. Ridicule will be more fully explained afterward: the prefent chapter is appropriated to the other emotion.

Rifible objects are fo common and fo well underftood,

underſtood, that it is unneceſſary to con-
ſume paper or time upon them. Take the
few following examples.

Falſtaff. I do remember him at Clement's inn,
like a man made after ſupper of a cheeſe-paring.
When he was naked, he was for all the world like a
forked radiſh, with a head fantaſtically carved upon it with a knife.

Second part, Henry IV. *act* 3. *ſc.* 5.

The foregoing is of diſproportion. The
following examples are of ſlight or imaginary misfortunes.

Falſtaff. Go fetch me a quart of ſack, put a
toaſt in't. Have I liv'd to be carried in a baſket,
like a barrow of butcher's offal, and to be thrown
into the Thames? Well, if I be ſerv'd ſuch another trick, I'll have my brains ta'en out and butter'd, and give them to a dog for a new-year's
gift. The rogues ſlighted me into the river with
as little remorſe as they would have drown'd a
bitch's blind puppies, fifteen i' th' litter; and you
may know by my ſize, that I have a kind of alacrity in ſinking: if the bottom were as deep as hell,
I ſhould down. I had been drown'd, but that the
ſhore was ſhelvy and ſhallow; a death that I abhor;

for

for the water fwells a man: and what a thing
fhould I have been, when i had been fwell'd ?   I
fhould have been a mountain of mummy.

Merry wives of Windfor, act 3. fc. 15.

Falftaff. Nay, you fhall hear, Mafter Brook,
what I have fuffer'd to bring this woman to evil
for your good.   Being thus cramm'd in the bafket, a couple of Ford's knaves, his hinds, were
call'd forth by their miftrefs, to carry me in the
name of foul cloaths to Datchet-lane.   They took
me on their fhoulders, met the jealous knave their
mafter in the door, who afk'd them once or twice
what they had in their bafket.   I quak'd for fear,
left the lunatic knave would have fearch'd it; but
Fate, ordaining he fhould be a cuckold, held his
hand.   Well, on went he for a fearch, and away
went I for foul cloaths.   But mark the fequel, Mafter Brook.   I fuffer'd the pangs of three egregious
deaths: firft, an intolerable fright, to be detected
by a jealous rotten bell-weather; next, to be compafs'd like a good bilbo, in the circumference of a
peck, hilt to point, heel to head; and then to be
ftopt in, like a ftrong diftillation, with ftinkingcloaths
that fretted in their own greafe.   Think of that, a
man of my kidney; think of that, that am as fubject to heat as butter; a man of continual diffolution and thaw; it was a miracle to 'fcape fuffoca-
tion.

tion.   And in the height of this bath, when I was
more than half-ftew'd in greafe, like a Dutch difh,
to be thrown into the Thames, and cool'd glow-
ing hot, in that furge, like a horfe-fhoe ; think of
that ; hifling hot ; think of that, Mafter Brook.

Merry wives of Windfor, act 3. fc. 17.

C H A P.

C H A P. VIII.

Refemblance and Contraft.

HAVING difcuffed thofe qualities and circumftances of fingle objects that feem peculiarly connected with criticifm, we proceed, according to the method propofed in the chapter of beauty, to the relations of objects, beginning with the relations of refemblance and contraft.

Man being unavoidably connected with the beings around him, fome acquaintance with their nature, their powers, and their qualities, is requifite for regulating his conduct. As an incentive to acquire a branch of knowledge fo effential to our well-being, motives alone of reafon and intereft are not fufficient. Nature hath providently fuperadded curiofity, a vigorous propenfity which never is at reft. It is this propenfity which attaches us to every new object * ; and in

* See chap. 6.

particular incites us to confider objects in the way of comparifon, in order to difcover their differences and refemblances.

Refemblance among objects of the fame kind, and diffimilitude among objects of different kinds, are too obvious and familiar to gratify our curiofity in any degree. The gratification lies in difcovering differences among things where refemblance prevails, and in difcovering refemblances where difference prevails. Thus a difference in individuals of the fame kind of plants or animals is deemed a difcovery, while the many particulars in which they agree are neglected : and in different kinds, any refemblance is greedily remarked, without attending to the many particulars in which they differ.

A comparifon however may be too far ftretched. When differences or refemblances are carried beyond certain bounds, they appear flight and trivial ; and for that reafon will not be relifhed by one of tafte. Yet fuch propenfity is there to gratify paffion, curiofity in particular, that even among good writers, we find many comparifons too flight to afford fatisfaction. Hence the frequent

inftances

inftances among logicians, of diftinctions without any folid difference : and hence the frequent inftances among poets and orators, of fimiles without any juft refemblance. With regard to the latter, I fhall confine myfelf to one inftance, which will probably amufe the reader, being a citation not from a poet nor orator, but from a grave author writing an inftitute of law.   " Our ftudent " fhall obferve, that the knowledge of the " law is like a deep well, out of which " each man draweth according to the " ftrength of his underftanding.   He that " reacheth deepeft, feeth the amiable and " admirable fecrets of the law, wherein I " affure you the fages of the law in former " times have had the deepeft reach.   And " as the bucket in the depth is eafily drawn " to the uppermoft part of the water, (for " *nullum elementum in fuo proprio loco eft* " *grave)*, but take it from the water it " cannot be drawn up but with a great " difficulty ;   fo,   albeit beginnings of " this ftudy feem difficult,   yet when the " profeffor of the law can dive into the " depth, it is delightful, eafy, and with-

" out

" out any heavy burden, ſo long as he
" keep himſelf in his own proper ele-
" ment *."   Shakeſpear with much wit ri-
dicules this diſpoſition to ſimile-making, by
putting in the mouth of a weak man a reſemblance much of a piece with that now
mentioned.

Fluellen. I think it is in Macedon where Alexander is porn : I tell you, Captain, if you look in
the maps of the orld, I warrant that you ſall find,
in the compariſons between Macedon and Monmouth, that the ſituaſions, look you, is both alike.
There is a river in Macedon, there is alſo more-
over a river in Monmouth : it is call'd *Wye* at Monmouth, but it is out of my prains what is the name
of the other river ; but it is all one, 'tis as like as
my fingers to my fingers, and there is ſalmons in
both. If you mark Alexander's life well, Harry
of Monmouth's life is come after it indifferent well ;
for there is figures in all things. Alexander, God
knows, and you know, in his rages, and his furies,
and his wraths, and his cholers, and his moods, and
his diſpleaſures, and his indignations, and alſo being
a little intoxicates in his prains, did, in his ales and
his angers, look you, kill his peſt friend Clytus.

* Coke upon Littleton, p. 71.

Gower.

Gower. Our King is not like him in that, he never kill'd any of his friends.

Fluellen. It is not well done, mark you now, to take the tales out of my mouth, ere it is made and finished. I fpeak but in figures, and comparifons of it: As Alexander kill'd his friend Clytus, being in his ales and his cups; fo alfo Harry Monmouth, being in his right wits and his good judgments, turn'd away the fat knight with the great belly-doublet; he was full of jefts, and gypes, and knaveries, and mocks: I have forgot his name.

Gower. Sir John Falftaff.

Fluellen. That is he: I tell you, there is good men porn at Monmouth.

K. Henry V. *act* 4. *fc.* 13.

Inftruction, no doubt, is the chief end of comparifon, but not the only end. In works addreffed to the imagination, comparifon may be employed with great fuccefs to put a fubject in a ftrong point of view. A lively idea is formed of a man's courage, by likening it to that of a lion; and eloquence is exalted in our imagination, by comparing it to a river overflowing its banks, and involving all in its impetuous courfe. The fame effect is produced by contraft. A man in profperity, becomes more fenfible

fible of his happiness, by oppofing his condition to that of a perfon in want of bread. Thus comparifon is fubfervient to poetry as well as to philofophy; and with refpect to both, the foregoing obfervation holds equally, that refemblance among objects of the fame kind, and contraft among objects of different kinds, have no effect. Such a comparifon neither tends to gratify our curiofity, nor to fet the objects compared in a ftronger light. Two apartments in a palace, fimilar in fhape, fize, and furniture, make feparately as good a figure as when compared; and the fame obfervation applies to two fimilar copartments in a garden. On the other hand, oppofe a regular building to a fall of water, or a good picture to a towering hill, or even a little dog to a large horfe, and the contraft will produce no effect. But refemblance, where the objects compared are of different kinds, and contraft where the objects compared are of the fame kind, have each of them remarkably an enlivening effect. The poets, fuch of them as have a juft tafte, draw all their fimiles from things that in the main differ

differ widely from the principal fubject; and they never attempt a contraft but where the things have a common genus and a refemblance in the capital circumftances. Place together a large and a fmall fized animal of the fame fpecies, the one will appear greater the other lefs, than when viewed feparately. When we oppofe beauty to deformity, each makes a greater figure by the comparifon.

Upon a fubject not only in itfelf curious, but of great importance in all the fine arts, I muft be more particular. That refemblance and contraft have an enlivening effect upon objects of fight, is made fufficiently evident; and that they have the fame effect upon objects of the other fenfes, will appear from induction. Nor is this law confined to the external fenfes. Characters contrafted, make a greater figure by the oppofition. Iago, in the tragedy of *Othello*, fays

He hath a daily beauty in his life,
That makes me ugly.

The character of a fop, and of a rough warrior,

rior, are no where more fuccefsfully contrafted than by Shakefpear.

Hotfpur. My liege, I did deny no prifoners;
But I remember, when the fight was done,
When I was dry with rage, and extreme toil,
Breathlefs and faint, leaning upon my fword;
Came there a certain Lord, neat, trimly drefs'd,
Frefh as a bridegroom; and his chin, new-reap'd,
Shew'd like a ftubble-land at harveft-home.
He was perfumed like a milliner;
And 'twixt his finger and his thumb he held
A pouncet-box, which ever and anon
He gave his nofe;—and ftill he fmil'd, and talk'd;
And as the foldiers bare dead bodies by,
He call'd them untaught knaves, unmannerly,
To bring a flovenly, unhandfome corfe
Betwixt the wind and his nobility.
With many holiday and lady terms
He queftion'd me: amongft the reft, demanded
My pris'ners, in your Majefty's behalf.
I then all fmarting with my wounds; being gal'd
To be fo pefter'd with a popinjay,
Out of my grief, and my impatience,
Anfwer'd, neglectingly, I know not what:
He fhould, or fhould not; for he made me mad,
To fee him fhine fo brifk, and fmell fo fweet,
And talk fo like a waiting-gentlewoman,

Of

Of guns, and drums, and wounds; (God fave the
      mark!)
And telling me, the fovereign'ft thing on earth
Was parmacity, for an inward bruife;
And that it was great pity, fo it was,
This villanous faltpetre fhould be digg'd
Out of the bowels of the harmlefs earth,
Which many a good, tall fellow had deftroy'd
So cowardly: and but for thefe vile guns,
He would himfelf have been a foldier.—

                 Firft part, Henry IV. *act* 1. *fc.* 4.

Paffions and emotions are alfo inflamed
by comparifon. A man of high rank
humbles the byftanders fo far as almoft to
annihilate them in their own opinion. Cæfar, beholding the ftatue of Alexander, felt
a great depreffion of fpirits, when he re-
flected, that now at the age of thirty-two,
when Alexander died, he had not performed one memorable action.

Our opinions alfo are much influenced
by comparifon. A man whofe opulence
exceeds the ordinary ftandard, is reputed
richer than he is in reality; and the character of wifdom or weaknefs, if at all re-

Vol. I.   Y y   markable,

markable, is generally carried beyond the truth.

The opinion a man forms of his prefent condition as to happinefs or mifery, depends in a great meafure on the comparifon he makes betwixt it and his former condition:

Could I forget
What I have been, I might the better bear
What I am deftin'd to. I'm not the firft
That have been wretched : but to think how much
I have been happier.

Southern's Innocent adultery, act 2.

The diftrefs of a long journey makes even an indifferent inn pafs current. And in travelling, when the road is good and the horfeman well covered, a bad day may be agreeable, by making him fenfible how fnug he is.

The fame effect is equally remarkable, when a man fets his condition in oppofition to that of others. A fhip toffed about in a ftorm, makes the fpectator reflect upon his own fecurity and eafe, and puts thefe in the ftrongeft light:

Suave,

Suave, mari magno turbantibus æquora ventis,
E terra magnum alterius fpectare laborem,
Non quia vexari quemquam eft jocunda voluptas,
Sed quibus ipfe malis careas, quia cernere fuave eft.
Lucret. l. 2. principio.

A man in grief cannot bear mirth.   It
gives him a more lively notion of his un-
happinefs, and of courfe makes him more
unhappy.   Satan contemplating the beauties of the terreftrial paradife, breaks out in
the following exclamation.

With what delight could I have walk'd thee round,
If I could joy in ought, fweet interchange
Of hill and valley, rivers, woods, and plains,
Now land, now fea, and fhores with foreft
  crown'd,
Rocks, dens, and caves! but I in none of thefe
Find place or refuge; and the more I fee
Pleafures about me, fo much more I feel
Torment within me, as from the hateful fiege
Of contraries: all good to me becomes
Bane, and in heav'n much worfe would be my ftate.
Paradife Loft, *book* 9. *l.* 114.

Gaunt. All places that the eye of heaven vifits,
Are to a wife man ports and happy havens.

Y y 2   Teach

Teach thy neceffity to reafon thus:
There is no virtue like neceffity.
Think not the King did banifh thee;
But thou the King   Wo doth the heavier fit,
Where it perceives it is but faintly borne.
Go fay, I fent thee forth to purchafe honour;
And not, the King exil'd thee.   Or fuppofe,
Devouring peftilence hangs in our air,
And thou art flying to a frefher clime,
Look what thy foul holds dear, imagine it
To lie that way thou go'ft, not whence thou
        com'ft.
Suppofe the finging birds, muficians;
The grafs whereon thou tread'ft, the prefence-
        floor;
The flow'rs, fair ladies; and thy fteps, no more
Than a delightful meafure, or a dance.
For gnarling Sorrow hath lefs power to bite
The man that mocks at it, and fets it light.
    Bolingbroke. Oh, who can hold a fire in his
        hand,
By thinking on the frofty Caucafus?
Or cloy the hungry edge of Appetite,
By bare imagination of a feaft?
Or wallow naked in December fnow,
By thinking on fantaftic fummer's heat?
Oh, no! the apprehenfion of the good
Gives but the greater feeling to the worfe.
        King Richard II. *act* 1. *fc.* 6.

            The

The appearance of danger gives fometimes pleafure, fometimes pain. A timorous perfon upon the battlements of a high tower, is feized with terror, which even the confcioufnefs of fecurity cannot diffipate. But upon one of a firm head, this fituation has a contrary effect. The appearance of danger heightens by oppofition the confcioufnefs of fecurity, and of confequence the fatisfaction that arifes from fecurity. The feeling here refembles that above mentioned occafioned by a fhip labouring in a ftorm.

This effect of magnifying or leffening objects by means of comparifon, is fo familiar, that no philofopher has thought of fearching for a caufe *. The obfcurity of the fubject may poffibly have contributed to their filence. But luckily in treating other fubjects, a principle is unfolded which will clearly account for this phenomenon. It

---

* Practical writers upon the fine arts will attempt any thing, being blind both to the difficulty and danger. De Piles, accounti g why contraft is agreeable, fays, " That " it is a fort of war which puts the oppofite parties in motion." Thus, to account for an effect of which there is no doubt, any caufe, however foolifh, is made welcome.

depends

depends upon the power of paffion to mo-
del our opinion of objects for its gratification *. We have had occafion to fee many illuftrious examples of this fingular
power of paffion ; and the prefent fubject
affords an additional inftance. That this is
the caufe, will evidently appear, by reflecting in what manner a fpectator is affected,
when a very large animal is for the firft
time placed befide a very fmall one of the
fame fpecies. The oppofition is the firft
thing that ftrikes the mind : the unufual
appearance gives furprife ; and the fpectator,
prone to gratify this emotion, conceives
the oppofition to be the greateft that can be.
He fees, or feems to fee, the one animal
extremely little, and the other extremely
large. The emotion of furprife arifing
from any unufual refemblance, ferves e-
qually to explain why at firft view we are
apt to think fuch refemblance more entire
than it is in reality. And it muft be obferved, that the circumftances of more and
lefs, which are the proper fubjects of com-

* Chap. 2. part 5.

parifon,

parifon, raife a perception fo indiftinct and
vague as to facilitate the effect defcribed.
We have no mental ftandard of great and
little, nor of the feveral degrees of any attribute; and the mind thus unreftrained, is
naturally difpofed to indulge its furprife to
the utmoft extent.

In exploring the operations of the mind,
fome of which are extremely nice and flip-
pery, it is neceffary to proceed with the utmoft circumfpection. And after all, feldom it happens that fpeculations of this kind
afford any ftrong conviction. Luckily, in
the prefent cafe, we have at hand facts and
experiments that fupport the foregoing theory in a fatisfactory manner. In the firft
place, the oppofing a fmall object of one
fpecies to a great object of another, produces not, in any degree, that effect of contraft, which is fo remarkable when both objects are of the fame fpecies. There is no
difference betwixt thefe two cafes that pro-
mifeth to have any influence, but only that
the former is common, the latter rare. May
we not then fairly conclude, that furprife
from the rarity of appearance is the caufe
of

of contraſt, when we find no ſuch effect where the appearance is common? In the next place, if ſurprife be the ſole cauſe of the effects that appear in making a compariſon, it follows neceſſarily that theſe effects will vaniſh ſo ſoon as a compariſon becomes familiar. This holds ſo unerringly, as to leave no reaſonable doubt that ſurprife is the prime mover in this operation. Our ſurprife is great the firſt time a ſmall lapdog is ſeen with a large maſtiff: but when two ſuch animals are conſtantly together, there is no ſurprife; and it makes no difference whether they be viewed ſeparately or in company. We put no bounds to the riches of a man who has recently made his fortune. The oppofition betwixt his preſent and paſt ſituation, or betwixt his preſent ſituation and that of others, is carried to an extreme. With regard to a family that for many generations hath enjoyed great wealth, the ſame falſe reckoning is not made. It is equally remarkable, that a ſimile loſes its effect by repetition. A lover compared to a moth ſcorching itſelf at the flame of a candle, is a ſprightly ſimile, which by fre-

quent

quent use has lost all force.   Love cannot
now be compared to fire, without some degree of disgust.   It has been justly objected
against Homer, that the lion is too often introduced in his similes.   All the variety he
is able to throw into them, is not sufficient
to keep alive the reader's surprise.

To explain the influence of comparison
upon the mind, I have chosen the simplest
case, that of two animals of the same kind,
differing in size only, seen for the first time.
To complete the theory, other circumstances must be taken in.   And the next suppo-
sition I shall make, is where both animals,
separately familiar to the spectator, are
brought together for the first time.   In this
case, the effect of magnifying and diminish-
ing, will be found remarkably greater than
in that first mentioned.   And the reason
will appear upon analyzing the operation.
The first thing we feel is surprise, occasioned by the uncommon difference of two
creatures of the same species.   We are next
sensible, that the one appears less, the other
larger, than they did formerly.   This new
circumstance is a second cause of surprise,

and augments it fo as to make us imagine a
ftill greater oppofition betwixt the animals,
than if we had formed no notion of them
beforehand.

I fhall confine myfelf to one other fuppofition, That the fpectator was acquainted beforehand with one of the animals only, the
lapdog for example. This new circumftance will vary the effect. Inftead of
widening the natural difference by enlarging
in appearance the one animal and diminifh-
ing the other in proportion, the whole ap-
parent alteration will reft upon the lapdog.
The furprife to find it lefs than judged to be
formerly, will draw the whole attention of
the mind upon it ; and this furprife will be
gratified, by conceiving it to be of the moft
diminutive fize poffible. The maftiff in the
mean time is quite neglected. I am able to
illuftrate this effect by a very familiar example. Take a piece of paper or linen reckoned to be a good white, and compare it
with fomething of the fame kind that is a
pure white. The judgement we formed
of the firft object is inftantly varied ; and
the furprife occafioned by finding it not fo
white

white as was thought, produceth a hafty
conviction that it is much lefs white than it
is in reality. Withdrawing now the pure
white, and putting in its place a deep black,
the furprife occafioned by this new circumftance carries our thought to the other extreme, and we now conceive the original object to be a pure white. Thus experience
forces us to acknowledge, that our emotions
have an influence even upon our eye-fight.
This experiment leads to a general obfervation, That whatever is found more ftrange
or beautiful than was expected, is judged to
be more ftrange or beautiful than it is in reality. Hence it is a common artifice, to de-
preciate beforehand what we wifh to make
a figure in the eyes of others.

The comparifons employed by poets and
orators, coincide with the laft-mentioned
fuppofition. It is always a known object
that is to be aggrandized or leffened. The
former is effectuated by likening it to fome
grand object, or by contrafting it with one
that has the oppofite character. To effec-
tuate the latter, the method muft be rever-
fed. The object muft be contrafted with

Z z 2   fomething

something superior to itself, or likened to something inferior. The whole effect is produced upon the principal subject, which by this means is elevated above its rank or depressed below it.

In accounting for the effect that any unusual resemblance or contrast has upon the mind, I have hitherto assigned no other cause but surprise ; and to prevent confusion and obscurity, I thought it proper to discuss that principle first. But surprise is not the only cause of the effect described. Another cause concurs, which operates perhaps not less powerfully than surprise. This cause is a principle in human nature that lies still in obscurity, not having been evolved by any writer, though its effects are extensive. As it is not distinguished by a proper name, the reader must be satisfied with the following description. No man who studies himself or others but must be sensible of a tendency or propensity in the mind to complete every work that is begun, and to carry things to their full perfection. This principle has little opportunity to display itself upon natural operations, which are seldom left imperfect.

But

But in the operations of art it hath great
fcope; and difplays itfelf remarkably, by
making us perfevere in our own work, and
by making us wifh for the completion of
what is done by another. We feel a fenfible
pleafure when the work is brought to perfection; and our pain is not lefs fenfible
when we are difappointed. Hence our uneafinefs, when an interefting ftory is broke
off in the middle, when a piece of mufic
ends without a clofe, or when a building or
garden is left imperfect. The fame principle operates in making collections, fuch as
the whole works good and bad of any author. A certain perfon endeavoured to col-
lect prints of all the capital paintings, and
fucceeded except as to a few. La Bruyere
remarks, that an anxious fearch was made
for thefe, not on account of their value, but
to complete the fet *.

The

---

* The examples above given are of fubjects that can be
brought to an end or conclufion. But the fame uneafinefs is
perceptible with refpect to fubjects that admit not any conclufion; witnefs a feries that has no end, commonly called *an infinite feries*. The mind running along fuch a feries, begins
foon to feel an uneafinefs, which becomes more and more fenfible in continuing its progrefs.

An

The final cause of this principle is an additional proof of its existence. Human works are of no significancy till they be completed. Reason is not always a sufficient counterbalance to indolence : and some principle over and above is necessary, to excite our industry, and to prevent our stopping short in the middle of the course.

We need not lose time in describing the co-operation of the foregoing principle with surprise

An unbounded prospect doth not long continue agreeable. We soon feel a slight uneasiness, which increases with the time we bestow upon the object. In order to find the cause of this uneasiness, we first take under consideration an avenue without a terminating object. Can a prospect without any termination be compared to an infinite series ? There is one striking difference, that with respect to the eye no prospect can be unbounded. The quickest eye commands but a certain length of space; and there it is bounded, however obscurely. But the mind perceives things as they exist ; and the line is carried on in idea without end. In that respect an unbounded prospect is similar to an infinite series. In fact, the uneasiness of an unbounded prospect differs very little in its feeling from that of an infinite series ; and therefore we may reasonably conclude that both proceed from the same cause.

We next consider a prospect unbounded every way, as for example, a great plain, or the ocean, viewed from an eminence. We feel here an uneasiness occasioned by the want of an end or termination, precisely as in the other cases. A prospect
unbounded

furprife in producing the effect that is felt
upon the appearance of any unufual refemblance or contraft.   Surprife firft operates,
and carries our opinion of the refemblance
or contraft beyond the truth.   The principle
we have been defcribing carries us ftill farther;
for being bent upon gratification, it forces upon the mind a conviction that the refemblance
or contraft is complete.   We need no better
illuftration than the refemblance that is fan-

unbounded every way is indeed fo far fingular, as at firft to be
more pleafant than a profpect that is unbounded in one direction
only, and afterward to be more painful.   But thefe circumftances are eafily explained without breaking in upon the general theory.   The pleafure we feel at firft is a ftrong emotion
of grandeur, arifing from the immenfe extenfion of the object.
And to increafe the pain we feel afterward for the want of a
termination, there concurs a pain of a different kind, occafioned by ftretching the eye to comprehend fo great a profpect;
a pain that gradually increafes with the repeated efforts we
make to grafp the whole.

It is the fame principle, if I miftake not, which operates
imperceptibly with refpect to quantity and number.   Another's
property indented into my field gives me uneafinefs; and I am
eager to make the purchafe, not for profit, but in order to fquare
my field.   Xerxes and his army in their paffage to Greece were
fumptuoufly entertained by Pythius the Lydian.   Xerxes get-
ting a particular account of his riches, recompenfed him with
7000 Darics, which he wanted to complete the fum of four
millions.

cied

cied in some pebbles to a tree or an insect.
The resemblance, however faint in reality,
is conceived to be wonderfully perfect. This
tendency to complete a resemblance acting
jointly with surprise, carries the mind sometimes so far as even to presume upon future
events. In the Greek tragedy, intitled,
Phineides, those unhappy women, seeing the
place where it was intended they should be
slain, cried out with anguish, " They now
" saw their cruel destiny had condemned
" them to die in that place, being the
" same where they had been exposed in
" their infancy *."

This remarkable principle which inclines
us to advance every thing to its perfection,
not only co-operates with surprise to deceive
the mind, but of itself is able to produce
that effect. Of this we see many instances
where there is no place for surprise. The
first instance I shall give is of resemblance.
*Unumquodque eodem modo dissolvitur quo colli-
gatum est*, is a maxim in the Roman law that
has no foundation in truth. For tying and

---

* Aristotle, poet. cap. 17.

loosing

loosing, building and demolishing, are acts opposite to each other, and are performed by opposite means. But when these acts are connected by their relation to the same subject, their connection leads us to imagine a sort of resemblance betwixt them, which the foregoing principle makes us conceive to be as complete as possible. The next instance shall be of contrast. Addison observes *, " That the palest features look " the most agreeable in white; that a face " which is overflushed appears to advantage " in the deepest scarlet; and that a dark " complexion is not a little alleviated by a " black hood." The foregoing principle serves to account for these appearances. To make this evident, one of the cases shall suffice. A complexion, however dark, never approaches to black. When these colours appear together, their opposition strikes us; and the propensity we have to complete the opposition, makes the darkness of complexion vanish out of sight.

The operation of this principle, even

* Spectator, N° 265.

where there is no ground for furprife, is not
confined to opinion or conviction. So
powerful is it, as to make us fometimes proceed to action in order to complete a refemblance or contraft. If this appear obfcure, it will be made clear by the following inftances. Upon what principle is the
lex talionis founded other than to make the
punifhment refemble the mifchief? Reafon dictates, that there ought to be a conformity or refemblance betwixt a crime and
its punifhment; and the foregoing principle
impells us to make the refemblance as complete as poffible. Titus Livius, influenced
by this principle, accounts for a certain
punifhment by a refemblance betwixt it and
the crime, far too fubtile for common apprehenfion. Speaking of Mettus Fuffetius,
the Alban general, who, for treachery to the
Romans, his allies, was fentenced to be torn
to pieces by horfes, he puts the following
fpeech in the mouth of Tullus Hoftilius,
who decreed the punifhment. " Mette
" Fuffeti, inquit, fi ipfe difcere poffes fi-
" dem ac fœdera fervare, vivo tibi ea difci-
" plina a me adhibita effet. Nunc, quo-
                                    " niam

" niam tuum infanabile ingenium eft, at
" tu tuo fupplicio doce humanum genus,
" ea fancta credere, quæ a te violata funt.
" Ut igitur paulo ante animum inter Fide-
" natem Romanamque rem ancipitem gef-
" fifti, ita jam corpus paffim diftrahendum
" dabis *." By the fame influence, the
fentence is often executed upon the very
fpot where the crime was committed. In
the *Electra* of Sophocles, Egiftheus is dragged from the theatre into an inner room of
the fuppofed palace, to fuffer death where
he murdered Agamemnon. Shakefpear,
whofe knowledge of nature is not lefs profound than extenfive, has not overlooked
this propenfity :

Othello. Get me fome poifon, Iago, this night;
I'll not expoftulate with her, left her body and
her beauty unprovide my mind again; this night,
Iago.

Iago. Do it not with poifon; ftrangle her in
her bed, even in the bed fhe hath contaminated.

Othello. Good, good : The juftice of it pleafes;
　　　　very good.

Othello, act 4. *fc.* 5.

* Lib. 1. § 28.

3 A 2

Warwick.

Warwick. From off the gates of York fetch down
the head,
Your father's head, which Clifford placed there.
Inſtead whereof let his ſupply the room.
Meaſure for meaſure muſt be anſwered.

Third Part of Henry VI. *act* 2. *ſc.* 9.

Perſons in their laſt moments are generally
ſeized with an anxiety to be buried with
their relations.　In the *Amynta* of Taſſo,
the lover, hearing that his miſtreſs was torn
to pieces by a wolf, expreſſes a deſire to die
the ſame death *.

Upon the ſubject in general, I have two
remarks to add.　The firſt concerns reſemblance, which when too entire hath no effect, however different in kind the things
compared may be. This remark is applicable
to works of art only; for natural objects of
different kinds, have ſcarce ever an entire reſemblance. Marble is a ſort of matter, very
different from what compoſes an animal;
and marble cut into a human figure, produces great pleaſure by the reſemblance.
But let a marble ſtatue be coloured like a

* Act 4. ſc. 2.

picture,

picture, the resemblance is so entire as to produce no effect. At a distance, it appears a real person. We discover the mistake when we approach; and no other emotion is raised but surprise occasioned by the deception. The idea of resemblance is sunk into that of identity. The figure still appears to our eyes rather to be a real person than a resemblance of it; and we must make use of our reflection to correct the mistake. This cannot happen in a picture; for the resemblance can never be so entire as to disguise the imitation.

The other remark regards contrast. Emotions make the greatest figure when contrasted in succession. But then the succession ought neither to be precipitate nor immoderately slow. If too slow, the effect of contrast becomes faint by the distance of the emotions; and if precipitate, no single emotion has room to expand itself to its full size; but is stifled as it were in the birth by a succeeding emotion. The funeral oration of the Bishop of Meaux upon the Duchess of Orleans, is a perfect hotchpotch of chearful and melancholy representations
following

following each other in the quickeſt ſucceſſion. Oppoſite emotions are beſt felt in
ſucceſſion : but each emotion ſeparately
ſhould be raiſed to its due pitch, before another be introduced.

What is above laid down, will enable us
to determine a very important queſtion
concerning emotions raiſed by the fine arts,
viz. What ought to be the rule of ſuccſ-
ſion; whether ought reſemblance to be ſtu-
died or contraſt? The emotions raiſed by
the fine arts, are generally too nearly related to make a figure by reſemblance; and
for that reaſon, their ſucceſſion ought to
be regulated as much as poſſible by contraſt. This holds confeſſedly in epic and
dramatic compoſitions: and the beſt writers, led perhaps by a good taſte more than
by reaſoning, have generally aimed at this
beauty. In the ſame cantata, all the variety of emotions that are within the power
of muſic, may not only be indulged, but,
to make the greateſt figure, ought to be
contraſted. In gardening there is an additional reaſon for the rule. The emotions
raiſed by that art, are at beſt ſo faint, that
every

every artifice fhould be ufed to give them
their utmoft ftrength.   A field may be laid
out in grand, fweet, gay, neat, wild, melancholy fcenes.   When thefe are viewed
in fucceffion, grandeur ought to be contrafted with neatnefs, regularity with wildnefs, and gaiety with melancholy; fo as
that each emotion may fucceed its oppofite.
Nay it is an improvement to intermix in
the fucceffion, rude uncultivated fpots as
well as unbounded views, which in themfelves are difagreeable, but in fucceffion
heighten the feeling of the agreeable objects.   And we have nature for our guide,
who in her moft beautiful landfcapes
often intermixes rugged rocks, dirty marfh-
es, and barren ftony heaths.   The greateft
mafters of mufic, have the fame view in
their compofitions : the fecond part of an
Italian fong feldom conveys any fentiment ;
and, by its harfhnefs, feems purpofely contrived to give a greater relifh for the interefting parts of the compofition.

A fmall garden comprehended under a
fingle view, affords little opportunity for
this embellifhment.   Diffimilar emotions
require

require different tones of mind; and therefore in conjunction can never make a good
figure *. Gaiety and fweetnefs may be
combined, or wildnefs and gloominefs; but
a compofition of gaiety and gloominefs is
diftafteful. The rude uncultivated copart-
ment of furze and broom in Richmond
garden, hath a good effect in the fucceffion
of objects; but a fpot of this nature would
be infufferable in the midft of a polifhed
parterre or flower-plot. A garden therefore, if not of great extent, will not admit
of diffimilar emotions. And in ornamenting
a fmall garden, the fafeft courfe is to confine it to a fingle expreffion. For the fame
reafon, a landfcape ought alfo to be confined
to a fingle expreffion. It is accordingly a
rule in painting, That if the fubject be gay,
every figure ought to contribute to that e-
motion.

It follows from the foregoing train of reafoning, that a garden near a great city,
ought to have an air of folitude. The foli-
tarinefs again of a wafte country ought to

* See chap. 2. part 4.

be

be contrasted in forming a garden; no temples, no obscure walks; but *jets d'eau*, cascades, objects active, gay, and splendid. Nay such a garden should in some measure avoid imitating nature, by taking on an extraordinary appearance of regularity and art, to show the busy hand of man, which in a waste country has a fine effect by contrast.

It may be gathered from what is said above *, that wit and ridicule make not an agreeable mixture with grandeur. Dissimilar emotions have a fine effect in a flow succession; but in a rapid succession, which approaches to co-existence, they will not be relished. In the midst of a laboured and elevated description of a battle, Virgil introduces a ludicrous image, which is certainly out of its place:

Obvius ambustum torrem Chorinæus ab ara
Corripit, et venienti Ebuso plagamque ferenti
Occupat os flammis: illi ingens barba reluxit,
Nidoremque ambusta dedit.

Æn. xii. 298.

* Chap. 2. part 4.

The following image is not lefs ludicrous,
nor lefs improperly placed.

Mentre fan quefti i bellici ftromenti
Perche debbiano tofto in ufo porfe,
Il gran nemico de l' humane genti,
Contra i Chriftiani i lividi occhi torfe:
E lor veggendo à le bell' opre intenti,
Ambo le labra per furor fi morfe:
E qual tauro ferito, il fuo dolore
Verfo mugghiando e fofpirando fuore.

Gierufal. cant. 4. *ft.* 1.

It would however be too auftere, to banifh altogether ludicrous images from an e-
pic poem.   This poem doth not always
foar above the clouds.   It admits great variety; and upon occafions can defcend even
to the ground without finking.   In its more
familiar tones, a ludicrous fcene may be introduced without impropriety.   This is
done by Virgil * in defcribing a foot-race;
the circumftances of which, not excepting
the ludicrous part, are copied from Homer †.   After a fit of merryment, we are,

* Æn. lib. 5.
† Iliad, book 23. l. 879.

it

it is true, the lefs difpofed to the ferious and fublime : but then, a ludicrous fcene, by unbending the mind from fevere application to more interefting fubjects, may prevent fatigue, and preferve our relifh entire.

3 B 2   C H A P.

C H A P. IX.

Of Uniformity and Variety.

WHEN I apply myself to explain u-
niformity and variety, and to show
how we are affected by these circumstances, it appears doubtful what method ought to be followed. I foresee several difficulties in keeping close to my text;
and yet by indulging a range, such as may
be necessary for a clear view, I shall certainly incur the censure of wandering.—Be
it so. One ought not to abandon the right
track for fear of censure. The collateral
matters, beside, that will be introduced,
are curious, and not of slight importance in
the science of human nature.

The necessary succession of perceptions,
is a subject formerly handled, so far as it
depends on the relations of objects and their
mutual

mutual connections *. But that subject is not exhausted; and I take the liberty to introduce it a second time, in order to explain in what manner we are affected by uniformity and variety. The world we inhabit is replete with things not less remarkable for their variety than their number. These, unfolded by the wonderful mechanism of external sense, furnish the mind with many perceptions, which, joined with ideas of memory, of imagination, and of reflection, form a complete train that has not a gap or interval. This tide of objects, in a continual flux, is in a good measure independent of will. The mind, as has been observed †, is so constituted, " That it can by no effort " break off the succession of its ideas, nor " keep its attention long fixt upon the " same object." We can arrest a perception in its course; we can shorten its natural duration, to make room for another; we can vary the succession by change of place or amusement; and we can in some mea-

* Chap. 1.
† Locke, book 2. chap. 14.

sure

fure prevent variety, by frequently recalling the fame object after fhort intervals: but ftill there muft be a fucceffion, and a change from one thing to another. By artificial means, the fucceffion may be retarded or accelerated, may be rendered more various or more uniform, but in one fhape or other is unavoidable.

The rate of fucceffion, even when left to its ordinary courfe, is not always the fame. There are natural caufes that accelerate or retard it confiderably. The firft I fhall mention depends on a peculiar conftitution of mind. One man is diftinguifhed from another, by no circumftance more remarkably than the movement of his train of perceptions. A cold languid temper is accompanied with a flow courfe of perceptions, which occafions dulnefs of apprehenfion and fluggifhnefs in action. To a warm temper, on the contrary, belongs a quick courfe of perceptions, which occafions quicknefs of apprehenfion and activity in bufinefs. The Afiatic nations, the Chinefe efpecially, are obferved to be more cool and deliberate than the Europeans: may not the

the reason be, that heat enervates by exhausting the spirits? A certain degree of cold, such as is felt in the middle regions of Europe, by bracing the fibres, rouses the mind, and produces a brisk circulation of thought, accompanied with vigour in action. In youth there is observable a quicker succession of perceptions, than in old age. Hence in youth a remarkable avidity for variety of amusements, which in riper years give place to more uniform and more sedate occupation. This qualifies men of middle age for business, where activity is required, but with a greater proportion of uniformity than variety. In old age, a slow and languid succession makes variety unnecessary; and for that reason, the aged, in all their motions, are generally governed by an habitual uniformity. Whatever be the cause, we may venture to pronounce, that heat in the imagination and temper, is always connected with a brisk flow of perceptions.

The natural rate of succession, depends also in some degree upon the particular perceptions that compose the train. An agreeable

able

able object, taking a ftrong hold of the mind, occafions a flower fucceffion than when the objects are indifferent. Grandeur and novelty fix the attention for a confiderable time, excluding all other ideas ; and the mind thus occupied feels no vacuity. Some emotions, by hurrying the mind from object to object, accelerate the fucceffion. Where the train is compofed of connected objects, the fucceffion is quick. For it is fo ordered by nature, that the mind goes eafily and fweetly along connected objects *. On the other hand, the fucceffion muft be flow where the train is compofed of unconnected objects. An unconnected object, finding no ready accefs to the mind, requires time to make an impreffion. And that it is not admitted without a ftruggle, appears from the unfettled ftate of the mind for fome moments after it is prefented, wavering betwixt it and the former train. During this fhort period, one or other of the former objects will intrude, perhaps oftener than once, till the attention be fixt entirely upon

* See chap. 1.

the

the new object. The same observations are applicable to ideas suggested by language. The mind can bear a quick succession of re- lated ideas. But an unrelated idea, for which the mind is not prepared, takes time to make a distinct impression; and there- fore a train composed of such ideas, ought to proceed with a slow pace. Hence an e- pic poem, a play, or any story connected in all its parts, may be perused in a shorter time, than a book of maxims or apothegms, of which a quick succession creates both confusion and fatigue.

Such latitude hath nature indulged in the rate of succession. What latitude it indul- ges with respect to uniformity we proceed to examine. The uniformity or variety of a train, so far as composed of external ob- jects, depends on the particular objects that surround the percipient at the time. The present occupation must also have an influ- ence; one is sometimes engaged in a multi- plicity of affairs, sometimes altogether va- cant. A natural train of ideas of memory is more circumscribed, each object being linked, by some connection, to what pre-

cedes

cedes and to what follows it. Thefe connections, which are many and of different
kinds, afford fcope for a fufficient degree of
variety; and at the fame time prevent any
excefs that is unpleafant. Temper and conftitution alfo have an influence here, as well
as upon the rate of fucceffion. A man of a
calm and fedate temper, admits not willing-
ly any idea but what is regularly introduced
by a proper connection. One of a roving
difpofition embraces with avidity every new
idea, however flender its relation be to
thofe that go before it. Neither muft we
overlook the nature of the perceptions that
compofe the train; for their influence is not
lefs with refpect to uniformity and variety,
than with refpect to the rate of fucceffion.
The mind ingroffed by any paffion, love or
hatred, hope or fear, broods over its object, and can bear no interruption. In
fuch a ftate, the train of perceptions muft
not only be flow, but extremely uniform.
Anger newly inflamed eagerly grafps its object, and leaves not a cranny in the mind
for another thought than of revenge. In
the character of Hotfpur, this ftate of mind

is

is reprefented to the life; a picture remarkable for high colouring as well as for ftrictnefs of imitation :

Worcefter. Peace, coufin, fay no more.
And now I will unclafp a fecret book,
And to your quick-conceiving difcontents
I'll read you matter, deep and dangerous;
As full of peril and advent'rous fpirit
As to o'erwalk a current, roaring loud,
On the unfteadfaft footing of a fpear.
   Hotfpur. If he fall in, good-night.   Or fink or
      fwim,
Send danger from the eaft into the weft,
So honour crofs it from the north to fouth;
And let them grapple.   O! the blood more ftirs
To roufe a lion than to ftart a hare.
   Worcefter. Thofe fame Noble Scots,
That are your prifoners——
   Hotfpur. I'll keep them all.
By Heav'n, he fhall not have a Scot of them:
No, if a Scot would fave his foul, he fhall not;
I'll keep them, by this hand.
   Worcefter. You ftart away,
And lend no ear unto my purpofes;
Thofe prif'ners you fhall keep.
   Hotfpur. I will; that's flat:
He faid, he would not ranfom Mortimer:

Forbad

Forbad my tongue to fpeak of Mortimer :
But I will find him when he lies afleep,
And in his ear I'll holla *Mortimer!*
Nay, I will have a ftarling taught to fpeak
Nothing but *Mortimer*, and give it him,
To keep his anger ftill in motion.

 Worcefter. Hear you, coufin, a word.

 Hotfpur. All ftudies here I folemnly defy,
Save how to gall and pinch this Bolingbroke:
And that fame fword-and buckler Prince of
  Wales,
(But that I think his father loves him not,
And would be glad he met with fome mifchance),
I'd have him poifon'd with a pot of ale.

 Worcefter. Farewel, my kinfman, I will talk
  to you,
When you are better temper'd to attend.

    Firft part, Henry IV. *act* 1. *fc.* 4.

Having viewed a train of perceptions as
directed by nature, and the variations it is
fufceptible of from different neceffary caufes, we proceed to examine how far it is
fubjected to will ; for that will hath fome
influence, more or lefs, is obferved above.
And firft, the rate of fucceffion may be retarded by infifting upon one object, and
         propelled

propelled by difmifling another before its time. But fuch voluntary mutations in the natural courfe of fucceffion, have limits that cannot be extended by the moft painful efforts. The mind circumfcribed in its capacity, cannot, at the fame inftant, admit many perceptions; and when replete, it has no place for new perceptions till others be removed. For this reafon, a voluntary change of perceptions cannot be inftantaneous; and the time it requires fets bounds to the velocity of fucceffion. On the other hand, the power we have to arreft a flying perception, is equally limited. The longer we detain any perception, the more difficulty we find in the operation; till, the difficulty becoming unfurmountable, we are forced to quit our hold, and to permit the train to take its ufual courfe.

The power we have over this train as to uniformity and variety, is in fome cafes very great, in others very little. A train fo far as compofed of external objects, depends entirely on the place we occupy, and admits not more or lefs variety but by change of place. A train compofed of ideas of memory,

mory,

mory, is ftill lefs under our power. Objects which are connected, afford the mind an eafy paffage from one to another. They fuggeft each other in idea by the fame means; and we cannot at will call up any idea that is not connected with the train *. But a train of ideas fuggefted by reading, may be varied at will, provided we have books in ftore.

This power which nature hath given us over our train of perceptions, may be greatly ftrengthened by proper difcipline, and by an early application to bufinefs. Its improved ftrength is remarkable in thofe who have a ftrong genius for the mathematics: nor lefs remarkable in perfons devoted to religious exercifes, who pafs whole days in contemplation, and impofe upon themfelves long and fevere penances. It is not to be conceived, what length a habit of activity in affairs will carry fome men. Let a ftranger, or let any perfon to whom the fight is not familiar, attend the Chancellor of Great Britain through the labours but of one day,

* See chap. 1.

during

during a seffion of parliament : how great
will be his aftonifhment! what multiplicity of law-bufinefs, what deep thinking,
and what elaborate application to matters of
government ! The train of perceptions
muft in this great man be accelerated far
beyond the common courfe of nature. Yet
no confufion nor hurry ; but in every article
the greateft order and accuracy. Such is
the force of habit ! How happy is man, to
have the command of a principle of action,
that can elevate him fo far above the ordinary condition of humanity * !

We are now ripe for confidering a train
of perceptions with refpect to pleafure and
pain : and to this fpeculation we muft give
peculiar attention, becaufe it ferves to explain the effects that uniformity and variety
have upon the mind. A man is always in
a pleafant ftate of mind, when his perceptions flow in their natural courfe. He feels
himfelf free, light, and eafy, efpecially after any forcible acceleration or retardation.
On the other hand, the refiftance felt in
retarding or accelerating the natural courfe,
excites a pain, which, though fcarcely felt

* This chapter was compofed in the year 1753.

in

in fmall removes, becomes confiderable toward the extremes. An averfion to fix on any fingle object for a long time, or to take in a multiplicity of objects in a fhort time, is remarkable in children; and equally fo in men unaccuftomed to bufinefs. A man languifhes when the fucceffion is very flow; and, if he grow not impatient, is apt to fall afleep. During a rapid fucceffion, he hath a feeling as if his head were turning round. He is fatigued, and his pain refembles that of wearinefs after bodily labour. External objects, when they occafion a very flow or a very quick fucceffion, produce a pain of the fame fort with what it felt in a voluntary retardation or acceleration : which fhows that the pain proceeds not from the violence of the action, but from the retardation or acceleration itfelf, difturbing that free and eafy courfe of fucceffion which is naturally pleafant.

But the mind is not fatisfied with a moderate courfe alone : its perceptions muft alfo be fufficiently diverfified. Number without variety conftitutes not an agreeable train. In comparing a few objects, uniformity

mity is agreeable : but the frequent reiteration of uniform objects becomes unpleasant.
One tires of a scene that is not diversified;
and soon feels a sort of unnatural restraint
when confined within a narrow range,
whether occasioned by a retarded succession or by too great uniformity.   An excess
in variety is, on the other hand, fatiguing.
This is even perceptible in a train composed
of related objects : much more where the objects are unrelated; for an object, unconnected with the former train, gains not admit-
tance without effort; and this effort, though
scarce perceptible in a single instance, becomes by frequent reiteration exceeding
painful.   Whatever be the cause, the fact
is certain, that a man never finds himself
more at ease, than when his perceptions
succeed each other with a certain degree,
not only of velocity, but also of variety.
Hence it proceeds, that a train consisting
entirely of ideas of memory, is never painful by too great variety; because such ideas
are not introduced otherwise than according
to their natural connections*.   The plea-

* Chap. 1.

fure of a train of ideas, is the moſt remarkable in a reverie ; eſpecially where the imagination interpoſes, and is active in coining
new ideas, which is done with wonderful
facility. One muſt be ſenſible, that the ſe-
renity and eaſe of the mind in this ſtate,
makes a great part of the enjoyment. The
caſe is different where external objects enter
into the train ; for theſe, making their appearance without any order, and without
any connection ſave that of contiguity,
form a train of perceptions that may be extremely uniform or extremely diverſified ;
which, for oppoſite reaſons, are both of
them painful.

Any acceleration or retardation of the natural run of perceptions, is painful even where
it is voluntary. And it is equally painful
to alter that degree of variety which nature
requires. Contemplation, when the mind
is long attached to one thing, ſoon becomes
painful by reſtraining the free range of perception. Curioſity and the proſpect of advantage from uſeful diſcoveries, may engage a man to proſecute his ſtudies, notwithſtanding the pain they give him ;
and

and a habit of clofe attention, formed by frequent exercife, may foften the pain. But it is deeply felt by the bulk of mankind, and produceth in them an averfion to all abftract fciences. In any profeffion or calling, a train of operation that is fimple and reiterated without intermiffion, makes the operator languifh, and lofe his vigor. He complains neither of too great labour nor of too little action; but regrets the want of variety, and his being obliged to do the fame thing over and over. Where the operation is fufficiently varied, the mind retains its vigor, and is pleafed with its condition. Actions again create an uneafinefs when exceffive in number or variety, though in every other refpect agreeable. This uneafinefs is extremely remarkable, where ftrict attention muft be given, at the fame time, to a number of different things. Thus a throng of bufinefs in law, in phyfic, or in traffick, diftreffeth and diftracts the mind, unlefs where a habit of application is acquired by long and conftant exercife. The exceffive variety is the diftreffing circumftance; and the mind fuffers

3 D 2   grievoufly

grievously by being kept constantly upon the stretch.

With relation to involuntary causes disturbing that degree of variety which nature requires, a slight pain affecting one part of the body without variation, becomes, by its constancy and long duration, almost insupportable. The patient, sensible that the pain is not increased in degree, complains of its constancy more than of its severity, that it ingrosses his whole thoughts, and gives admission to no other object. Pain, of all feelings, seizes the attention with the greatest force; and the mind, after fruitless efforts to turn its view to objects more agreeable, must abandon itself to its tormentor. A shifting pain gives less uneasiness, because change of place contributes to variety. An intermitting pain, suffering other objects to intervene, is not increased by reiteration. Again, any single colour or sound often returning, becomes disagreeable; as may be observed in viewing a train of similar apartments painted with the same colour, and in hearing the prolonged tollings of a bell. Colour and sound found varied within certain limits, though without any order, are agreeable ; witneſs a field variegated with many colours of plants and flowers, and the various notes of birds in a thicket. Increaſe the number or variety, and the feeling becomes unpleaſant. Thus a great variety of colours, crowded upon a ſmall canvas or in quick ſucceſſion, create an uneaſy feeling, which is prevented by putting the colours at a greater diſtance either of place or time. A number of voices in a crowded aſſembly, a number of animals collected in a market, produce an unpleaſant emotion ; though a few of them together, or all of them in a moderate ſucceſſion, would be agreeable. And becauſe of the ſame exceſs in variety, a number of pains felt in different parts of the body, at the ſame inſtant or in a rapid ſucceſſion, make an exquiſite torture.

The foregoing doctrine concerning the train of perceptions, and the pleaſure or pain reſulting from that train in different circumſtances, will be confirmed by attending to the final cauſe of theſe effects. And as I am ſenſible that the mind, inflamed with
ſpeculations

speculations of this kind so highly interesting, is beyond measure disposed to conviction, I shall be watchful to admit no argument nor remark but what appears solidly
founded. With this caution I proceed to
the inquiry. It is occasionally observed a-
bove, that persons of a phlegmatic tempe-
rament, having a sluggish train of perceptions, are indisposed to action ; and that
activity constantly accompanies a brisk motion of perceptions. To ascertain this fact,
a man need not go abroad for experiments.
Reflecting upon things passing in his own
mind, he will find, that a brisk circulation
of thought constantly prompts him to action ; and that he is averse to action when
his perceptions languish in their course.
But man by nature is formed for action, and
he must be active in order to be happy.
Nature therefore hath kindly provided a-
gainst indolence, by annexing pleasure to a
moderate course of perceptions, and by making every remarkable retardation painful.
A slow course of perceptions is attended
with another bad effect. Man in a few
capital cases is governed by propensity or
instinct ;

inftinct ; but in matters that admit deliberation and choice, reafon is affigned him for
a guide. Now, as reafoning requires often
a great compafs of ideas, their fucceffion
ought to be fo quick, as readily to furnifh
every motive that may be neceffary for ma-
ture deliberation. In a languid fucceffion,
motives will often occur after action is com-
menced, when it is too late to retreat.

Nature hath guarded man, her favourite,
againft a fucceffion too rapid, not lefs carefully than againft one too flow. Both are
equally painful, though the pain is not the
fame in both. Many are the good effects
of this contrivance. In the firft place, as
the bodily faculties are by certain painful
fenfations confined within proper limits, beyond which it would be dangerous to ftrain
the tender organs, Nature, in like manner,
is equally provident with refpect to the nobler faculties of the mind. Thus the pain
of an accelerated courfe of perceptions, is
Nature's admonition to relax our pace, and
to admit a more gentle exertion of thought.
Another valuable purpofe may be gathered,
from confidering in what manner objects
are

are imprinted upon the mind. To make such an impreffion as to give the memory faft hold of the object, time is required, even where attention is the greateft; and a moderate degree of attention, which is the common cafe, muft be continued ftill longer to produce the fame effect. A rapid fucceffion then muft prevent objects from making impreffions fo deep as to be of real fervice in life; and Nature accordingly for the fake of memory, has by a painful feeling guarded againft a rapid fucceffion. But a ftill more valuable purpofe is anfwered by this contrivance. As, on the one hand, a fluggifh courfe of perceptions indifpofeth to action; fo, on the other, a courfe too rapid impels to rafh and precipitant action. Prudent conduct is the child of deliberation and clear conception, for which there is no place in a rapid courfe of thought. Nature therefore, taking meafures for prudent conduct, has guarded us effectually from precipitancy of thought, by making it painful.

Nature not only provides againft a fucceffion too flow or too quick, but makes the middle courfe extremely pleafant. Nor is

this

this middle courfe confined within narrow
bounds.   Every man can naturally without
pain accelerate or retard in fome degree the
rate of his perceptions ; and he can do this
in a ftill greater degree by the force of habit.
Thus a habit of contemplation annihilates
the pain of a retarded courfe of perceptions ;
and a bufy life, after long practice, makes
acceleration pleafant.

Concerning the final caufe of our tafte for
variety, it will be confidered, that human
affairs, complex by variety as well as number, require the diftributing our attention
and activity, in meafure and proportion.   Nature therefore, to fecure a juft diftribution
correfponding to the variety of human affairs, has made too great uniformity or too
great variety in the courfe of our perceptions equally unpleafant.   And indeed, were
we addicted to either extreme, our internal
conftitution would be ill fuited to our external circumftances.   At the fame time, where
a frequent reiteration of the fame operation
is required, as in feveral manufactures, or a
quick circulation, as in law or phyfic, Nature,
attentive to all our wants, hath alfo provided

ded for thefe cafes. She hath implanted in
the breaft of every perfon, an efficacious
principle, which leads to habit. By an ob-
ftinate perfeverance in the fame occupation,
the pain of exceffive uniformity vanifheth;
and by the like perfeverance in a quick circulation of different occupations, the pain
of exceffive variety vanifheth. And thus
we come to take delight in feveral occupations, that by nature, without habit, are not
a little difguftful.

A middle rate alfo in our train of perceptions betwixt uniformity and variety, is not
lefs pleafant, than betwixt quicknefs and
flownefs. The mind of man thus conftituted, is wonderfully adapted to the courfe of
human affairs, which are continually chan-
ging, but not without connection. It is e-
qually adapted to the acquifition of knowledge, which refults chiefly from difcovering refemblances among differing objects,
and differences among refembling objects.
Such occupation, even abftracting from the
knowledge we acquire, is in itfelf delightful,
by preferving a middle rate betwixt too great
uniformity and too great variety.

We

We are now arrived at the chief purpofe
of the prefent chapter; and that is to examine how far uniformity or variety ought
to be ftudied in the fine arts. And the
knowledge we have obtained, will even at
firft view fuggeft a general obfervation, That
in every work of art, it muft be agreeable to
find that degree of variety which correfponds
to the natural courfe of our perceptions;
and that an excefs in variety or in uniformity, muft be difagreeable by varying that natural courfe. For this reafon, works of art
admit more or lefs variety according to the
nature of the fubject. In a picture that
ftrongly attaches the fpectator to a fingle object, the mind relifheth not a multiplicity of
figures or of ornaments. A picture again reprefenting a gay fubject, admits great variety
of figures and ornaments; becaufe thefe are
agreeable to the mind in a chearful tone.
The fame obfervation is applicable to poetry
and to mufic.

It muft at the fame time be remarked,
that one can bear a greater variety of natural
objects than of objects in a picture; and a
greater variety in a picture than in a defcrip-

tion,

tion. A real object prefented to the view, makes an impreffion more readily than when reprefented in colours, and much more readily than when reprefented in words. Hence it is, that the profufe variety of objects in fome natural landfcapes, neither breed confufion nor fatigue. And for the fame reafon, there is place for greater variety of ornament in a picture, than in a poem.

From thefe general obfervations I proceed to particulars. In works expofed continually to public view, variety ought to be ftudied. It is a rule accordingly in fculpture, to contraft the different limbs of a ftatue, in order to give it all the variety poffible. Though the cone in a fingle view be more beautiful than the pyramid; yet a pyramidal fteeple, becaufe of its variety, is juftly preferred. For the fame reafon, the oval in compofitions is preferred before the circle; and painters, in copying buildings or any regular work, endeavour to give an air of variety by reprefenting the fubject in an angular view: we are pleafed with the variety without lofing

fight

fight of the regularity. In a landfcape reprefenting animals, thofe efpecially of the
fame kind, contraft ought to prevail. To
draw one fleeping another awake, one fitting another in motion, one moving toward
the fpectator another from him, is the life
of fuch a performance.

In every fort of writing intended for a-
mufement, variety is neceffary in proportion
to the length of the work. Want of variety
is fenfibly felt in Davila's hiftory of the civil
wars of France. The events are indeed important and various : but the reader lan-
guifheth by a tirefome uniformity of character; every perfon engaged being figured a
confummate politician, governed by intereft
only. It is hard to fay, whether Ovid difgufts more by too great variety or too great
uniformity. His ftories are all of the fame
kind, concluding invariably with the trans-
formation of one being into another. So
far he is tirefome with excefs in uniformity.
He alfo fatigues with excefs in variety, by
hurrying his reader inceffantly from ftory to
ftory. Ariofto is ftill more fatiguing than
Ovid, by exceeding the juft bounds of variety.

riety. Not satisfied, like Ovid, with a succesfion in his stories, he distracts the reader by jumbling together a multitude of unconnected events. Nor is the Orlando Furiofo lefs tirefome by its uniformity than the Metamorphofes, though in a different manner. After a story is brought to a crifis, the reader, intent upon the cataftrophe, is fuddenly fnatched away to a new story, which is little regarded fo long as the mind is occupied with the former. This tantalizing method, from which the author never once fwerves during the courfe of a long work, befide its uniformity, hath another bad effect: it prevents that fympathy which is raifed by an interefting event when the reader meets with no interruption.

The emotions produced by our perceptions in a train, have been little confidered, and lefs underftood. The fubject therefore required an elaborate difcuffion. It may furprife fome readers, to find variety treated as only contributing to make a train of perceptions pleafant, when it is commonly held to be a neceffary ingredient in beauty of whatever kind; according to the

definition,

definition, " That beauty confifts in uni-
" formity amidft variety." But after the
fubject is explained and illuftrated as above,
I prefume it will be evident, that this definition, however applicable to one or other
fpecies, is far from being juft with refpect
to beauty in general. Variety contributes
no fhare to the beauty of a moral action,
nor of a mathematical theorem; and numberlefs are the beautiful objects of fight that
have little or no variety in them. A globe,
the moft uniform of all figures, is of all the
moft beautiful; and a fquare, though more
beautiful than a trapezium, hath lefs variety
in its conftituent parts. The foregoing definition, which at beft is but obfcurely expreffed, is only applicable to a number of objects in a group or in fucceffion, among
which indeed a due mixture of uniformity
and variety is always agreeable, provided
the particular objects, feparately confidered,
be in any degree beautiful. Uniformity a-
midft variety among ugly objects, affords no
pleafure. This circumftance is totally o-
mitted in the definition; and indeed to
have mentioned it, would at firft glance
                                                fhow

fhow the definition to be imperfect. To define beauty as arifing from beautiful objects blended together in a due proportion of uniformity and variety, would be too grofs to pafs current; as nothing can be more grofs, than to employ in a definition the very term that is propofed to be explained.

APPENDIX to Chap. IX.

Concerning the works of nature.

IN natural objects, whether we regard their internal or external ftructure, beauty and defign are equally confpicuous. We fhall begin with the outfide of nature, as what firft prefents itfelf.

The figure of an organic body, is generally regular. The trunk of a tree, its branches, and their ramifications, are nearly round, and form a feries regularly decreafing from the trunk to the fmalleft fibre. Uniformity is no where more remarkable
than

than in the leaves, which, in the fame fpecies, have all the fame colour, fize, and
fhape.   The feeds and fruits are all regular
figures, approaching for the moft part to the
globular form.   Hence a plant, efpecially
of the larger kind, with its trunk, branches,
foliage, and fruit, is a delightful object.

In an animal, the trunk, which is much
larger than the other parts, occupies a chief
place.   Its fhape, like that of the ftem of
plants, is nearly round ; a figure which of
all is the moft agreeable.   Its two fides are
precifely fimilar.   Several of the under parts
go off in pairs ; and the two individuals of
each pair are accurately uniform.   The fingle parts are placed in the middle.   The
limbs, bearing a certain proportion to the
trunk, ferve to fupport it, and to give it a
proper elevation.   Upon one extremity are
difpofed the neck and head, in the direction
of the trunk.   The head being the chief
part, poffeffes with great propriety the chief
place.   Hence, the beauty of the whole figure, is the refult of many equal and pro-
portional parts orderly difpofed ; and the
fmalleft variation in number, equality, pro-

VOL. I.   3 F   portion,

portion, or order, never fails to produce a
perception of uglineſs and deformity.

Nature in no particular ſeems more profuſe of ornament, than in the beautiful colouring of her works. The flowers of
plants, the furs of beaſts, and the feathers
of birds, vie with each other in the beauty
of their colours, which in luſtre as well as
in harmony are beyond the power of imitation. Of all natural appearances, the colouring of the human face is the moſt exquiſite. It is the ſtrongeſt inſtance of the
ineffable art of nature, in adapting and pro-
portioning its colours to the magnitude, figure, and poſition, of the parts. In a word,
colour ſeems to live in nature only, and to
languiſh under the fineſt touches of art.

When we examine the internal ſtructure
of a plant or animal, a wonderful ſubtility of
mechaniſm is diſplayed. Man, in his mechanical operations, is confined to the ſur-
face of bodies. But the operations of nature are exerted through the whole ſubſtance, ſo as to reach even the elementary
parts. Thus the body of an animal, and
of a plant, are compoſed of certain great
                                    veſſels ;

veſſels; theſe of ſmaller; and theſe again
of ſtill ſmaller, without end ſo far we can
diſcover. This power of diffuſing mechaniſm through the moſt intimate parts, is peculiar to nature; and diſtinguiſhes her operations, moſt remarkably, from every work
of art. Such texture, continued from the
groſſer parts to the moſt minute, preſerves
all along the ſtricteſt regularity. The fibres of plants are a bundle of cylindric ca-
nals, lying in the ſame direction, and parallel or nearly parallel to each other. In
ſome inſtances, a moſt accurate arrangement of parts is diſcovered, as in onions,
formed of concentric coats one within
another to the very centre. An animal
body is ſtill more admirable, in the diſpoſition of its internal parts, and in their order
and ſymmetry. There is not a bone, a
muſcle, a blood-veſſel, a nerve, that hath
not one correſponding to it on the oppoſite
ſide of the animal; and the ſame order is
carried through the moſt minute parts. The
lungs are compoſed of two parts, which are
diſpoſed upon the ſides of the thorax; and
the kidneys, in a lower ſituation, have a

3 F 2   poſition

position not lefs orderly. As to the parts
that are fingle, the heart is advantageoufly
fituated nigh the middle. The liver, fto-
mach, and fpleen, are difpofed in the up-
per region of the abdomen, about the fame
height: the bladder is placed in the middle
of the body; as well as the inteftinal canal;
which fills the whole cavity by its convo-
lutions.

The mechanical power of nature, not
confined to fmall bodies, reacheth equally
thofe of the greateft fize; witnefs the bodies
that compofe the folar fyftem, which, however
large, are weighed, meafured, and fubjected to
certain laws, with the utmoft accuracy. Their
places around the fun, with their diftances,
are determined by a precife rule, correfponding to their quantities of matter. The
fuperior dignity of the central body, in refpect of its bulk and lucid appearance, is
fuited to the place it occupies. The globular figure of thefe bodies, is not only in
itfelf beautiful, but is above all others fitted
for regular motion. Each planet revolves
about its own axis in a given time; and
each moves round the fun, in an orbit
nearly

nearly circular, and in a time proportioned
to its diſtance. Their velocities, directed
by an eſtabliſhed law, are perpetually chan-
ging by regular accelerations and retarda-
tions. In fine, the great variety of regular
appearances, joined with the beauty of the
ſyſtem itſelf, cannot fail to produce the
higheſt delight in every perſon who can
taſte deſign, power, or beauty.

Nature hath a wonderful power of connecting ſyſtems with each other, and of
propagating that connection through all her
works. Thus the conſtituent parts of a
plant, the roots, the ſtem, the branches,
the leaves, the fruit, are really different
ſyſtems, united by a mutual dependence on
each other. Thus in an animal, the lym-
phatic and lacteal ducts, the blood-veſſels
and nerves, the muſcles and glands, the
bones and cartilages, the membranes and
viſcera, with the other organs, form diſtinct
ſyſtems, which are united into one whole.
There are, at the ſame time, other connections leſs intimate. Thus every plant is
joined to the earth by its roots; it requires
rain and dews to furniſh it with juices; and

it

it requires heat to preferve thefe juices in fluidity and motion. Thus every animal, by its gravity, is connected with the earth, with the element in which it breathes, and with the fun, by deriving from it cherifh-ing and enlivening heat. The earth fur-nifheth aliment to plants, thefe to animals, and thefe again to other animals, in a long train of dependence. That the earth is part of a greater fyftem, comprehending many bodies mutually attracting each other, and gravitating all toward one common centre, is now thoroughly explored. Such a regular and uniform feries of connections, propagated through fo great a number of beings and through fuch wide fpaces, is wonderful: and our wonder muft increafe, when we obferve this connection propagated from the minuteft atoms to bodies of the moft enormous fize, and widely diffufed, fo as that we can neither perceive its begin-ning nor its end. That it doth not termi-nate within our own planetary fyftem, is certain. The connection is diffufed over fpaces ftill more remote, where new bodies and fyftems rife to our view, without end. All fpace is filled with the

works

works of God, which, being the operation
of one hand, are formed by one plan, to
anfwer one great end.

But the moft wonderful connection of
all, though not the moft confpicuous, is
that of our internal frame with the works
of nature. Man is obvioufly fitted for contemplating thefe works, becaufe in this
contemplation he has great delight. The
works of nature are remarkable in their u-
niformity not lefs than in their variety; and
the mind of man is fitted to receive pleafure
equally from both. Uniformity and variety are interwoven in the works of nature
with furprifing art. Variety, however
great, is never without fome degree of u-
niformity; nor the greateft uniformity,
without fome degree of variety. There is
great variety in the fame plant, by the different appearances of its ftem, branches,
leaves, bloffoms, fruit, fize, and colour;
and yet when we trace this variety through
different plants, efpecially of the fame
kind, there is difcovered a furprifing uniformity. Again, where nature feems to
have intended the moft exact uniformity,

as among individuals of the same kind,
there still appears a diversity, which serves
readily to distinguish one individual from
another. It is indeed admirable, that the
human visage, in which uniformity is so
prevalent, should yet be so marked as to
leave no room for mistaking one person for
another. The difference, though clearly
perceived, is often so minute as to go beyond the reach of description. A corre-
spondence so perfect betwixt the human
mind and the works of nature, is extremely
remarkable. The opposition betwixt variety and uniformity is so great, that one
would not readily imagine they could both
be relished by the same palate; at least not
in the same object, nor at the same time.
It is however true, that the pleasures they
afford, being happily adjusted to each other,
and readily mixing in intimate union, are
frequently produced in perfection by the
same individual object. Nay further, in
the objects that touch us the most, uniformity and variety are constantly combined;
witness natural objects, where this combination is always found in perfection. It is
for

for that reafon, that natural objects readily form themfelves into groups, and are agreeable in whatever manner combined : a wood with its trees, fhrubs, and herbs, is agreeable : the mufic of birds, the lowing of cattle, and the murmuring of a brook, are in conjunction delightful ; though they ftrike the ear without modulation or harmony. In fhort, nothing can be more happily accommodated to the inward conftitution of man, than that mixture of uniformity with variety which the eye difcovers in natural objects. And accordingly, the mind is never more highly gratified than in contemplating a natural landfcape.

End of the FIRST VOLUME.